YESTERDAY IS DEAD

YESTERDAY IS DEAD

By Stuart Cloete

SMITH & DURRELL · NEW YORK

1940

Introduction

I AM THE MAN in the street. My point of view is prejudiced by my upbringing and the circumstances of my life. My opinion is divided between that which I know to be possible and that which, though I know it to be possible, I cannot believe. I know Germany may win the war. I cannot believe that England can be defeated. I know that London is being partially destroyed, and may be completely destroyed, but I cannot reconcile my memories of London with the destruction of London; my memories of Paris with the slavery of Paris; my knowledge of the last war with the maiming and death of women, children and old people in this one. My intellect tells me there is little difference between a young man with his arms blown off and a young girl with her arms blown off, but I do not believe my intellect.

This book was written to clarify my own mind, to try to create some kind of order, to find some kind of sequence in the events of the last few years. But my mind refuses to be clarified. My mind and my heart are opposed to each other. This book began as a search for cause and effect; as an effort to find reason. We demand reason. If the flame of our civilization and humanity is to be snuffed out we want to know the breath that has blown

v

it out with such facility. We demand reason. We demand cause and effect and rationality—a relation between the event and the circumstances that lead up to the event. Superficially, they are not hard to find, but below the superficial reasons lies the basic reason for this physical disaster which is the spiritual and psychological vacuum of the materialistic age in which we live, and the only answer to the vast and palpable forces of evil which have arisen to destroy us is the vast and palpable force of good that must arise to oppose and vanquish it.

THOSE PEOPLE have a belief in evil that cannot be met by toleration, by apathy, by cynicism or wishful thinking. Men must either rise up in righteous anger or they must lie down before the juggernaut of expediency. They must either be ready to sacrifice themselves, their lives and fortunes, for what may appear to be an abstraction or they must be ready to worship this strange new god of force in abject slavery.

I am the man in the street. I speak without authority. I write what I feel, what I know, what I have read here and there, what I have picked up. In this I am like every man in every street.

These are my views, my feelings—as such they are of no value; their significance lies in how near they are to the views and feelings of others—those countless others in the streets of America, in the little towns, on the farms and in the great cities. It is to them, the men and women in the streets, that this book is dedicated. To them and to my mother who died before it all began.

Contents

YESTERDAY IS DEAD

Chapter One

Today

THE MAN IN THE STREET is uneasy. Things have not worked out as they should have done. He does not know what is the matter but he is clear that something is wrong.

The man in the street is simple. His life is simple. It is centered round his home and his work. His home includes his wife and family, or his parents. His work is a way of obtaining money with which to run his home and is something more besides, being intimately related to his pride. It is the outward and visible sign of his place in the world. He says with pride— "I am a riveter, or a carpenter, or an accountant, or a doctor. I have a wife and two children. I have a home in New Jersey."

These things are all part of him. He could, until recently, count on them. He could say with some degree of probability where he would be next month, next year even. His life was based on the illusion of continuity. It was based on the fact that barring certain mishaps, such as an automobile accident or the bankruptcy of the company he worked for, life would go on in a way not greatly different from the way it had always gone.

Now he is less certain. Now he does not know where he will be next year. He does not know how the shape of things will have changed. And he does not know whom to ask. He is uncertain about the church. There must be something wrong with a church that does not condemn war. He is uncertain about his member of Parliament in England, his deputy in France, his senator in America. There must be something wrong with a government that allows these things to happen. Yet it is his government. He put it in. He is ruled by it. It is his church. He worships in it.

Next he turns to books. They are by experts, yet each tells him something different. He is convinced that there must be an answer . . . a way of living that would put all this right. He inclines to something positive, becomes an Oxford Grouper, a Christian Scientist, a communist, or a fascist—these are panaceas for spiritual unease. All, once the shock of joining them is over, the conversion as it were, offer a clear set of rules for living.

The man in the street does not like to think things out. He is not equipped by his education to do so. That is why he reads the papers, listens to the radio, goes to the movies. These activities are substitutes for actual thought processes. They fill in the gaps of time that occur between the necessary activities of his life, and act as a sedative to his anxieties. If the papers say there will be no war, as the English papers said up to September 1939, he is convinced that there will be no war. He need not worry. He can clean the car or mow the grass in the yard in peace. He is lulled by the professional lullabyers—the politicians he elected because their platform agreed with his wishful thinking; the newspapers that publish the articles he wishes to read, as a means of selling him their papers. Any unpalatable truth is a lie—is propaganda.

In England, before the invasion of Poland, anyone who said there would be war was described as an anti-Nazi, anti-German —one of those who wanted to stir up trouble, and was immediately classed as a communist.

War was too terrible to contemplate—so there would not be war. That was what Mr. Chamberlain was there for—to keep the English out of war; and when war came, there was never any question of defeat. Anyone who suggested such a possibility was a defeatist, a traitor, and possibly a Nazi agent.

Defeat was too terrible to think about—so it was not thought about. The idea that Hitler would not have started the war unless he had at least a chance of winning was discounted. Hitler was a bluffer, he was without resources. The Allies had called his bluff. Besides, there was internal trouble in Germany; the Third Reich had not enough food, no credit, and the material they had was defective. Much of it had broken down in the Austrian Anschluss and was entirely unable to stand up to war conditions.

Business must go on as usual. Business through appeasement, through weakness, but business anyhow. Anyone who told the truth was a propagandist and was assisting in Hitler's war of nerves. The way to deal with a war of nerves was to take no notice of it . . . to carry on. God was in His heaven. The allied general staffs were in entire and brotherly accord. Mr. Chamberlain was Prime Minister and everything was being done to insure the security of Great Britain and the integrity of the British Empire.

"Business as usual," and the party squabbles that accompanied it, account for the defeat of France and the danger of Great Britain.

It is the cry of the reactionary, of the business executive who hides his head in the ledgers of a past prosperity. Business is not as usual, and it never will be as usual again. These days represent the death throes of civilization as we knew it, or the birth agony of a new civilization that is, as yet, unknown. The future will either be vastly worse than anything at present conceived possible or, spread over a long period, infinitely better than was conceived possible.

Reconstruction is not panic. Precaution is not fear. A change of living standards, provided men keep their spiritual freedom, will in no way interfere with the pursuit of happiness. Universal service, the service of men to their country, and their fellow men, may even bring men to realize that they have fellow men; that they owe service. The Civil War united the forty-eight states of America under one flag, the threat of war today may unite the American people into one nation.

Disillusioned by the results of the last war, by the men who came back, by the graves of those who did not, democracy has lost its ideals in the wilds of a spurious materialism, in a frantic rushing back and forth in the pursuit of money which, without sufficient evidence, is assumed to be capable of buying contentment. People demanded happiness as a right, and because they could not get it, took excitement as a substitute.

The writers . . . Dos Passos, Remarque, Hemingway, Sir Philip Gibbs, Richard Aldington, and Gilbert Frankau, have been blamed for the attitude of modern youth. Perhaps this is right, or perhaps it is only superficially right. It seems possible that the resentment of those writers, that their disillusion, which apparently they have passed on by their work, was due less to the war, their wounds, and the death of their friends, than to the attitude of the civilians who had seen no fighting and the profiteers who had made fortunes out of their sufferings. The soldiers who knew war were against disarmament, were against appeasement, were against the financial interests which, for gain, jeopardized the safety of their children.

Men are ready to fight today, Frenchmen, Englishmen, Americans; but no one must profit by their fighting. There must be no cry of "business as usual." Let the home fires burn, but let them burn dimly. Let the sacrifice be spread widely—over every man, woman, and child. Let the country work, and stand breathless, as the young men fight.

Country after country has fallen because of "business as usual"; because of lack of sacrifice, because the people of those countries shied away from any leader who suggested any change. Change presupposed the possibility of war. There would be no war. There must be no change. Change meant regimentation which was, in itself, a denial of democracy. . . .

Where by chance a legislator who was honest got into office because, presumably, his electorate considered him the best man among them; because they considered his personal capacity higher than their normal average capacity, he was put under pressure by that electorate as its political whims changed from day to day. He was not the best man. The man whose judgment they trusted . . . whose leadership they were content to follow. He was their mouthpiece, their servant . . . not their leader. He was not left to function but was continually conditioned by the mass hysteria of his followers.

Today a political leader must not lead. He must anticipate the desires of his electorate—and what is easier? They demand not service, not sacrifice, not solidarity; but less work, more money, and greater facilities for enjoyment.

*　　*　　*

There are two ways of facing the present. One way is to face it realistically—that is to say pessimistically, and the other is to avoid all possible contact with reality. This is becoming increasingly difficult. On the radio a dance tune is faded into war news, garnished and softened by reference to cool drinks, refrigerators, and loans on motor cars, but nevertheless war news. The papers and even the magazines are full of war. The war, therefore, has arrived spiritually on this side of the Atlantic. It is at the back of everyone's mind, perhaps even more at the back of those minds that avoid all mention of it than of those who are ready to face it.

The tragedy is not the war. It is the failure of democracy—its weakness, its vacillations, its lack of integrity, its materialism and apathy. Its complete inability to relate cause and effect, or to see that the terrifying events of today, and still more terrifying events of tomorrow, are the direct outcome of past events. That National Socialism is political evolution, just as total war is military evolution. Most people still think, wishfully, that evolution must be progress: and fail to see that, by certain standards, National Socialism is progress.

Words . . . real words have been robbed of their virtue and cheapened by the rhetorical platitudes of politicians who have talked of freedom, of individual liberty, of free speech, of the pursuit of happiness till these words have lost their value. Yet we live by words. By the spoken word, the written word. We live by argument, by controversy. It is the capacity for speech that makes man human; for free speech that makes him civilized. Today, in all continental Europe, there is no free speech.

It is not merely the destruction of life that matters. Taking a wide view and considering man as a species, there is little need of anxiety. Man like every other animal invariably increases up to the limit of subsistence, doubling his numbers, under favorable conditions, in twenty-five years. The loss lies in the loss of learning, both actual through the destruction of books; and potential, in the destruction of those who would write them, and the conditioned education of the children of today.

Education has been confused with erudition, civilization with swift transport, religion with subscriptions, love with sexual intercourse, happiness with excitement. Man has in these last years been taught to live vicariously, to demand material things, to think of luxuries as necessities and demand them as a right.

Government has become a system of wholesale charity and any government that did not subscribe to this policy of bread and circuses was thrown out. The professional politician is little more than a panderer. He is elected on the basis of what he can get for the community; he covers his inadequacy with a striptease of palliatives—the forty-hour week, doles of all kinds, unearned pensions—and never dares to tell the truth on any subject, even if he is well informed enough to know it. The truth is not wanted. The political platform is based, as the cheap newspapers are based, on giving the public what it wants. This is pseudo-democracy in its last and dying phase. This is the democracy of appeasement, of cowardice; of houses and classes, divided among themselves. The giant of democracy is fat, somnolent—soft with material prosperity; he jumps when the dictators crack the whip, and cowers behind their broken promises.

The failure of democracy is due to the failure of democracy. The success of democracy, if it is to succeed, must be through the success of democracy. . . . Through liberty, fraternity, and equality—through justice. Yet these great words, for which thousands have died, have been so prostituted by cheap orators that the sharp spear of their meaning is dulled. That they, the principles for which our fathers died, are called propaganda . . . war mongering.

War, as those know who have seen it, is terrible. But today we have ultimate cynicism—we must live better than our fathers, and dare not die so well.

We demand freedom without service. We demand our individual liberty, but refuse, voluntarily, to serve the state. We refuse to accept the corollary of free choice and free living, we do not acknowledge that for these freedoms, and because of them, we must be ready to die freely.

The state must give, but what is the state? Is not the state the people themselves? Is it not the government—of the people, by the people, for the people? And if so why should the people hesitate? Why should they evade their responsibilities? Why should they cheat the state without moral scruple, as though it were a corporation?

For seven years the National Socialists gave up butter for guns. Now they have got the butter and are selling the guns. What we have spent in amusements alone would have built an army, an air force, and a navy. There would have been no necessity to sacrifice anything but amusement, the films, the radio, the football and baseball games, horse racing. But these again are bread and circuses . . . they are the great lullers . . . the great soporifics which have kept us from thinking—which have allowed us no time for thinking; the great creators of demand which, by the meretricious materialism they encourage, are going to destroy us. It is they who have created the illusion of happiness by possession, as opposed to the happiness of renunciation and simplicity. Built up by business, the democracies will be torn down by business.

The Small Town, where a man was known to his fellows, has become a subject for jokes. The farmer and the peasant, whose realism surpasses that of the urban sophisticate, are subjects for jokes. The man who is ready to die for his country, the woman whose moral standards are unimpaired, are also subjects for jokes. Sentiment has been replaced by sentimentality. Sex has replaced love, money has replaced tradition, vulgarity has replaced manners.

Time has become the handmaid of efficiency, and time is saved at great risk, for no purpose. Great music, canned like meat, has been swung and syncopated for popular consumption; great pictures, cheaply reproduced, have, by their use in advertising, become mentally associated with soap and tooth paste. Great emotions have been prostituted on the films; foreign countries have been brought, complete in color and with sound, to Main Street; and the continued showing of the horror and destruction of war has so confused us that we are now unable to feel the genuine, having been so conditioned by the synthetic.

The greatest instruments of pleasure and education have been used to prevent pleasure and education; have been used to dull thought instead of to encourage it; and to arouse, not the desire for a better life, but an envy for more luxurious living. Without personal risk, at the cost of twenty-five cents, anyone can, within two hours, shoot tigers in India, make love to a film star, and kill a gangster. Personal values which are important because they are individual are merged into a thought pattern originating in Hollywood. A young girl no longer kisses her lover. She wants to kiss him as Danielle Darrieux kisses Charles Boyer. That is—she wants to look like Danielle Darrieux while she is kissing her lover. The important part—the kiss—is forgotten. And the girl herself is lost in the celluloid pattern of her dreams.

Nothing new is left in the world—no surprise. Everything has been brought too near; and perspective, which can only be born of time, is utterly distorted by vicarious experience. Curiosity for life, the mainspring of youth, has been too easily satisfied. Love, death, war, flood, and fire are no longer interesting. The actual is now only a duplication of the fictional. The change in the youthful attitude is due, in great part, to this disillusion, to satiation by inferior material, of its natural impulses. Why seek when you can find everything without effort? Why read when you can listen by turning a switch in the living room? Why think? Indeed, why live at all?

The world is too full of things you cannot do. Too full of things you cannot have. Youth has been trained to think of success in terms of things. To imagine that it must start where its parents left off. To believe that life, through the fact of their having been born, owes them something.

Youth is not to be blamed for the world it lives in. It is merely that the tempo of the modern world is too fast for modern man; that the opportunities are too great, the developments too great, the disappointments too great, for those who demand happiness without suffering in its pursuit and for those who want, but are unready to pay the price.

Who are the people? Who is the man in the street? What man? What street? Does it mean you and me? or does it mean someone else? Some other curious, composite man, who lives in some other curious, composite street? Or does it mean just nothing at all? Do the words liberty, equality, fraternity mean anything today? or are they just words that are inscribed on coins, and above the doors of public buildings?

And where is the man who considers others equal to himself, who feels that other men are his brothers, who is ready to agree that liberty, except for himself, is a good thing? Is everything right because it is conceivable that it might be worse? Do we cherish the things we are accustomed to for this reason alone?

It is easy to talk of duty. But it remains undefined. It remains something that we think should apply to other people. For the rich it means that there should be no strikes, that the workers should work, and be glad they have the opportunity. For the poor it means that the rich should be milked of their wealth.

We talk of faith, but who has it? We talk of Christianity, but who is Christian? What have the churches done since the last war? Has the Pope excommunicated every Catholic soldier who fought? Have the priests and ministers died at their altars for their beliefs? Believers in after-life, have they dared to die? Is it possible that they were afraid of the great issues who condemned the small? Is it possible that the churches, who condemned the publican and the sinner, were themselves not clear about right and wrong?

Why was the war "phony" for so long? Why was there no enthusiasm for it? Only because its ends were not clear—the war aims unclarified. Theoretically, the war was to destroy National Socialism and fascism. But actually, there remained a suspicion in the heart of the man in the street, that composite man, who walks his composite street, that the war was an effort to retain the *status quo* at best; and at the worst, that it was a reactionary battle whose aim was to put back the clock. There could be little enthusiasm for such a cause. No one promised a "brave new world." They promised it last time and, thanks to President Wilson, we nearly got it; but the others, again mythical figures of composite statesmen, politicians, and the representatives of vested interests, were too strong for Wilson. Today with our backs to the wall we British are fighting. Fighting desperately against an aggressor that they, our own statesmen who were governing for us, and by us, have built up. Already this spirit is apparent in defeated France. Already, the men in the streets are looking for scapegoats, asking why they were not told the truth. Why were they treated like children? Asking what was the significance of this party system, that because of its fear of losing popularity, never tried a really constructive policy, that never, because it had nothing to put in its place, dared to tear down a part of its own political structure?

The day of palliatives . . . of political lady bountifuls . . . has passed. A new world must be constructed. A new world, based on the old truths that still live. It is useless for those in authority to say that this, or that, is utopian and impossible. If eighty million people can be conditioned to the creed of National Socialism and war, other millions can certainly be led along the path of true democracy and peace.

* * *

We have confused the inconceivable with the impossible. We have thought in terms of faith and morality and good will, assuming these to be natural, instead of considering mechanics alone. We have, because of our upbringing, refused to face the power of power alone, of evil, consolidated by the might of a great state and co-ordinated by a genius. We have said, "This could not be done" merely because we ourselves could not do it. And then it was done. There was never anything except a moral inhibition which prevented it from being done, or will prevent new things from being done. We have looked back at history and said that no one has ever conquered the world; therefore it will never be conquered. This is wishful thinking. Aircraft, employed as they are, have made anything possible. They have changed the map of the world. England is no longer an island, it has become a peninsula separated by a moat from France and the Low Countries. Both the Suez and Panama Canals may, for practical purposes, cease to exist.

We have said that no dictator has ever been able to pass on his power. But National Socialism is not a dictatorship. It is a religion vested in a corporation. It is, in spite of what is written and said about it, structurally sound, eugenically sound, and politically sound. It has reduced a nation to a state of farmyard efficiency; by sterilization and elimination it aims to produce the super man and the worker—a brave new world indeed and, whatever we choose to think, a possibility.

We have said that no nation can be held in subjection forever or even for a long period, but this again is wishful thinking. Why can it not be if sufficiently brutal methods are used? What is there mechanically impossible about putting every man and woman with a university education, or who pays income tax, against a wall and shooting them? That would leave the leaderless and intimidated proletariat to work for their new masters. The intellectual, that is to say, the educated man, is alone able, by virtue of his education, to organize or lead. Eliminate him as a class and there is no hope for the rest.

It has been said that the will of the masses must prevail by sheer weight of numbers, but this again is false. The masses, even if organized, cannot with scythes and axes defy a minority armed with quick firing weapons of precision. In looking back to history for our examples we have forgotten to look forward. That history repeats itself is true, but it repeats itself only approximately. The form changes, and the form today is governed by volume of fire capable of such rapid movement that all resistance becomes futile. Nor is it certain that the distant future will bring about revolutions in conquered countries. Young children will be educated and conditioned to the new régime; knowing nothing else they will believe in it.

Adolf Hitler, the corporal, the painter, has extracted parts of every creed, of every political system, of every psychological theory, and has welded them into a national religion. He has dug up the old Teuton gods from their forest graves; he has seen visions like the Maid of Orleans; he has gone into the wilderness and wrestled with devils.

The sexuality of Freud, Malthus' theory of population, and the mathematical certainty of Euclid have all been used. He has studied Machiavelli in his intrigues; Napoleon in his campaigns; American advertising in his propaganda; Al Capone, in his methods of gang warfare; Torquemada in his inquisition; Fouché in his secret service; Greek mythologoy in his Trojan horse methods; the Jesuits in his training of children; Mendel in his breeding of storm troopers; Charles Darwin in his belief in the survival of the fittest.

Hitler is a genius whose future actions will be limited only by mechanical possibility. The man who, while we shivered at the ghost of communism, built up under our very eyes the monstrosity of National Socialism.

Uninterested in our political systems, we have lived and trusted our rulers. The common man, the man in the street, wants only to live his life. He is a man of good will. By means of taxes he employs the police to take care of him at home, and his government, with its army, navy, and diplomats, to take care of him abroad. His views are parochial, his hopes centered on his home, his children, and his neighbors; and because of this, because of his tolerance and good will, he falls an easy prey. His upbringing and education have led him away from fact, have made him hide his eyes from the unpleasant, have made him believe, without logical reason, that in the end things will come right.

What is happening today is the result of defective thinking, itself the result of defective academic education, which has aimed at producing practical men—business men. No one has listened to the dreamers. No one has listened to H. G. Wells, to Sinclair Lewis, to Hendrik van Loon, to Jack London, to Conan Doyle, to Ernest Hemingway, to Aldous Huxley, to Jules Verne. No one believed, once they got over their scare, that the Orson Welles program, where the United States was attacked by men from Mars, would be duplicated so terribly, so accurately, or so soon in Holland.

Why should they have listened? These men were novelists, actors, writers of fiction, and practical men do not read fiction or go to the theater. They listen to no voice crying in the wilderness. Their aim is to produce and to sell to any buyer. Sales of armaments, like those of any other commodity, produce more sales, produce competitive buying which is endless. Rumors of wars send stocks up and down for the fishers of the troubled waters of high finance. Hitler was backed by the great interests of his own and other countries. Without them he could have achieved nothing, because of them he may achieve everything.

The Germans believe that they are fighting a holy war. They are inspired. Already victorious in other battles, with a warlike tradition behind them, with officers and non-commissioned officers trained in Spain, they are comparable only to such picked troops as those of Mahomet, Oliver Cromwell, Napoleon, and Gustavus Adolphus.

We have been led, by propaganda, to believe that there was much internal dissension in Germany. This is a myth. That trouble existed is certain, but its importance was vastly exaggerated. The German government may even have offered the subterranean forces facilities, not by direct help, but by non-interruption, to strengthen this belief in the outer world.

Herr Hitler has succeeded in the greatest double bluff ever thought of. He wrote in a book what he was going to do. Because he wrote it no one believed him. Because no one believed him he was able to do it. The only lie he told was the only truth he told . . . that about Russia. So within the double bluff was another double bluff.

This is no time for optimism or pessimism. It is no time for talking. It is the time for thought, followed by action. America may, within a short time, be the last great democracy in the world. A democracy that lies naked, sprawling between two oceans. This is no time for the isolationists to argue. Before long they may be isolated utterly—a triumph of isolation.

England alone remains, and England's greatest hour is upon her. Softened by the prosperity of a century of progress, weakened by the last war, perhaps exhausted and ruined by this one, she will arise, if she survives, purified by sacrifice and the common danger that all have shared. The weakness of England lay in her plutocratic aristocracy; in the government, from Downing Street, of an Empire that she half despised. It lay in the immense inherited incomes, the residue of an old landed aristocracy bolstered up by rich marriages, and in the number of its institutions that were tied, by their traditions, to a vanished past.

The strength of England lies in those Englishmen who are never seen, the millions who work in the factories and fields; in the yeomen of England, in England's lesser and impoverished gentry. It lies in the stolidity of the English temperament which, at this time, appalls the American observer. In great hours great men arise. The last war was not great enough. Nevertheless, the combinations of blood and circumstance that produced Marlborough, Cromwell, Wellington, and Nelson still exist. The Men of Dunkerque prove it.

That the English continue to have tea at half past four, and to play golf on weekends is amazing, but it is not new. Sir Francis Drake continued to play bowls after the Spanish Armada had been sighted. At these times, when war is prosecuted by attacks on the whole nation, this stolidity may prove the final factor which will bring England victory. A great nation, at its greatest in disaster, through its utter inability to understand it. There is no final British effort. There is only England; and the belief of Englishmen in England. On this, perhaps, depends the future of the world; of this new world that is in the making. It is the fight between what we term "progress" and "human nature" for a new adjustment.

This is not a war, as wars are conceived. It is the emergence of an angry humanity from a world of bureaucracy, of red tape, of mechanical development, whose burden it can no longer bear. Humanity is tired of disorder, of unnecessary unhappiness. The Germans are fighting for a totalitarian order which, in essence, is that of the capitalist civilization, simplified into a single national organism. The democracies are fighting for new democracy—of a kind that has not yet been tried. They are fighting for the abstract virtues of equality, liberty, and brother-hood.

There can be no question of the clock being put back. Twenty years have been wasted in the attempt and all the time the clock that beats in men's hearts went on.

These are the chimes we hear—the hour is about to strike.

Chapter Two

World Sickness

THE WORLD IS SICK, and what we are calling a war is not a war. It is a revolution. It is the penultimate, and most obvious, of a series of symptoms. It is the result of frustrations whose roots run back into history—to the signing of the Magna Charta, to the Boston Tea Party and the fall of the Bastille.

The causes of this war are not the historic causes, any more than, in 1914, the murder at Sarajevo was the cause of the first world war. This war is due to the immense dissatisfaction of man, who feels that a Utopia is not impossible; who demands, without knowing it, that his potentialities for personal happiness be given a chance. It is the development of personal grudges into national ones. It is logically and psychologically explicable. It springs from the writings of Voltaire, Rousseau, Stuart Mill, Robert Owen, Karl Marx, Spinoza, Sigmund Freud, Emile Zola, Tolstoi, Samuel Butler, Thomas More, Charles Dickens, D. H. Lawrence, Abraham Lincoln, and the others who believed that the conditions of life should be made to fit man, and not that man should be forced into the conditions of life.

With the age of mechanical progress the population of Western Europe increased to the limit of its subsistence. The aristocratic principle was replaced by the plutocratic, which later assumed the somewhat ineffectual disguise of democracy.

The great landowners gave place to great mill owners. There was a flow of skilled agricultural labor from the country to the towns where their skill and rural culture were lost. Machines were what counted. Men were machine tenders . . . machine fodder. Towns grew rapidly. Business prospered. The death and birth rates rose; and new social strata, layers in the cake of the modern social pyramid, were formed.

Before this period there were great aristocrats . . . a lesser aristocracy, the squirearchy from which the officers of the army and navy and politicians and judiciary were drawn. There were merchants, tradesmen, and working men—laborers. Doctors had no social standing. They were still rising out of the barber stage. Men of letters existed only by patronage, and painters only by sycophancy. Now came the great factory owners; the great owners of slum property, among whom was the church. The middlemen, the prototype of the modern business man and broker, who, having nothing to do with production, occupy themselves with the handling and distribution of commodities that they never see. Changes had been a slow, an imperceptible graduation of class, of work, of population drift; of social, national, and political adjustment through the centuries. A methodical, progressive evolution—from the family to the tribe; from the tribe to the nation under military leaders, who became kings and surrounded themselves with a hereditary aristocracy, that later, by reason of birth and inherited wealth, rather than competence, obtained power out of all proportion to its gifts of leadership.

Aristocracy was destroyed in France in 1789, in the United States of America in 1776 and 1865, in Russia in 1917, in Germany in 1918, in Spain in 1936, in efforts of those countries to achieve democracy by violence.

In England it is being destroyed by attrition today.

Democracy is essentially the principle of "equality" against that of "vested interest." It embodies in its theory such ideas as free trade . . . the league of nations . . . a single currency . . . a universal language . . . an alliance between the peoples of the world . . . a more just distribution of wealth.

This radicalism has always been opposed by the ruling classes who are, broadly speaking, international. A parallel was the Latin-speaking Roman Catholic Church of the middle ages, which had great wealth, controlled all art and learning, and by its wealth and the diversity of its interests, was the greatest single temporal power. The upper class have the means and leisure to travel freely. They have knowledge, either due to their superior education, or because they have hired it in the open market. Most of them speak two or more languages, many have estates in several countries and all have by investment, many interests abroad. These foreign interests have to be protected, not by professional armies, but by whole nations in arms. And the units of the nation, the men in the streets, have begun to understand the processes of high finance. The taxi driver, and the mechanic are beginning to wonder how the loss of an oil well in Irak, or a plantation in Malaya, will affect his life. He finds that it does not affect his life. He finds that he is expected to do the fighting while someone else reaps the benefit. He realizes that public education, general franchise, the abolition of slavery and child labor have all been opposed by great sections of the ruling classes. He has come to see through the system that kept the worker, the common man, in ignorance and subjection; to understand how, when this could not be done by force, it was done more subtly, by means of such drugs as the radio, the cinema—by the encouragement of drinking and gambling; by religion, and above all by giving him a defective education. That is, an education which while it discouraged thought, encouraged purchasing.

The money barons had replaced the robber barons. The employee had replaced the man at arms; the free Negro had replaced the slave, but the system had not been changed. There

remained the *haves* and the *have nots*. But the great guarantee
of their passivity had gone when Charles Darwin published the
Origin of Species.

With disbelief in the Old Testament came disbelief in the
New. Came the knowledge that Jesus Christ would today end,
as He did two thousand years ago, on the Cross. Came also the
doubt that it really was easier for a camel to pass through the
eye of a needle than for a rich man to enter the Kingdom of
God. Came even a doubt of heaven—of God. There seemed so
little evidence of either. The common man began to see that
perhaps a heaven, less complex perhaps but more homely than
that promised him from the pulpit, could be produced while he
yet lived, in his own house, among his own people. He began to
associate cause with effect, and then to examine cause. He began
to see that everything was controversial; that there was no absolute; that right and wrong were largely geographical; that sin
was now associated with sex only, and not with dishonesty, or
the bearing of false witness, or slander—not with cruelty, or
vanity, or hypocrisy, or gluttony, or selfishness. That justice, if
it could not be bought, could at least be influenced by money.

Here then is the final issue—the tension. This is the deep,
hidden psychological cause of the war, as opposed to the superficial historical reasons. This war, this revolution is due to a
general unexpressed feeling against plutocracy; against the present system of capitalism and exploitation. The system that has
on the one side led to National Socialism, and on the other, to
the apathy and distrust of their leaders which characterizes the
democracies.

They were being ruled by the men of Munich—the appeasers.
They knew, in their hearts, that they were being ruled by men
who had failed utterly either to appease the enemy, or to prepare for war with him. They went back in their minds to the
failures of the last ten years. . . . The failure of sanctions
against Italy, the failure of non-intervention in Spain, the failure in Manchukuo, the betrayal of Czecho-Slovakia . . . the

promises that had been made to them about their own preparedness. They saw that the government believed that a victory for
Haile Selassie might prove awkward. Black men are not supposed to beat white men. Even if black men are right. And there
was the precedent. The British Empire had been built up by
such conquests. It was said, cynically, that if Abyssinia was
worth anything we would have had it long ago. And the film
Rhodes that was showing at the time is supposed to have been
cut several hundred feet so that the public should not have its
heart wrung by seeing British Tommies mow down Matabele
warriors with machine guns.

They, the people, the men of England and France, were sent
again in 1939 to fight without equipment; to fight tanks and
aircraft with rifles. They were sent to fight the finest mechanized
army in the world with bladders tied to sticks. Their fathers had
been betrayed before them. Their fathers had been fed words,
starved of ammunition, told to fight a war to end war; to fight
to make the world secure, and their home a home for heroes.
They knew what had happened to those heroes. How they
starved in gutters. How they had been mocked for fools by
lesser men.

A nation has a collective mind and memory. It has an inarticulate, but cumulative passion, that harbors for generations a resentment that has never been openly expressed.

War . . . then let us fight the war!

Why did they not fight it? Is it not possible that those in
charge of operations were not sure whether they would fight or
not? It is one thing to arm a nation—another to disarm it. The
Russian soldiers marched back with their rifles in '17—the Germans with their rifles in '18.

The collective mind of modern man is no different from the
collective mind of primitive man . . . it demands leadership,
and courage and integrity from that leadership. There is a psychology of war . . . a bigness and a littleness. It is the ultimate
primitive. Man succeeds in preserving his sanity in war only

by throwing back; by utilizing his capacity for adjustment in reverting to the atavistic instincts that lie buried within the depths of his personality. A fighting man demands the illusion, at least, of a just cause; requires the certainty of national solidarity behind the lines; requires that the fires of a terrible idealism be lit and kept burning, in order that he may die. He must at least think that it is for his personal and group advantage that he fights. He must have something to look forward to in the event of his survival, and a certainty that his dependents will not suffer by his death.

It was these factors which were missing from the democracies at the outbreak of the war. It is these factors which are now coming into being. It is they that made Dunkerque possible, they that allow captains to go down with their ships at sea. But it is also these factors that will prevent, forever, the return of those conditions which made this war possible. There may be other wars, even worse wars; there may be other conditions, even worse conditions, but they will not be the same war or the same conditions.

Communism was an effort towards a religion of humanitarianism. The failure of communism was due less to its principles than to the application of those principles. Begun in violence it continued in violence. Those who lived by the sword perished by the sword. National Socialism and fascism were efforts towards a national religion. Also violent, they reached their present success, despite their defects, by the mechanistic excellence of their methods.

Communism failed in Russia because the Russian people were not ripe for communism. National Socialism succeeded in Germany because the German people were ripe for National Socialism.

It is impossible to divorce the Nazi party from Germany, or to assume that the German people in no way share the responsibility of that party. Herr Hitler is Germany. He represents it not only as Fuehrer, as Chancellor, as dictator, but psychologically. He is German historically, and it is to history that he goes for his theories . . . for his idea of the conquering horde, and the superiority of the Nordic type.

There can be no question of Hitler's genius. It is apparent even in the way that he disguised it. He is the first man to co-ordinate all knowledge into one terrible machine for war. Most of his principles are German, but some he borrowed: the principles of Machiavelli, the Italian student of statecraft, the Jesuit principles of education . . . "give us a child till it is five," and their assumption that the end justifies the means. From the Roman Catholic Church he borrowed his world-wide organization, his theory that a German was always a German wherever he might be.

The strength of National Socialism is the wide base of its appeal. A youth movement, it derides the wisdom of age as fear. As a youth movement, it created pride of race, of conquest, of physical strength, and a new code of morals.

By conditioning, it arrested the intellectual development of youth at puberty and diverted the two main streams of youthful energy; its idealism was turned into nationalism, its brutality into permitted sexual activity for the privileged, and into war. It had the charm of absolute simplicity. There was no subject that could be argued. Everything was laid down. Everything was certain.

Here again it was a movement calculated to appeal to youth, by removing youth's uncertainties. Strength through joy gave joy through strength, and produced young men capable of forced marches, and young women capable of war work in the fields. Hardship, rationing, sacrifice, all appeal to youth. And youth finally becomes mature . . . fixed in the principles acquired in youth.

Out of disgrace and disaster Herr Hitler has led his nation to success by every means at his disposal, the means of repression, false news, censorship, forged documents, public and private blackmail, national and international assassination. These means have, so far, been justified to the people he leads by the ends attained. Two years ago Hitler had his chance to be the greatest hero of the world—the man who brought Europe permanent peace. But he would have none of it. The world was too fair. He has stretched out his hand to take it.

The National Socialists assume that the democracies have none of the qualities that lead to a permanent political structure. They assume, with some justice, that the idea of freedom is relatively new—that dictatorship, tribe leadership, by an individual, is normal, and that the only way to world peace is by world conquest, and by the domination of the peoples of the world by a superior people. They regard themselves as the chosen instruments of this new and realistic civilization. Considered on the basis of physical and mechanical efficiency, it is even conceivable that they are right. But man does not live by bread alone. In the final issue, it is the spiritual values that count. Few men have died to protect their possessions. Many have died when their ideals and beliefs were threatened. The man who fights for his home is not fighting for his household goods. He is fighting for his hearth and threshold which are sacred.

Man, despite what is said to the contrary, is not a rational animal. He is rational only with his head, and he lives by his heart. He finds it impossible to believe, though he knows it to be true, that it is only by the grace of God he was not born of a different race or creed—yet he will fight for his race or creed. He will fight for his political beliefs, though in most cases, his beliefs are those of his parents, and have never been considered objectively on their merits alone.

It is this, the religious, the spiritual side of life which has been ignored, or become lost in a maze of money-making, money-spending, of labor and thought-saving devices, of government protection and economic wet nursing.

*   *   *

Historically, the present period began with the violation of

Belgian neutrality in 1914. That was the beginning of the present epoch . . . the beginning of national armies and the break-up, not only of established knowledge, but knowledge itself. Economists said that the war could not last. It lasted four years. Today there are no economists, there are only manipulators of currency and goods who hope for the best while they try out their theories on a basis of trial and error. World credit, like personal credit, is based on confidence. The credit followed the confidence, and disappeared with the confidence. The written word ceased to be binding as soon as those who wrote it were strong enough to take it back. New words came into being —the language of euphemism and sophistry . . . the pact . . . non-intervention . . . non-belligerence . . . absolute neutrality . . . assistance short of war . . . protective custody.

Patriotism either died of exhaustion, or was resuscitated in the form of a reactionary and ruthless nationalism. Brute force that for hundreds of years had been decently clad in the uniform of the fighting services, appeared naked, sword in hand. Parade uniforms were abandoned, armaments built up, and the glamor of the mounted soldier gave place to the mechanic of death, in asbestos overalls and goggles. He was not a soldier. He was a trained technician. An exterminator.

It was impossible that these public acts, these national renunciations of principle, should not affect private lives and morals. The gangster, the blackmailer, and the defaulter could find moral support in the actions of whole nations. Right and wrong were blurred into expediency. If a thing worked it was good. If a thing did not work it was no good. Utility replaced beauty. Movement replaced contemplation. Civilization was confused with rapid transport—with air conditioning. Manners, evolved over generations, as a means of pouring oil on the troubled waters of social intercourse, were abandoned. Morals, in a world that was in flux, became looser and looser in an effort to keep up with the times. Youth was blamed, but modern youth was bearing the burden imposed on it by age. It became more and more frustrated because it bore it reluctantly and fought for outlets, for new methods, new ways of life, because, without being able to state its case fully, without, perhaps, actually knowing that what it fought for was survival, under conditions that changed so swiftly as to make every adjustment obsolete before it could become practice. In one place it swore never to fight, even in the defense of its country; in another it was ready to die in battle. These views are in no way opposed to each other. They are the same view. Something must be gained. It could be gained either by fighting or not fighting. They represented the opposite poles of Hitler and Gandhi; but represented also the factual necessity for change.

The modern girl or boy of the popular magazines is no different from the boy or girl of any other period. Human nature remains only too static. It is probable that people are neither less good nor less bad, than they ever were. Neither more, nor less moral. It is only intellectually that mankind has changed. By literacy, vast masses have become infinitely susceptible to the half truths of propaganda. And because of rapid transport and the swift transmission of news events, wars, famines, and disasters can no longer be isolated or kept from the masses who read the papers or own radios.

The questions of the day are no longer academic, nor can they be answered academically. Modern education, tied like a can to the dog's tail of imperfect fact, has failed completely in its function of preparing young men and women for life, or even for the earning of a livelihood. Manual labor has been despised, yet it is by manual labor, by the two basic industries of mining and farming that we live. People are no longer clear about the difference between necessity and luxury, between leisure and pleasure. They must continue to move because they are afraid to stand still. They have forgotten that civilization is an attitude of mind. A man is civilized when his mental equipment is such that he can dispense wtih material things . . . with amusements or possessions. But as such he is, in direct ratio to his civilization, a non-purchaser and as such anathema to progress seen in the light of gadgets.

These facts, these questions, these uncertainties are intimately tied to a world situation which has produced men as widely diverse as Gandhi, Hitler, and Henry Ford. That at other periods men as different as these have lived in different parts of the world, is possible, but at no time has the ordinary man known about them, and had to decide, with an inadequate education, between their merits.

Hitler is not to blame. He is no more to blame than a storm in summer that brings flood and devastation. He was created by the circumstances of our time. He may even prove, in fifty years, or five hundred years, to have been a benefactor. Disaster, seen in relation to time, may cease to be disaster. It is possible that without the advent of a Hitler the world would not have progressed; that a false democracy would have merged into civil wars whose magnitude would have made the present war seem small. It is possible that Hitler's coming will open the eyes of men to their own potentialities and weld them into a United States of Men. Only by the threat to our liberties do we appreciate them. Only after the storm do we know calm; only after effort, rest. It is possible that man has gone as far as man can go under the existing conditions. Yet at this moment we are concerned with the immediate present, and the immediate future. At this moment we are concerned to the exclusion of all else with the man Hitler.

*   *   *

Adolf Hitler is less a genius than a phenomenon. He is the greatest of those men of destiny who have been born with exactly the right gifts, at exactly the right time. He represents, not man as we know man, but a mathematical improbability in man's shape. The concatenation of circumstances that, by their interplay, produced him are incalculable. There have been no "Ifs" with Hitler. He has, by his particular gifts, been able to forestall events and juggle with providence, to subordinate, not merely the bodies of men, but their minds. Man is the most terrible of animals and Hitler the most terrible of men. Not in his person . . . no man could be entirely terrible who inspires such devotion . . . but in his singleness of purpose, in his beliefs, in his ability to deal with humanity on the basis of those natural laws, from which man, for two thousand years, has been trying to free himself, in his creed which appeals to the body by means of the emotions. Strength through joy is Goethe's conception of Faust, brought from the drama into the million homes of the German Reich.

Hitler is an artist, a painter, and a man of imagination. As an artist he has seen human nature in its light and shadow; has seen the failure of the light, and by an immense distortion has reversed all values. He saw it was easier to weld a nation together by hatred than by love. He saw that man is ruled by his belly and not by his head. He saw that man can be influenced by political advertising in the form of reiterated slogans. He understood that suffering demands a scapegoat, and misery a leader. He knew the power of words, of oratory. The power of sex, the influence of music, the effect of drama, and pseudo-religious mysticism. He solved the question of thought by parades and propaganda which gave no time for thought. He felt the public need of masochism and sacrifice, as much as its need for sadism and debauchery. He gave it both. He combined the saturnalia with asceticism, and built up a religion whose strength lies in its fantastic paradoxes. He sought the Heel of Achilles in every man, in every nation. Each had its weakness, some special hate . . . some special desire. To obtain Czecho-Slovakia he gave a piece of it to Poland. To obtain Poland he gave a piece of it to Russia.

Above all, Hitler has been logical. Above all he has been truthful.

With the statement that fact is stranger than fiction comes the conclusion that, when it is stranger than fiction, it is taken as fiction. Herr Hitler has been the soul of truth, the soul of honesty. He has done all things he has said he would do, and to them, for good measure, has added a number of things that he said he would not do.

He has, by his honesty, bluffed the world into disaster. He stated what he would do . . . he wrote it in his best seller . . . he screamed it hysterically from the Sportspalast. And then he did it.

It occurred to no one that as he was going to do it, he was clever enough to say so. Herr Hitler stands today as the greatest truth teller in the world. He said what he was going to do. He did what he said he was going to do . . . a triumph of veracity. Even when informed by their own agents that he had the power to carry out his threats, the democracies refused to believe it . . . a triumph of incredulity, of hard-boiled business men fooled by an Austrian painter. The Pound Sterling and the Dollar made such armaments as were reported impossible—made war impossible. Though they had been seen, been counted, they were still impossible. If the democracies who were wealthy were unable to afford such armaments, how could Germany, which was bankrupt, afford them?

But the armaments were there and the war is here. Economists refuted the possibility on the grounds that civilization could not stand a war, that the economic structure would collapse. Then the economists turned round. Having first said there would not be war because it would change everything, and the financial structure of the world would be unable to bear the strain, now that war has come they say that, despite the war, nothing will change. They failed to see that a man could look beyond civilization; could by the mechanics of civilization destroy the civilization that had brought those mechanics about. That a man could envisage a world without economics.

The academic mind stuck to facts, looked back into the past for precedents instead of into the future for dreams. Now the future is mortgaged because initiative, unbacked by university diplomas, has been strangled at birth; because ideas have died through lack of nourishment; because genius has been silenced by the amorphous mass of public ignorance.

Irrevocably, the clock turns. As we say now, *now* is gone; and the *now,* which has just gone, may even be too late.

The English had Churchill who warned them. They had T. E. Lawrence whose heart they broke. The United States had General Billy Mitchell. France had men . . . but what could they do? An Englishman could write to the London Times . . . his letter, if it was published, would lie between that of a man who objected to girls smoking openly in railway carriages, and one from a woman who complained about the difficulties of getting servants.

The few who believed Hitler a danger were called alarmists, war mongers, because knowing that war was coming they wished to prepare for it. Their writings were suppressed. They could get no hearing. Today, when they write again they are called defeatists. Realism is confused with fear . . . integrity with disloyalty.

The old school-tie loyalty to incapable colleagues, and silence about incompetence in high places due to misplaced schoolboy inhibitions about sneaking, has led to this world tragedy of unpreparedness.

In the last five years it is the democracies that have been lied to. It is the democracies that have been betrayed, not the German people.

It was the democracies who boasted of the freedom of their press when it was controlled. Herr Hitler acknowledged that his press was controlled. The people knew it and trusted him. He told the truth.

It was the democracies who told their people that all was well when it wasn't. Hitler told them all was not well, that they must sacrifice their butter for guns. He told the truth.

It was the democracies who told their people that the defense programs were being speeded up when they had cut their American order for planes in half, when they had no reserve of trained pilots, when only on May the 18th did France order a twelve-hour day in the aviation industry, and England increase its working hours from eight to ten.

Hitler told his people that every nerve was being strained to achieve the ends that he considered necessary. Hitler told the truth.

Hitler was derided as an upstart, a corporal, the son of a small official. He was never seen as he really was, as no doubt he saw himself—as an avenging angel, a deliverer.

He was derided as an ascetic, as a vegetarian, as a lunatic. His integrity was never seen, nor his singleness of purpose. His complete and fanatical ruthlessness, which made him able to destroy his friends, if they stood in the way of his purpose. The democracies never saw how calculated his actions were, how he answered their every argument.

The Maginot line . . . magnificent, except that it was never completed on the flanks owing to a ninteenth century belief in the inviolability of neutral nations, was answered by the Siegfried line. He never meant to use the Siegfried line. He even advertised its defects to comfort the democracies. By his treatment of the Jews he obtained great wealth, trained his people to brutality, exercised his secret police, and eliminated those who were against him by accusing them of having Jewish blood. By his hatred of communism he got loans from the democratic capitalists who saw in communism a menace. By his concentration camps he broke the spirit of all who were not with him and sent streams of refugees into other countries to complicate their administration and to carry with them, in the tide of their progress, the fifth columnists he needed. Czecho-Slovakia was a trial of strength; the Anschluss a practice march to try out his mechanized transport; the Spanish war a training ground for pilots and material; Poland a field day with live ammunition.

Norway the first test of his infiltrated legions and parachutists.
The Germans have not been deceived by their Fuehrer. Their
confidence has not been misplaced.

*   *   *

Adolf Hitler has been underestimated because of his social
position, because of his asceticism, his diet, his height, and his
method of doing his hair. But what have these things to do with
genius? They are utterly irrelevant. Yet they were used by a
mentally defective press to amuse the people they should have
tried to rouse.

Above all Hitler was despised for being a painter. Practical
men, men of business, do not understand artists, their way of
life or their dreams . . . they fear them. Had Hitler been a general instead of a corporal, had he even been to a university, had
he been a princeling or a duke, he would have been taken seriously.

Perhaps there is still time. Perhaps the ideal of democracy, of
free thought, free worship, free speech, of Christianity, not of
creed or dogma, but the genuine Christianity of Jesus Christ can
still stand against Hitler's mechanized culture, his regimented
spirit, and his desire to enslave mankind. But in the ever-
changing kaleidoscope of political events the neo-pantheism of
the National Socialist movement has been forgotten.

Confronted by fact—by German intervention in Spain; by
the Austrian Anschluss; by the incorporation of Czecho-Slovakia
into the Reich—the democracies refused to see, or were unable
to see, the fanaticism that made such things possible. Fundamentally National Socialism is anti-Christian. Not merely anti-
Christian in the sense that it refuses to recognize what has come
to be known as Christianity, but un-Christian, in that it is a complete denial not only of the letter but of the spirit of Christianity.

National Socialism is an aristocratic religion. It is based on
Herrschaft . . . a ruling class within a ruling race. Christianity

began as a religion of slaves, a religion of the workers who, because their lives were so miserable, were promised a new life after death. National Socialism approaches very nearly to the Mithraic cult with its phallic bias, its bulls, stallions, lions, and wild boars; with its conception of Ceres and spawning women. It has been forgotten that wherever the Roman legions paused there was an altar set up to Mithras . . . that for four hundred years the Mithraic cult challenged Christianity. Its emblem, the bull with Mithras stabbing it, and full blades of wheat growing out of its wound, was a world symbol. This was a warrior's religion, a religion for the plunderers of goods and women, of the men who came with fire and sword and left their bastards behind them. It has been forgotten that the Germans are a nation of warriors.

That is the war that is going on today. Is the world to be Christian and peaceful? Or is it to be pantheistic and savage? For this also is an ideal. The warrior with his woman, with his sons fighting at his side for their tribe, is more impressive, more spectacular than the farmer tilling his soil or the student crouched over his books. Politically, the warrior is the best platform. It is easier to appeal to the primitive in man which is positive; to his desire for conquest, for women, for power, than to his spiritual aspirations which are nebulous and ill-defined.

Women have a great part in this world situation. The democracies have raised women to an approximate equality with men. They may even have raised them higher than they wished. It is probable that women, in the mass, are less susceptible to civilization than men. Their point of view is more subjective and practical.

The totalitarian states have degraded women to their most elementary function as the bearers of children and a pleasure medium for men. This suits a warlike tradition. Virility means force. It means the forcing of one will on another. According to the dictators, the men of the democracies have been emasculated by their women—are exploited by them. It is only amazing that the women, in the earlier phases of totalitarianism, did not react more strongly against it, or that the women of the democracies, having their vote, have done so little to justify it. Perhaps women are indeed passive and men aggressive.

It is in these facts that lies the unseen danger of the National Socialist principle. In its appeal to the hidden depths of human nature, to the things that are so vehemently denied because we are afraid to acknowledge their truth, National Socialism runs with the dark hidden tide of hidden behaviorism. It idealizes the herd instinct. It makes use of the modern sexual preoccupation. It allows, in the name of the nation, a disciplined licentiousness. It uses the vocabulary of the stable, the farm, the latrine, and the brothel in its propaganda. It has gone back, beyond the sophistications of risqué humor, into the nightborn phantasies of men, into their Freudian dreams of debauchery.

None of this has been recognized because of the fears that such thoughts engender. The Church, conscious of its own faults, did not dare to act. The statesmen were silent because of the unease such truths would have caused in a populace already restless and desiring change, or because they were without the intellectual equipment to understand them.

Why was the truth about the concentration camps held back officially till after the war had started? Why was German and Italian intervention in Spain denied officially? Was it because they, the rulers, had not been officially informed of its existence, when every child in England and France knew what was going on? Or was it simply because national feeling, the good feeling of the inarticulate masses of the democracies would have demanded war? And war would then, as it will now, inevitably lead to revolution. Those in the saddle were, and are, afraid of the people they rule. At all cost those people must be blinded, must be held in restraint, or the system of democratic government would prove to be the failure that it is.

There could be no greater failure than that of France. No greater betrayal than the abandonment of Paris. Of what value the casket when the jewel has gone? The jewel of freedom has gone from Paris. What greater monument could there be to democracy than a ruined Paris? In what greater mausoleum could the body of freedom lie?

Chapter Three

"This Tyranny"

THE CONCEPTS OF LIBERTY, of freedom, are based on faith—on justice; on the knowledge that within the state, laws operate according to the constitution of that state; and externally according to the rules of international law—the Hague convention, the Geneva convention, and the treaties and pacts established between nations to control their actions.

Centuries were required to build up this national and international faith—to establish credits, to establish citizen and guild rights. Roman law, English common law, the Code Napoleon, were things hardly arrived at. The scales of justice came from ancient Egypt; the modern concept of right and wrong from the ten commandments of Moses, the rights of man from the Magna Charta.

Tyranny is a system that denies these rights, and substitutes the will of a despot for the legal processes of a nation.

Today the world is threatened by a despot, by a nation of despots, who already have silenced the voice of continental Europe. There is no voice from Europe now. It has become the new dark continent—its millions are silenced and enslaved, its cities destroyed, its people threatened with starvation. And throughout the world, personal life, that is, a life based on the illusion of continuity and on the continued possession of material objects, has disappeared.

Last year in Poland, Holland, Belgium, France, Norway, Luxemburg, Denmark, and England, it was reasonable to assume that you would still be living at home with your wife and children in 1941. It was reasonable to assume that your property and investments were safe . . . that whatever happened elsewhere, nothing could happen here. That life, as one knew it, would go on more or less unchanged, or at most subject to such gradual change that it would pass almost unnoticed.

That was yesterday . . . the period between two wars. That was the beautiful dream that lasted twenty-two years.

Today is the awakening. There is no more personal life. Life itself is threatened and security has gone. From Gibraltar to Japan there is no personal life. In America alone it remains, precariously balanced on the outcome of the battle now in progress. Because of one man millions are homeless—how many dead? A strange paradox, that in a civilized world only savages remain content—the natives of Africa, the head hunters of Malaya, the Australian aborigines, the Indians and Bush Negroes of the Amazon.

For two thousand years man has fought bitterly to raise himself above his geological heredity. Two thousand years of struggle have led him back to where he began.

Every animal passes through, in its beginnings, the phases of its evolution. A young elephant has hair like a mammoth; the foetus of a bear cannot, at one time, be distinguished from that of a dog, or the human foetus from that of a monkey. Babies can support their weight with their hands; boys are cruel, belligerent, and destructive by nature until conditioned, by the circumstances in which they live, into humanity and kindness.

Herr Hitler has arrested the mental process of a nation at the Neanderthal stage. He has trained children, who are brutal by nature, into further brutality; he has taught them the art of destruction, which comes easily to a child. He has put them into planes and told them to destroy.

Civilization is against nature. It is an immense effort. We think too loosely of nations being civilized because they eat with a knife and fork, or drive an automobile. Civilization is an attitude of mind that concerns itself more with abstract conceptions than with practical necessities. Brutality, gang law, are natural. Herr Hitler has gone back to nature, to the vast natural reservoirs of evil from which mankind has endeavored to free itself for centuries.

Civilization, like democracy or free trade, must be universal to succeed. Always, in history, civilization has gone down before the uncivilized because it was civilized. Man, though few will recognize it, is the most savage animal on the surface of the earth. He has mastered all other animals. He has exterminated them. He has fought continuously with the beasts and his own kind. He remains intrinsically bloodthirsty, savage, selfish, and intractable.

The conception of liberty is not natural. It is a phenomenon that has cropped up only at intervals in Greece, in Venice, in Switzerland, in America, France, and England. Right and justice are, in the natural scheme, no more significant than wrong or injustice. Strength is all that counts in the ultimate natural struggle.

Whether the democratic or the totalitarian forces win, the devil has been unloosed: the Dhjin is out of the bottle. Herr Hitler's total war is a war of fear. He has unleashed terror and destruction to achieve his ends. Terror and destruction beget their like; fear breeds fear, horror breeds horror. Evil has become palpable, the miasma of a blood lust clouds the eyes of mankind.

What will begin, on the part of the democracies, as righteous indignation, if victory comes to them, will end as sadistic revenge. Herr Hitler began this war against women and children, against the old; against historic architectural beauties that are an integral part of the culture of the nations to whom they belong; but Herr Hitler cannot end it. This is a Biblical war—a war of extermination; and righteous men, roused to hatred, are in no way different from evil men. As it began so will it end, in hatred, in rivers of blood, in devastation.

The fleeing babes of Europe will grow up hating. They will teach their children to hate everything German. Prophets will arise. Calm men will be goaded by the women into actions that will gain momentum as the wheel of evil spins.

Can the men of devastated Europe be calmed? Can they be persuaded to stay their hands? Could they even be seduced into making peace with such a man as Hitler; with a people who, from the beginning of time, have overrun all Europe with their hordes? Can the women be silenced? Can the destroyed cities and the dead rise up in the twinkling of an eye, to reassure them? Will there not be for years the gaunt specters of shattered towns and cities to remind them? Will not the children playing, for years, find bleached skulls in the hedgerows?

At first it was Herr Hitler and the Nazis. Then it became apparent that Herr Hitler represented the people of the Reich, and they became the enemy. Now both Herr Hitler and the German people have become no more than a symbol—the figurehead of the ship of evil which sails the seas of man's latent bestiality.

The devil took Herr Hitler to a high place and tempted him, offering him all the countries of the world. Where Our Lord put Satan behind Him, Herr Hitler took him by the arm and said, "Show me the way. . . ."

Those who have denied God may find Him, for if God has remained invisible, Lucifer is abroad. Thus may the world be saved, drawn back from dogma and schism, to the religion of humanity and love, by fear. The Golden Calf has grown into an ox. It is time that the ox was slaughtered.

The choice lies between might and right. Between accepting the yoke of servitude, necessary even in a free country to co-ordinate it for its own protection, or the spiked collar of slavery. Your home is your own only if you are ready to fight for it. Your body is your own only if you are ready to lay down your life. Those who will not fight will find themselves physically dispossessed. Those who will not die are, already, spiritually dead.

The ultimate natural struggle is now taking place. The struggle between ruthless material strength and spiritual strength. On the organization of its spiritual strength, on the unselfishness, not of the nation as an abstract idea, but of every man and woman within the nation, does the safety of England and America, and the future existence of democracy and freedom rest.

Either way, win or lose, the impress of National Socialism is on the world with controlled currency, and trade by barter. Money has ceased to have meaning, except as convenient counters, within national boundaries. And the trade of the future will be based on values that are apparently arbitrary. A ton of copper is, under old conceptions of value, worth more than a ton of cotton, but to a nation with a surplus of either, they are, in point of fact, worth nothing, their only value being what can be got for them. You can't make a copper kettle with cotton and you can't make a cotton sheet with copper.

On a desert island a ham would be worth an unlimited number of dollars because the ham will sustain life, and the dollars are useless without a complex organization of shops, manufacturers, and trade behind them. It is therefore useless to think that the conditions of free trade and business that have grown up in a pre-war civilization can continue. The old order has gone forever. It is not now a question of how many industries will be government controlled but of how few will not be.

The revolution has occurred. That it has occurred silently behind the smoke screen of war; that it has occurred without panoply, as part of a wartime economy, is in a sense its own justification. Already, bankrupt countries have been forced into a system that shows the greatest efficiency and the least waste.

There is no possibility of denial that the pre-war democracies were, economically, in the hands of a few groups who controlled their world policy, and gave some justification to the charge of plutocracy that was leveled at them. These interests worked silently. They were behind the scenes, but their effect on international affairs and policy was enormous. Corporations, banks, insurance companies, affiliations of industrial groups, were the actual rulers, the anonymous rulers, of the democracies.

It is probable that their power has gone for good. As the rich and leisured, as a class, have gone. The old social, economic, and political structure has been superseded.

For good or evil the world is in flux, and will remain in flux, taking various forms, governed by expediency, until it finally cools, and crystallizes into a shape that is at present unguessable. It may take five years, or five hundred, before anything approaching order comes out of this world chaos; before public life, which is the aggregate of millions of individual lives, assumes a more or less permanent form. It is probable that the whole legal system, the system of traditional morals and ways of life, will be changed either suddenly by a disastrous occurrence, or slowly, in the years to come. It is certain that every change will be fought by those reactionaries whose material possessions and positions would be affected by such a change. It is equally certain that no reactionary movement can succeed. The best that can be hoped for is a slow socialistic progress that will allow time for adaptation, rather than the swift and bloody change of revolution.

Too much has come out in this war. The radio, the newspapers, and the magazines have given us too much information about mismanagement in high places, for the general public ever to be lulled into co-operation with the forces and interests that controlled the pre-war world.

The man in the street is clear that it is up to him to win this war—if he can. This applies equally to the common man in Germany and the common man in the democracies. It is a fight to a finish.

Victory, when it comes, may not be the proof of justice, or right and wrong, as we conceive them, but only of the efficacy of one system and the failure of the other.

If nations are unable to adjust their small differences, if they are going to be unable to weld themselves, by their democratic ideal, into a solidarity at least comparable to that of the totalitarian states, they will fall beneath the onslaught of those states.

England has put her liberties in pawn. She has chosen a leader. That is probably the only answer there is, for to cling to the lesser rights in these days, is to lose the great ones. No one, except the few who were favored by it, is prepared to state that the pre-war civilization was completely good and without fault. It worked by trial and error, by an approximation, which took some wealth away from those who had a great deal and gave it, as a palliative, to those who were destitute. Not enough was taken from the rich to change their ways of life, and not enough was given to the poor to do more than alleviate their penury.

Taxation was based on a percentage scale without regard to actual values in terms of goods. The ratio of taxation was considered in terms of figures instead of terms of comfort. A man with $50,000 a year could be taxed $30,000 without losing any real comforts. He would lose only luxuries. Whereas a man with $1000 a year if taxed $10 would have to forego some necessity.

There is a very definite upward curve of comfort, in the lower income groups, for every hundred dollars increase per annum; but the curve becomes less steep as the income, beyond a certain point, is raised. Increase in luxury is substituted for increase in comfort, then in super luxury, and finally there comes a point where nothing further is attainable since everything is available. These differences could be illustrated in women's coats . . . no coat at all . . . cloth coat . . . cloth coat with fur collar . . . fur coat, lapin, fur coat, muskrat . . . mink . . . supermink . . . Russian sable . . . chinchilla. The difference in comfort value between muskrat and Russian sable negligible.

Comfort, with its corollary of contentment, is important. Luxury, with its corollaries of snobbery, competition, and waste is useless. Human values are dependent on human service rather than on incomes, which may be derived from inherited wealth, or even from activities that are, in the widest sense, anti-social, ranging from respectable armaments manufacture to political rackets and illicit drug traffic.

Men are not born equal. The struggle for life is continuous, but men are born, and by that fact alone, entitled to shelter, subsistence, and some measure of happiness. Possibly a combination of birth control and sterilization of the unfit will become necessary. It is a natural law that the simplest organisms increase the fastest since they have the highest death rate; but science, in the form of child welfare, has upset this natural and brutal selection, and general franchise has given the simplest organism power equal to that of the more complex, and the numerical power to outvote it. Considered objectively and without sentimentality, this is a paradox that would be tolerated in no business.

Physical and mental fitness remains of paramount national importance. Not marriage, but who shall bear children, is a question of national importance, since the unfit and the misfit become national charges. A sound illegitimate child, provided it does not suffer from the stigma of its birth, is of more national value than a moron born in wedlock.

These are bitter fundamental truths—the truths of the farm yard and the laboratory, that have become incorporated in the eugenic policy of the Reich. They are truths that will become, in a different form, embodied in the laws of all countries in the future. They existed in a minor form in Scandinavia. Marriage itself, which has been taken out of its sphere as the association of a man and a woman for their mutual benefit and the production of children, and has been put into the economic sphere, is unquestionably breaking under the strain of modern life. Divorce, which has been, and is, considered immoral, is actually a sign of a high morality—desire for perfectionism and a refusal to tolerate the brutality implied in a life contract where the partners have come to hate each other. America, where divorces are common, has a higher moral standard than England where they are rare.

These questions, apparently irrelevant, are tied up in the revolution that is going on today, not only on the battlefields of Europe and Asia but in the minds of men. Solitary battles are being fought out by the men in the streets who are trying everywhere to reconcile practice with precept—and to whom, at last, the vast gaps between *what is* and *what ought to be* are being bridged by *what is possible*. So much is possible when the artificial barriers of tradition and accepted usage are torn down that men are aghast at the stupidities that they have tolerated for so long.

The legal defense of a criminal has been turned into immunity for that criminal, in most cases, where he has the money and the power to evade the processes of the law. Medical help is dependent for its efficacy largely on the economic status of the patient. Political corruption has been accepted as a necessity of government and has permeated the whole social and economic democratic structure. The corruption of the French politician, the French press, and even the French army, undermined the Third Republic of France. It had seeped through the whole mass of the people till everyone was corrupt and demanded percentages and donations as a right. Every French cook demanded five percent for every purchase; every taxi driver was a blackmailer in a small way; every doorkeeper could be bought. It was a rot that demoralized the nation.

In England the remnants of the great caste system were not corrupt, but effete and tied by tradition to an Empire no longer willing to be ruled from Downing Street. In addition, the enormous vested interests of England were so diversified that their control with inadequate and pacific statesmen at the head of affairs was impossible.

But in England, in France, and in America there were, and are, men who, living in the democracies, were ready to betray them. They were men who said, "Better Chamberlain and Daladier"; who would rather make peace by appeasement and dishonor than face a war which would change things. They are the men who, now that Chamberlain and Daladier have gone, say, better Hitler than true democracy. They are the jackals who tore down Reynaud and who, if they can, will tear down Churchill; who, in America, say better Hitler than President Roosevelt.

These men, standing high in the government, prove Herr Hitler's contention that a plutocracy controls democracy; prove that God and Mammon cannot be served at one and the same time, that the right hand cannot point one way, and the left, another.

The democracies have been betrayed because they were ready to prefer the flesh-pots of an industrialized Egypt to the ideals of democracy to which they gave lip service. Deluded by riches, they have thought in terms of riches without service, leaving service without riches to fools and visionaries. They have denied the truth, and stuffed their fingers into their ears when they heard it.

They cannot in any circumstances deny that the truth was told them. They can only affirm that they did not hear the still small voices that called . . . the voices of Churchill, of Reynaud, of de Gaulle, and of Roosevelt. But these men called to duty. They called away from self-interest and self-indulgence, and the few who heard them looked back and were paralyzed, were turned, like Lot's wife, into pillars of salt.

Today there is no sense of duty, there is only a sense of gain, a desire for self-fulfillment. Even the churches have been afraid to cry out against a change in values. The church, allied to business and vested interest, supports the system of palliatives and half measures. The church is regimented, and is employed as an instrument of the established order, as much as the police. And yet what has the church to do with the established order? The church has only to do with right and wrong. It should not be concerned with property or interest. The church should live by virtue of its impartiality, instead of dying, stifled, under the weight of its possessions.

We know now that there were men, interests, that refused in the earlier stages of British and French preparation to place large orders for armaments abroad, who preferred to take the risk of unpreparedness, and keep the work at home, in their own factories. For those men, those interests, thousands of Englishmen and Frenchmen have died—their lives thrown away in the effort to stem steel with flesh and blood. Those men who died were the simple men, the common men, the men in the streets.

It was these interests that toyed with appeasement, that were, because of immediate profits, ready to sell the future of their peoples. It was these interests that built up Hitler by loans and were, on the eve of war, about to float another German loan. It was they who sabotaged the Russian alliance in the vain hope that Russia and Germany would destroy each other. These were the men, the interests, who introduced wishful thinking into the realms of diplomacy, and insulted the integrity of the people they represented by not believing those people capable of hearing the truth, or sacrificing themselves to support the free constitutions under which they lived.

World issues cannot be reduced to a profit and loss account. The gains and losses which are in the balance cannot be computed in millions of pounds sterling, in milliards of francs, in billions of dollars. The place for the money changers is not in the temple of freedom. Nor are the fluctuations of the stock market a true gauge for the temper of a people.

For many years politicians have been considered as out of the ordinary stream of life. Few have been respected, but people did not want to be bothered with politics. Politics was an apparently necessary, though not very savory, evil. An opposition was a check on the activities of the party in office—such a check that it prevented that party from taking any step which might prove unpopular for fear of putting a weapon into the hands of their political opponents. Politics had become a profession, often a last resort for those who had failed in making an economic success of other professions. There was the interesting phenomenon that, whatever happened, the same names remained in headlines of the papers. The posts were changed, but the names were the same.

Today the word politician stinks—it has acquired a stigma, a connotation that will cling to it forever. Today the common people must become politically minded, must know what is going on, must refuse to be spoon-fed. They must unite in the great issues and leave the small to take care of themselves.

That this will happen is inevitable—the only question is will it happen in time? For time is now the vital factor. Not merely time for rearmament, for hypothetical preparedness by the voting of large sums of money for this or that, but for a national solidarity of all classes, all religions, all ages into a national whole, vowed to the principles of freedom, even at the cost of comfort and of life itself. Only those prepared to die have the right to live.

* * *

Modern German literature has fully explained the aims of the German Reich. Nor is this new. Their heroes are Barbarossa . . . Frederick the Great . . . Moltke . . . Bismarck. Frederick the Great who said, "War is a trade in which the least scruple would spoil everything." Of his own people Heine said: "Christianity—and this is its greatest merit—has occasionally calmed the brutal German lust for battle, but it cannot destroy that savage joy. And when once that restraining talisman, the

Cross, is broken . . . the old stone gods will rise from unre-
membered ruins and Thor will leap to life at last and bring
down his gigantic hammer on the Gothic cathedrals. . . ."

"This is no mere fantasy. . . . The thought always precedes
the act as the lightning the thunder. . . ."

"Never doubt it; the hour will come."

The Germans have gone further than any other people in
advertising their intentions. In *Mein Kampf* by Adolf Hitler,
in *Raum und Volk* by Professor Banse, in Alfred Rosenberg's
Der Mythus des Zwanzigsten Jahrhunderts.

In each case when the English translations are not expurgated
of those passages likely to arouse alarm, the rights of free trans-
lation are denied by the German publishers under the international copyright laws. Nevertheless students translated them,
and placed the information in the hands of the authorities, who
apparently had no time to consider them—just as they found
no time to consider the reports of their military attachés or
secret agents. There will, when the time comes, be found no
lack of information pigeon-holed in the foreign offices and
chancelleries of what was Europe. The information existed. It
was available; but beside the information, there also existed men
who were unwilling to stir the public from its lethargy. There
would have been danger of panic. Business, that strange new
god, would have been dislocated by a national demand for
armaments, for protective alliances—even an alliance with Russia. The fact that the one thing Germany could not stand was
a war on two fronts, was lost in the terrible capitalist bogey of
an alliance with a communist state. Russia has never been a real
danger. The country is too big, too occupied with its own problems and development. Nor has communism ever been a serious
danger except in the event of serious reaction and repression.
Nor is it possible to ignore communism, or its principles, despite
the fact that it is now discredited, by assuming that it does not
exist. It is an interesting sidelight on modern democratic civilization that everything unpleasant—cancer, venereal disease, re-

form of the marriage laws, drunkenness, crime, and prostitution—are all ignored as major problems. Modern politics appear to be related to the art of conjuring—the skeletons in the national cupboards are replaced by the rabbits that come out of the politicians' hats.

Were the English people told that Ewald Banse said: "We confess that it gives us pleasure to meditate on the destruction that must sooner or later overtake this proud and seemingly invincible nation, and to think that this country which was last conquered in 1066 will once more obey a foreign master"? It was something they should have known. Why were they not told?

* * *

The National Socialist movement can only be understood by a close study of its bible. German foreign policy has followed almost exactly the program laid down in *Mein Kampf*. The German people read and believe in it more fervently than Christians read, or believe in, the Bible.

There are no heretics or half-believers in Germany—Adolf Hitler is the true Holy Ghost, the Messiah. He is the reincarnation, not only of God, but the embodiment of the true German spirit. He believes that "Nature knows no political boundaries, and that the strongest in courage is her favorite child to whom she promises the right to exist as master. That the German sword must win soil for the German plough." He believes that "An alliance whose object is not a future war is senseless and useless."

He has forbidden the reading of the Old Testament and produced, under the sponsorship of Reich Bishop Ludwig Mueller, and Bishop Weidemann of Bremen, a revised edition of the New Testament in which the words of Jesus Christ are twisted to fit into the conceptions of the new national philosophy. *Blessed are the meek for they shall inherit the earth,* has been paraphrased as *Happy is he who is always a good comrade; he will make his way in the world.*

It has even been officially stated that a man who thinks he can reconcile National Socialism with Christianity is neither a true Christian nor a true National Socialist. Such Christianity as is at present tolerated within the boundaries of the Third Reich is a sop to the public opinion of Italy and the United States, and to the older inhabitants both of Germany and the conquered states. To allow them something, some spiritual comfort, does little harm provided they are not permitted to teach their faith to their children. These men and women who still believe in God, who still, in the secret recesses of their souls, are not satisfied that Herr Hitler is really the Holy Ghost, will die off and be replaced by children brought up in the new faith.

Hitler is a believer in attrition—the attrition of souls by repression; the attrition of free thought by propaganda; the attrition of hostile populations and individuals by starvation. Even the blockade of Europe may fit into his scheme. The people of the Reich will not starve at first. The others will starve and by their deaths, not only may living room for the inhabitants of the Third Reich become available, but the problem of the disposal of the earlier inhabitants of those lands may have been accomplished by his enemies. Such as survive would inevitably hate those who starved them, and favor the Germans who kept them just alive by feeding them on such foodstuffs as were not needed within the borders of the Reich.

The foundation of the successful organization of the National Socialist regime is its ruthless logic. Its comprehension of first causes, and its development of cause and effect into an organized weapon of repression and rewards. The good Nazi can do no wrong. The good man who does not belong to the party can do no right. Justice is what serves the interests of the German nation. "The law and the will of Adolf Hitler are one."

In the press of events the German and Italian children have been forgotten. The millions of babies who march with little flags in their hands singing "Heil Hitler . . . to arms . . .

Germany awake . . ." The millions who pass through the various conditioning phases that will turn them out standardized products of the world's greatest war machine. It is this scientific conditioning that has produced the fanatical fury of the German soldier of today. It is his belief that death on the battlefield is to be regarded as a longed-for conclusion of life. Every book, every song, continually repeats the words—sword, blood, fury, hate, battle, death, glory. The children are reared with blood-clouded minds; with no ideal beyond a brutal Nordic conception of themselves as supermen, or as the mothers of supermen.

Nazi education consists of training first the body to endurance, then the character to further endurance, to that last ounce which only discipline can supply, and finally the intellect, to rationalize the whole, into a mystic belief in the ultimate ends of the Aryan race.

Children of six go to the Grundschule, at ten they go to the Oberschule for eight years. Then comes compulsory labor service followed by two years military service . . . after that they may go to the university or directly to work. But by that time their wills have been broken. They are machines, the instruments of anyone of superior rank. That is the danger of discipline— the blind obedience that is so thoroughly inculcated that it obeys rank without principles or scruple. It knows nothing but the orders of its immediate superior.

In addition to the schools a child has to attend, it also has civic responsibilities. At four, a boy child joins the Kindschaft, at ten the Jungvolk; and at fourteen, the Hitlerjugend. A further development is the Adolf-Hitler-Schule, where those showing exceptional merit and having the correct physical configuration and pigmentation, are trained to be leaders. As a beautiful girl in England or America hopes she will be able to go on the films, so does a blond blue-eyed boy hope to go to the leaders' school. At the age of twenty-five the picked members of these schools enter another phase of their education. They are advanced to one of the Leader-Colleges for three and a half years. These men are a selected aristocracy, picked as race horses are picked, for looks and possible performance. They are tested as race horses are tested, for their endurance, and capacity, under the rigorous conditions of their training. While they are attending this school they are required to marry; and should a cadet of one of these colleges be cashiered for misbehavior, he is immediately put to death as are his young wife and children. He has learnt too much to be allowed to live. These leaders are still in the making. The first will complete their education in 1955 though it is said that owing to the exigencies of the present situation, their education is being forced.

National Socialism divides the inhabitants of the Reich into three main categories. Foreigners, subjects, Jews, Poles; foreigners who happen to be born in Germany; and citizens. A subject is on the same footing as a foreigner, except that he is without the rights that a foreigner can claim as the citizen of some other state. The subject is without rights. He is a slave, a beast of burden, utterly at the mercy of the caprice of his masters. But not every German born of pure German parents is a citizen. He must be German in mind and in spirit. He must go through his labor and army service, and then, if he is physically fit and has a good political record, he will receive his citizen rights, and the diploma which entitles him to marry. Should he fail in any way, he can at any time be deprived of his rights and reduced to the status of a subject.

A German girl is brought up with one idea . . . that of motherhood. She remains a subject until her marriage with a citizen or the birth of her first child.

There is only one aim in Germany—only one end. The boys must be trained as soldiers, the girls as mothers of soldiers. Their minds, crushed by this iron discipline, derive a sense of security in the solidarity of their organizations, and the universal creed of the state. *Esprit de corps* attains its greatest heights by such mass suggestion. *One Fuehrer . . . One Reich . . . One people.* The spirit of comradeship makes, theoretically, the whole eighty million people of Germany into one great family. It includes every German outside the Reich—every man and woman and child of German blood wherever they are, and whatever their other allegiances. They, those other distant brothers, are the keys that will unlock the world to Germany. They are the forerunners of German culture; of German trade and of German conquest.

Chapter Four

The Result of Circumstance

NOTHING IS FORTUITOUS, neither democracy nor National Socialism, nor fascism, nor communism. They have all sprung up to fill some spiritual and political vacuum. They must all be considered in this light, as part of the world process—none is final since there is no finality.

Like, dislike, fear, and admiration are all equally irrelevant when considering a process. Fact must be accepted, as change must be accepted; and truth, overlaid by dogma, tradition, and custom, must be uncovered till its values are again laid bare. Basic facts that have been repudiated because they are unpleasant must be faced and dealt with by action, instead of blindness and wishful thinking.

There can be only two sides to the question of democracy. Those who are not actively for it are, by their passivity, against it. The hope that things will pass, or that they are not as bad as they seem, is false. Things will not pass; and are even worse than they seem if we do not, willfully, blind ourselves to them. If we have not, in the last twenty-five years, become so inured to horror that it has lost its meaning; unless our imagination is so blunted that we cannot visualize the march of the refugees; the terror of Dunkerque, or its heroism; the fury of the battle of England and its implications.

Even the names of these battles . . . the Battle of Flanders . . . the Battle of France . . . the Battle of England have the ring of finality, the ring of total war, of extermination.

It is hopeless to imagine the possible resurrection of the defeated nations unless England holds out. Nations today can be blotted out, by starvation, by sexual segregation, by sterilization, by despair, and by forced mass migrations. They can, within a generation, be utterly absorbed, their language and culture utterly destroyed. There are no historical precedents for today. There may in other times have been an equal will for destruction, but there was not the mechanical means of destruction, or the mechanical means of holding enslaved peoples in subjugation.

It is not generally realized on what a slender numerical thread the culture of a country stands. In the English *Who's Who* there are forty thousand names—that is, one thousand persons per million are sufficiently prominent to be included. These men and women are statesmen, members of Parliament, doctors, engineers, officers in the army and navy, lawyers, writers, painters, musicians, sculptors. . . . They are the leaders of the country in all fields. Double it, that is eighty thousand. Double that again—a hundred and sixty thousand. . . . Say two hundred and fifty thousand . . . a quarter of a million . . . make it a million, and you have the whole culture of England. All the business men, all the professional men. The American percentage is probably about the same and it is on these men that the ultimate issue, the culture and government of any country, depends. If they are good the government is good. If they are bad, then it is bad. Their position is due to the temper, and nature, and taste of the people in those countries. To their taste, to their toleration of graft and corruption, or in their lack of toleration, and insistence on high standards. Supply, even the supply of prominent men and leaders, is dependent on demand. The demand for politicians everywhere is slackening— they have even ceased to entertain—as the defects of government by party politicians have become public knowledge, ventilated by disaster.

Monarchy has probably received its final blow, and such kings as are left, remain more or less powerless hereditary presidents—focal points for national solidarity, anchors, which in some curious way reconcile the anomalies of the present with the historic grandeurs of the past.

The King of England represents an immense spiritual value, a belief that surpasses the material fact of his existence. The king can do no wrong. The king, in a way, represents on earth a kind of godly function—a kind of immortality that exists within, and because of, the crown. For the king cannot die. As one king expires another takes his place. The king is dead . . . long live the king. By virtue of this, English monarchy produces clarity, and lack of confusion in the minds of Englishmen. Kings, who once represented the most autocratic form of government, now represent not only free constitutional government, but the one strand that remains constant, whatever form that government should take.

The concepts of liberty—liberty of thought, of expression, of worship—are equally possible in a constitutional monarchy or in a republic. Liberty and true democracy seem synonymous; without the one the other is impossible. But these words, though they are so often used, are rarely thought of except as words. They are removed from their context of service.

There is probably no country in the world with a greater sense of individual rights, citizen rights, than the United States of America; but, to many, individual freedom is interpreted as the right to individual license. The purchase and carrying of guns, and the playing of radios without regard to people in the vicinity, are equally regarded as rights, and their infringement resented.

The scale of human values in the United States seems to include extra notes at the top and bottom of the scale. There are at once greater idealists and more brutal murderers. There is more genius and more illiteracy. There are more factions, religions, races, and isms than anywhere else in the world. There are anti-Semites, anti-Roman Catholics, anti-Negroes, anti-Germans, anti-British.

There are the great financiers and captains of industry; there are the workers employed by those industries; and there is an immense middle class that hides its ideological confusion by a cynical hard-boiled attitude towards everything—reaction, communism, and political corruption. Occasionally this section of the American people combines and cleans up such situations as have become intolerable. Then it relaxes again and the evils which have been driven under ground slowly raise their heads and the cycle recommences. The issues of law and order, of crime, of the color question, have never been faced in all their aspects and ramifications. The private citizen is helpless against rackets that lead to the highest places and yet it is, in the end, the private citizen, the man in the street, who suffers most and who, if he could co-ordinate his efforts, would be able to stamp out the indirect taxation he pays in poor law enforcement.

Individual freedom has been considered possible without service to the state—producing an anomaly, in which each man does the best be can for himself without regard to others. Freedom which should be a bond, a religion, has developed into a philosophy of personal isolation and "go-getting." So far has this gone that there are admirers of Hitler's methods, just as there were admirers of the gangsters from whom he drew his inspiration.

The government by the people is not respected by the people, which, on analysis, means that the people have lost their own self-respect. The gross evasions of income tax by the rich and the "gimme" attitude of the poor are both examples of this outlook. That these factors were present in other democracies in no way improves matters. It only makes them worse when the enslavement of those democracies, because of these defects, is considered.

Charity cannot replace justice, nor can sentimentality replace sentiment, or the pursuit of money be reconciled with patriotism, when money is made in such a way that it is contrary to the best interests of the country. The pursuit of happiness is not a personal matter, for no happiness can be purchased at the expense of others. Complete freedom is complete anarchy. The apparent failure of democracy is due to too many freedoms in matters which concern the general public and too few in those which concern the individual alone. The carrying of arms is a public danger. So is the ease with which the violators of traffic laws evade punishment. Whereas birth-control and the free choice of parenthood, is the most personal of all decisions.

Modern legislation in the democracies has been towards liberty—has been on the whole "labor" or "leftist," but the objection to a "leftist" movement is that it produces an economy which only "rightists" can run. Communism, and the state control implied by communism, is the forerunner of dictatorship, just as "big business" and its implication of combines and corporations, is the forerunner of plutocracy. Thus, extreme reaction produces communism and extreme communism produces reaction. Nothing could have been more reactionary or autocratic than the Czarist rule of Russia; nothing more communistic than the rule of Lenin; nothing more reactionary than the rule of Stalin.

The organization of German labor, from its first social insurance laws of 1883 and the reintroduction of guilds in 1897, was the beginning of a system under which German labor organizations became something not far short of organs of state administration. Even before the World War Germany had a planned economy—it had subsidies, state assistance. Trade penetration, particularly in South America, was part of the imperial scheme of peaceful penetration throughout the world. Even then, a sphere of influence was recognized as tantamount to a mandate, or protectorate, and as a kind of halfway state towards that end.

The post-war situation in Germany, during the Weimar Republic, was comparable to that of the French Republic under Blum—the workers demanded more money for less work. And the government, owing to the power of the labor groups, was coerced into trying to achieve this impossibility. On the one hand, the workers resented any reduction in wages or the lengthening of hours. On the other, the employers, seeing disaster ahead, attacked the government for its failure to reduce wages and lengthen working hours.

Assailed equally on both sides—by the extreme leftists, and extreme rightists, by the communists and conservative reactionaries—the government was bound to fall. Its policy of trying to please everyone ended in its pleasing no one, and in leaving a vacuum which the National Socialist order has so ably filled.

Freedom is contrary to the German thought pattern. The German demands safety, the protection of insurance societies, of bunds, guilds, clubs. The German is not an individualist. He likes to have things forbidden because by this other things are implicitly permitted. Life, in all its functions, is in one sense complicated by restrictions but, in another, simplified to the level of the kindergarten—confusion, even the confusion of thought, which is always controversial, is something the German tries to avoid.

He likes sacrifice. Its barbarity and fanaticism appeal to his sense of the dramatic and, lacking cynicism, he imagines sacrifice must serve some useful purpose. It is said that all the German wants is to work and live out his life. In this he is like every other man, but he is prepared to relegate authority further than other men, and it is this faculty for unthinking obedience which creates the German menace.

The National Socialist regime has merely accelerated all that was German; accelerated it to such a furious pace that the machine, were it to halt, would rip itself out of its foundations. Militarism, the Teuton dream of world conquest, of German superiority, of slavish devotion to naked power, now spins so swiftly that more and more must be done to keep it moving. The machine must not stop, for in all Germany there is nothing left to prime it again.

The German attitude of mind is the logical result of a series of historic processes that go back to the cold pre-dawn hour of civilization . . . back to the black Teuton forests where the German gods lie—untamed, undead. By the accident of time and place, by the developments of science, Adolf Hitler has been able to step into a position that was made for him by these historic circumstances; by the hereditary psychosis of the German race, and the vast unrest of a world already shattered by the first world war and the near collapse of the mechanistic plutocracy which caused it.

By means of the radio and the press, by means of his oratory, by means of his own very lack of education, Hitler has been able to strike into the hidden roots of German folklore, into the hearts, the minds, and the blood of the German people.

It is to blood and not to brains that he appeals. It is blood and sacrifice that he demands. These are his. He plays on German emotion as a violinist plays on his instrument. He is one with the instrument. Like a centaur, he is one with the horse he rides, indistinguishable from it. If he is victorious, the world will go down trampled beneath the hoofs of the German stallion. If he loses, that horse must be destroyed. The horse is the military soul of Germany. Hitler and the Nazi party are only the head of the horse. The body is German youth, in millions, reared to destruction by Hitler, whose mind, untrammeled by academic knowledge, was free to think of vast achievements undisturbed by the forces which an educated man would have known were against him.

Hitler's education ended when he was thirteen. It ended at the age when the immature boy's mind is interested in heroes. He dreams of heroes, he sees himself as a hero—as a deliverer.

An artist, thinking in abstract terms, Adolf Hitler identified himself with heroes of the German tradition. He resented the fact that he was an Austrian and went back to history to prove to his own satisfaction that the Germans and Austrians were one people. He saw Germania as Andromeda and himself as Perseus. He could cut Germania's bonds. He would marry Germany. He would see visions. He saw them. He went into high places and saw the countries of the world below him, spread out within the reach of his hand. He would give them to Germania . . . his wedding gift.

In all this there was the overcompensation of the unsuccessful son of a small official; combined with envy of the rich that soon, as he gained power, became hatred. An overcompensation that, because he was not German, he would give Germany more than any of her sons had done. An overcompensation for the hatred he had for his father; for his failure to get into the school where he wished to study painting. An overcompensation for his love of his mother, which was great enough to deny him the love of other women, canalized his energy into a political program of world conquest, and world order according to his own concept.

He studied . . . he read omnivorously. And he had a strangely selective mind. He was able to take from everything he read, observed, or was told, just that part which would be useful to him. The Nazi creed, and the development of the Nazi ideology contain traces of almost every culture, of almost every religion, and political formula. Each useful idea was removed from its context and welded into a solid, fantastically practical and workable whole.

Among its most basic principles was that of "the accomplished fact," the *fait accompli*—a method of looking round for national stables whose doors were not locked, stealing the horse, changing the brand, and then taking the matter to court himself, which immediately put the horse owner in the wrong. His "abused minority" plan supplied horses in almost every country.

But his development was not immediate. From his small be-

ginnings, he has gone logically forward, step by step. He has
never looked back. His contempt of the masses comes from inti-
mate knowledge of those masses, when he starved among them
in Vienna. He saw their stupidity, their gullibility, their suscep-
tibility to leadership, and their venality. His first party—the
"National Socialist Workers" party—was composed of restless,
unhappy men, the dregs of the German Republic. It was to
these "have nots," whose nebulous aims he crystallized, that
Hitler appeared as a savior. He wanted neither a return of
Hohenzollerns nor to strengthen the republic. The communists,
whom he hated, had destroyed the tradition of royalty, and he
knew enough of Germans to know that a republic was not really
to their liking. The republic was an accident due to the anarchy
of revolution. Law had broken down, the Emperor had fled;
there was nothing to do except to proclaim a republic. The German Republic was a political accident. It sprang up overnight
like a mushroom after rain. It had no roots. It never flowered.

President Wilson's mistake in 1917, when he declared that
the United States of America was not at war with the German
people but only with their government, was duplicated last year
when Great Britain asserted that she was not at war with the
German people but only with the National Socialist party.
Germany is a military country, with a military tradition, and a
worship of those formulae that create discipline of mind and
body. The German does not feel safe unless he is regimented
and ordered. Then he knows that someone is in control and is
relieved from the necessity of individual thought or choice. It
is this spirit that caused the students of the Berlin university
to cry that they were ready to "spit on freedom."

Hitler saw that peace of mind essential to all men could be
achieved in Germany by enclosing the mind in the steel box
of restraint. But though the box was steel, he padded it with
slogans, doctrines, and such a censorship that only the outer
world knew of its existence.

Within the ideology of National Socialism it was and is

possible for people to live contentedly if they are willing to be told what to do and think, willing to be herded to work, and to be sent on holidays, as cattle are driven from field to field. Such content is bovine content. It is the submission of mass matter to the minority mind, which is the Nazi machine, whose power rests in its armed forces both civil and military, in its creed of ruthlessness, in its suppression of justice, and denial that the word "mercy" has meaning. Such contest could be gained only when there was a single party, dominated by a single man, whose doctrine was everlasting and infallible . . . unchangeable.

Hitler kindled the fire by his singleness of purpose, his oratory, and his appeal to hatred. A born master of the art of expediency, he was quick, from the beginning, to see how everything could be turned in his favor by the simplest means. Means so simple that no one had thought of them before—a distorted psychology, an appeal to buried instincts of mankind, to their avarice, their lusts, and greed. He has re-created Valhalla, where gather the battle dead. The great hall of five hundred and two score doors, where a thousand can march in abreast to feast to the glory of Odin, served by the battle maidens till the crowing of cocks is heard, when they go out to fight again till noon, then returning to feast once more, their new wounds healed, till in the never-ending combat of the following dawn they are renewed.

He studied dramatic entrances . . . the use of flags, of flood lights . . . the art of keeping people on edge by making them wait . . . the appeal of marches, songs, and patriotic music. He found that an audience which would remain unmoved at eleven in the morning could be swayed to the highest pitch of passion at eleven at night. The night, and the things of the night, he made his servants.

Deutschland über Alles . . . Wessel's last greeting to the Germany of tomorrow . . . the cavalry march of Frederick the Great . . . Lutzow's *Wide Verwegene Jagd* . . . all served their turn.

Flags, regimental colors, gigantic storm troopers in uniforms standing like granite, Teuton gods. He played on his own simplicity—"I was a corporal". . . . The plainness of his dress, typical of his inversion of accepted values, made him stand out, by its dullness, in the brightest assembly. His emphasis on comradeship, his identification of himself with the mystic past, with the German Reich, and the German people, led the German people to identify themselves with him and with the Reich.

Not only has he great gifts of oratory, he has also immense endurance and can speak for hours, holding his audience— making them laugh or cry, love or hate, as he wills, leading them to fantastic heights by the auto-intoxication of their belief in him. Nothing is left to chance—even the desks from which he speaks have switches that indicate the effects he needs—more light, less light, spotlight, colored lights, music of different types. It is probable that even his inspiration, which cannot be denied, is produced by diet and fasting.

But basically, his success is due to the fact that a republic is contrary to the German tribal desire for panoply and hero worship. It is too ethical, too cerebral, and at the same time insufficiently mysterious for such an emotional people. It represented liberties that are contrary to their habits, and which they did not like. To the conservatives it was a Socialist regime that verged on the Bolshevik; to the workers, who had hoped for communism or neo-communism, it was conservative. And to the bureaucratic middle classes it was chaos, and an inflation which threatened their security.

No one had done anything to obtain a republic. No one understood or approved of a republic except those intellectuals who were subsequently eliminated.

The German people wanted an Adolf Hitler. They produced him. They are individually and collectively responsible for him. The will of the German people is still the unconscious urge of its psychological heredity. It is questionable if the majority of the people in the Third Reich consider the Nazi rule tyrannical.

To them it is the logical rule of a military state. And to them, a military state is the only kind of state. They are, more than any other people, the most capable of being hypnotized by the sight of marching men, inflamed by music, oratory, and appeals to their historic and ancient destiny.

The brutality of their system springs from roots in the national character; from their worship of strength and their sentimentality—sentimentality being the related opposite of brutality and sadism. It is sentiment that causes a man to risk his life to save a child. It is sentimentality that causes a mother to keep the nursery of a dead child intact with its crib, toys, feeding bottles, and clothes. The one is the ability to sacrifice oneself, the other the inability to sacrifice one's memories.

Of war and warriors there are two great concepts—that of the Chinese, whose civilization has probably yet to be equaled, and that of the Germans, who have never been really civilized. The Chinese despise war and the soldier. The Germans praise war and the soldier. These two concepts, like those of democracy and National Socialism, are irreconcilable.

The democratic compromise is that a citizen should be trained to arms, so that in case of necessity he can defend his rights. Compulsory military service is no more the forerunner of dictatorship than compulsory education, or the compulsory paying of taxes, or the enforcement of the traffic laws. It is, in a sense, a violation of the rights of a free man, that he should be compelled by law to do anything, even to drive on the right side of the road, or be forbidden to park his car opposite a hydrant. The democratic attitude was summed up before the Revolutionary War when Patrick Henry, speaking in the Virginia House of Burgesses said: "Is life so dear, or peace so sweet as to be purchased at the price of chains in slavery? Forbid it, Almighty God! I know not what course others may pursue, but as for me give me liberty or give me death."

Hitler's first problem was how far subversive, that is, democratic and socialist, ideals could be eradicated by violence. History showed that it could not be done. Russia had tried it for centuries. Brute force and violence could act only temporarily. What was put down by force in one place sprang up in another. Therefore force must be supplemented by a spiritual ideal. The new ideal must be inculcated to fill the place of the destroyed ideal. By this combination of force and spiritual education, the new state could be founded on lines that would be everlasting. A Reich that would go on for a thousand years —its principles immutable and unchanged.

It is completely possible that in the event of German victory this will happen. National Socialism is not rooted in the sand of a variable ideal. It is planted in the blood and clay of a great race. It is the logical outcome of profound racial characteristics insulated from contacts with the outside world . . . the world of ideas and theories. There is nothing to prevent this new civilization crystallizing and taking a final shape. It will require only from twenty to fifty years, and each year that passes will make it more probable. It requires only that those who remember other times shall die of old age, or other causes, and that a new generation shall be reared in the belief that this is the only natural way of life. To imagine anything else is wishful thinking, to hope for anything else unjustifiable optimism unless it is stopped by force.

National Socialism, which rose by force of arms, can only be destroyed by force of arms, either from outside the Germanic world, or from within it, or from without and within simultaneously. Starvation by blockade is force of arms. Famine, and pestilence which follows famine, are force of arms considered in terms of cause and effect. Propaganda is force of arms, for without force of arms to support the centers from which it issues, there could be no propaganda. The gradual tightening of the hostile stomach, the shrinking of its gut, by attrition, the gradual weakening by propaganda of the will to resist, the slow surrender to fear through bombing and nerve wars, and the final and terrible assault, the blood bath, are the ultimate ends.

There is actually nothing new in the National Socialist creed. All that is new is a mind capable of fitting the thousand pieces of this puzzle together and springing it on an astonished twentieth century.

Hitler knew that the assumption of the civilization of the world was entirely incorrect. On any basis, even that of table manners, it is the perquisite of a minority in those countries that are popularly considered civilized.

The peasant population of all countries remains very near to the soil. To them he gave a religion of the soil, of the farm, that they understood much more fully than any intellectual and mystic creed of behaviorism or ethics. To the working, urban masses, living from day to day, and from hand to mouth, who remain very near to rebellion at all times, he gave a Jewish scapegoat and the hope of escape into better economic circumstances. To the middle classes, the bourgeoisie, he gave the promise of economic and social security.

Incapable of reason, and without actual integrity on any level, Hitler saw the great working masses of his country, and of the world, as a ferment needing only the stimulus of a popular creed to drive them forward under his leadership. He saw that all classes believed in superstitions. Education failed entirely to remove beliefs inculcated by word of mouth, through the centuries, to children. Beliefs utterly without scientific foundation were clung to . . . superstitions about black cats, cross-eyed men, going under ladders, magpies, salt, the number thirteen, Friday, touching wood, a singing glass. He saw that men's beliefs were those with which they were brought up, that a man being a liberal, a conservative, a Democrat, a Roman Catholic, a Lutheran, a Mohammedan, was a matter of early environment and not conviction. He saw that great church festivals had had their dates changed to fit in with barbaric festivities whose importance was too deeply rooted in the depths of the human mind to be eradicated. He saw, in fact, that man, as the most intelligent animal, was the most trainable animal.

His psychologists, whose only justification for their researches in the muddy depths of the human soul was to lighten the burden of their bewildered patients, have turned their knowledge to the production of neuroses by terror. They have thought out, in their studies, surrounded by the books of great humanitarians, methods by which sane men and women can be driven mad.

His chemists have turned from production to destruction; and all science, that double-edged tool that man has forged so patiently, is pointed inwards, towards man—its creator. Engines designed to move men more swiftly from place to place, now only move death more quickly.

The great paradox has come about. Man, not great enough for the knowledge he has acquired, unable to apply it intelligently, has become the servant of his inventions. Where we imagined we had gone forward, we have gone back. And in the totalitarian countries, now all continental Europe, those who refuse to put their knowledge to the services that the state demands of them are destroyed, or made fugitive, hunted among the woods and mountains, or lost, after escaping to America, their nervous systems shattered.

The Library of Louvain has joined the University of Warsaw. Once again Louvain has been destroyed by the same men—or their sons. Seven hundred thousand books have followed the other books—the books burnt in the German marketplaces to make a holiday of learning for the people of the Reich.

Books do not burn easily. They have to be primed with gasoline or bombed with incendiary bombs. Seven hundred thousand books is a great number of books. The books were not cheap books. They were great books. They were bought by the pennies of the children in the United States. The German children put their pennies into the building of a pocket battleship.

Perhaps the German children were wise in this, their generation. Perhaps, after all, books are nothing . . . abstract thought nothing . . . beauty nothing.

What good are books to the illiterate, and who now will have time to read? Books make people think, and who now dares think? And this is not the end. More libraries, more museums, more universities will go up in flames. To implant the new culture the old must be destroyed. While books live and men have access to books the human spirit cannot die. When we can read what those who preceded us have suffered we ourselves are able to suffer. When we can read what they hoped we ourselves can hope.

The Library of Louvain was no accident. There was nothing fortuitous about it. Its destruction is part of a plan that has been considered to the last item, to the last nail that Herr Hitler is trying to drive into the coffin of our civilization.

Chapter Five

The Doubtful Mind

THE MAN IN THE STREET is bewildered by the mass of contradictory news he receives and must endeavor to co-ordinate; by the continuous and contradictory appeals to his emotions that he must somehow endeavor to rationalize. Countries he had hardly heard of become important suddenly, distances that he considered almost infinite become overnight hops by airplane. Maps that he was used to as a boy are unrecognizable, not only owing to the ever-varying changes of national boundaries, but by the actual method of their pictorial presentation. Today maps are presented, as they always should have been, by Mercator's projection, and West Africa is seen to be next door to Brazil and Greenland practically a part of Canada.

Men whose names he scarcely knew appeal to the common man directly over the radio. He becomes involved in world affairs wherever he lives. He finds that he has views, and that they change from hour to hour. He hears Senator Wheeler and thinks isolation is the thing. If he can stay isolated. He hears Churchill and becomes pro-English—"they are certainly up against it." He hears Hitler and is angry that Hitler should dare to talk to him like that in his own parlor. He hears pacifists and is all for peace. He hears interventionists and feels that intervention is necessary. He is told that the United States has nothing to intervene with even if it wanted to. And he becomes livid that so great a nation should have been so lax about its own defense. "Who is responsible . . . ?" He hears that some destroyers are so top-heavy that they dare not put to sea, that the guns at Panama are obsolete, that there is only one modern anti-aircraft gun in the whole country, that the army is smaller and less prepared and up-to-date than that of Switzerland.

He listens to the news analysts. He has his favorites among them. He gets to know their voices. He is annoyed when they have a holiday and feels defrauded. He hears American reporters talking from the capitals of Europe—all contradicting one another. He tries to imagine the conditions under which they work. He knows they can say only what they are permitted to say; that most of it is for enemy consumption. In the magazines he sees statistical pictures of little men, and little ships, and little tanks all arranged in rows, purporting to show the relative strengths of the contestants. He reads lead stories and editorials and articles about food reserves, oil reserves, man power, machine-tool production, and loses himself in the mathematical maze. If he could make up his mind he is not allowed to. He is given no time. There is his work during the day, there is a shelf to put up in the evening, or the grass to mow, and the baby is cutting its first tooth—that, for the moment, is more important than the war news. Yet he knows that the baby is not more important than Hitler, and he also knows that the baby is more important than Hitler. For a man lives from the inside to the outside. His immediate concern is himself, and those who are, by the circumstances of his life, a part of himself. It is only when world events threaten the events of the home that public and private interests converge into the mass opinion that demands action—protection, isolation, the enforcement of the Monroe Doctrine.

But if he cannot make up his mind, he is forced to think. He has to. For months he did not want to. It was over there. But

South America is not over there. The Caribbean is not over there. Canada is not over there. Alaska is not over there. They are all perilously close. And all this talk about the British navy. Why was he never told about it before? Surely he ought to have been told. And he ought to have been told that the Monroe Doctrine was an English idea. An arrangement between Canning and President Monroe. The ordinary man has worked hard to get his education. But a lot of things seem to have been kept from him. He begins to think back to the last war. A hundred and twenty-six thousand Americans killed. But twenty-four thousand are killed each year in automobile accidents. There was sabotage in the last war. There were American ships sunk by submarines a few miles off the American coast. Cape Cod was shelled, and all that happened while the British navy was afloat. Maybe America is not so far away from Europe after all. Maybe it would be better to fight while you still have friends rather than wait to fight alone.

He thinks of the Republican and Democratic conventions, the cheap oratory, the pretty girls, and wonders what they have to do with the present crisis. He thinks of England and France and wonders how democracy fitted in with their actions in Abyssinia, Spain, and China.

He thinks about democracy in general, an abstraction that he has accepted without really considering. You could do what you liked in a democracy, say what you liked, but was that all there was to it? How did it work? Did it work? The papers were giving a new significance to the Spanish rebellion. They said it was the first battle of the war. Things began to fall into a pattern. The battle of Spain . . . the battle of France . . . the battle of England . . . and the sideshows like Czecho-Slovakia, Poland, Holland, Belgium, and Norway . . .

He finds there is nothing new in Germany's interest in Spain, that Bismarck had referred to the "Spanish fly on the French flank," and that neutral Spain, under German influence in the last war, was a threat to the undefended French rear and to the British domination of the Atlantic and the Mediterranean as Bismarck's policy of an alliance with "one's neighbor's neighbor for purposes of encirclement" was put into force.

The Italian interest now coincides with the German. Control of southern Spain and Gibraltar is necessary if Mussolini's dream of Roman grandeur is to come true. A republican Spain would have been no assistance in a war of totalitarian aggression, therefore a republican Spain must cease to exist. The Nazis even referred to the Spanish civil war as Europe's war for supremacy in the Mediterranean. Nor was this secret in 1936. Sir Abe Bailey, the South African magnate, warned England that a Franco victory would turn the Mediterranean into an Italian lake and give Germany a hold on Spanish Morocco where, in 1911, there was nearly a war over the Agadir incident. In the last war three million tons of Allied shipping were sunk owing to Spain's pro-German neutrality and the use of her harbors by German submarines.

New Ceuta, opposite Gibraltar, has been heavily fortified, and Cadiz and Malaga are, to all intents and purposes, Axis forts whose guns are manned by German and Italian gunners. There are new bases, new forts behind Gibraltar, new airfields, and the Canary Islands menace the South Atlantic.

The ordinary man finds something strange in all this. In the fact that it was permitted. In the anomaly of a non-intervention that allowed intervention. Slowly it has seeped into his mind that the democracies might have, among their rulers, many whose traditions and personal interests make them prefer totalitarian methods to those of true democracy. What is now known only confirms that suspicion. The legitimate government of Spain was not communistic, but it was liberal and unaristocratic. It was a government of the people; had it not been, the people would not have fought as they did. Spain accepted the principle of non-intervention, and her subsequent bitterness was due to this principle becoming one-sided, and favoring the rebels to the detriment of the legitimate government.

Liberal Spain would have associated herself with the democracies of France and England who now are paying the price of their repudiation. A free Spain would have entered the United States orbit by throwing her influence, in the cause of freedom, into the struggle that is now taking place in South America. That there is no love for old Spain in the Latin-American countries is due to the residual hatred for the old, imperialistic Spain that exploited them. A rejuvenated, free Spain would have been welcomed. It is probable that now the harm is done, British agents are endeavoring to rouse Spain again, just as today they are using Haile Selassie in Abyssinia to foment a rebellion against the Italian conquerors whom they acknowledged so short a time ago.

Talks, formulae in the chancelleries of London and Paris for leaving Spain to Spaniards were followed by more talks, more formulae, and a press censorship that kept the people of England and France in ignorance of the actual facts until it was too late. The sympathies of the masses of England and France were with the Spanish government, but the business interests and the upper social strata of those countries were, tacitly at least, pro-Franco, pro-fascist. It was thought that the rebel generals, once they were in power, would be easily bought, and that the financial interests would be able to wean them from their allies in Germany and Italy. Here again was the delusion of money-power, and the fear of national freedom which induced a policy of appeasement, of peace at any price, that threw democratic Spain after Abyssinia and China, and led to the debacle of Czecho-Slovakia.

The German propaganda machine which described the Spanish government as Red was enlisted by the democracies to justify their apathy. The U.S.S.R. and Chile, Mexico, and Brazil alone had ambassadors in Madrid. The other countries were represented by consuls and the legations were filled with pseudo-refugees from Franco. The French Embassy at one time had two thousand who, while claiming the rights of asylum, were only waiting their chance to strike the republic in the back. It was in Spain that the term "fifth column" was coined.

Preoccupation with their financial interests prevented England and France from seeing the actual issue, that the Spanish war was part of the world revolution, part of the battle that is now being fought not merely between nations, but between conflicting ideologies. Not between nations, because in all nations there are sections of the public who favor fascism—the British Fascists under Mosley, the French Croix de Feu. There were similar groups in Belgium, in Holland, in Norway, in Denmark, in Poland. There are such groups in the United States and in the republics of South America. It is also conceivable that England and France did see the actual issue and refused help on that account.

The most dangerous Fascists are not aliens, they are nationals and they are violently patriotic. They believe in their countries, but not in the form of democratic government to which their countries have subscribed. Throughout the three years of German and Italian intervention in Spain no real effort was made to arrest it. The best that can be said is that it was connived at; the worst, that it was encouraged. Nor is the excuse that intervention, or rather the enforcement of non-intervention, would have precipitated a European war, sound. The war has come, a much worse war than would have come had the great democracies stood by their principles instead of considering only their pecuniary interests. Such men as Winston Churchill and Reynaud saw where non-intervention and appeasement would lead, but they were not followed. And now they, with those who would not listen to them, collectively, must pay the price. Reynaud, perhaps on the scaffold; Churchill leading his people grandly, towards what may be Britain's final battle.

There is something magnificent in the answer of a nation to the call of arms. This was apparent in Spain when men, women, boys, girls, and even children flung themselves into the cause that in their hearts they knew to be just. That spirit was lacking

in France. There was neither will enough nor confidence enough
to inspire the nation. The finest soldiers in the world have
good cause to consider themselves betrayed by their leaders, by
the lack of preparedness before the war, and the slowness of
preparations once it had begun, by a policy of defense that
threw away their greatest military asset—the "élan" that had
made them famous in attack. It is this same magnificence which
is becoming apparent in England. It is only by this spiritual
certainty, when it is added to good leadership and adequate war
material, that battles can be won. It would seem as if each
country had a soul deeply rooted within its soil, its culture,
and its traditions, and that national effort is only possible when
it is fully roused. Contemptuously described as mass hysteria,
it cannot be dismissed, any more than hysteria can be dismissed.
Both result from psychological causes, both are the escape of
steam that precedes the explosion. Both are signs that private or
public endurance has reached its limit.

It is almost universally the Spanish Episcopate identified itself
with reaction, even declaring that to vote conservative was to
vote for Christ, a slogan that would have astonished our Lord
who, in His time, was not considered a conservative. The Popular Front on earth was bracketed with hell-fire in the future by
priests whose mission should have concerned souls rather than
votes. Unquestionably, here and there, in all countries, humble
priests and ministers of religion have preached the pure word
of God, but these priests and ministers are not those who rise
highest in their respective churches. The church seeks temporal
power and the support of those who have it. It seeks collections,
tithes, and legacies, and it panders to those who can fulfill its
wants. The true missionary is overshadowed by the religious
spellbinder whose sophistries can convince his congregation of
their rectitude.

It is hard to understand how the Vatican can tolerate the substitution of German Neo-paganism for the religion of Jesus
Christ; very hard to believe that an organization so well-in-

formed as the Roman Catholic Church should be uninformed about the truth of the atrocities committed. Hard to believe that the Roman Catholic Church has not been influenced by its temporal possessions, its physical possession of the bodies and properties of men through its possession of their souls. With the democracies, the church outside of Spain was non-interventionist, while within the country it was violently pro-Franco. Non-interventionist it has remained, in spite of the bombings of cities, the machine-gunning of fleeing refugees, in spite of the breaking of written promises, of oaths, of betrayals. So that doubt of the church, not only the Roman Catholic Church, but the other churches, joins the march of doubts through the minds of men. Men still wish to believe in God, but they doubt the church. They wonder what the church has done in the last half century to justify its existence or its claims.

Spain clarified the position for the dictators. It paved the path to Munich. The democracies would not fight. Not only that, they were ready to welcome such forms of totalitarian propaganda as justified their refusal to fight. The German "Why Fight for Sudetenland?" was adopted in England and France as a God-sent slogan.

As Franco advanced, the fifth column went into action. The balconies of the cities, as they fell, were draped with royal standards of monarchist Spain, crucifixes, and holy images. The Beatas, the pious women, ran through the streets calling on Phalangist youths to "kill the heretics."

An order was published that it was the duty of every Spaniard to think like Franco, feel like Franco, and talk like Franco. And the Civil Guard, with their three-cornered, shiny hats, reappeared riding in pairs along the Spanish roads. Their brutalities, in the name of order, were not surpassed by those of the Moorish troops. A campaign for spurious purity was begun by the Church. Dancing, play clothes, bare legs, and cosmetics were forbidden. Divorce was abolished. Civil marriage was abolished. A cult for Spanish youth, similar in pattern to the

cults of Germany and Italy, was put into force with such slogans
as "Life is warlike, by land, sea, and air we build our empire."

A youth movement is an integral part of the totalitarian
scheme of education. Youth must be taught to obey, to revere
and not to think. Already there is a youth movement in France.
The Phalanx in Spain has complete control over the machinery
of the nation. It is not part of the state, or government. It is
the state and government, just as the National Socialist party
is the government of Germany, or the Fascist party is the
government of Italy. Against the party there is no option, no
appeal, no justice. There is only repression and obedience.

* * *

The policy of the British and French after Munich was to
stall at any price, while they built armaments. This policy was
continued even after the outbreak of war. Nothing was done to
start really active operations against the enemy. The Maginot
line was manned, small raiding operations took place, the blockade began, but the tempo was not that of war. National enthu-
siasms were curbed while the preparations went on. Given time,
there was no question that the resources of the allies, being so
much greater than the resources of Germany, would give them
victory.

Time was then the factor. And defense remained passive
while time passed. As time passed, the morale of the allies was
lowered, they were bored. The troops were bored, the civilians
were bored. It was all very uncomfortable, very annoying; above
all, it was not what they had been led to believe it would be.
Industry, satisfied that there was no hurry, settled down to make
what it could out of a long war.

England and France settled down to what they imagined to
be the siege of Germany. The rounding up of aliens, of communists and fascists, proceeded slowly. The Germans were
considered more sinned against than sinning. Capital which
dominated the Allied policy was frightened out of its wits. It

had interests in Germany, interests in France, in Holland, Denmark, Norway. It was afraid of Russia. It realized too late that this fear had made the war possible, since fear had caused the mismanagement of the Russian negotiations in August. Able to think of nothing, it waited, hoping for the best—for internal trouble in Germany, for a Czech revolution, for something, for anything, to happen. The reports from observers of the Polish campaign on the strength of the German mechanized units and air force were discounted. Poland was not a first-class power.

Almost as a gesture the democracies became dictatorships—nominally as the best way to organize against the dictatorships they were fighting, actually as a protection to business and a safeguard against internal trouble. The view still was that when it was over things would fall back into a pre-war pattern.

Then suddenly things changed. Germany took the initiative, marched into Belgium and Holland. Allied armies were decoyed into the Low Countries and trapped there. Other French armies cracked under disloyal and inefficient leaders. There were reshuffles, there was the epic of Dunkerque, there was the incredible break-up of France, there was the bitter knowledge that the policy of stalling for time had defeated itself by giving Germany the initiative, and allowing, at home, the growth of the illusion that there was no urgency. Defeatism spread. Reynaud, who had come too late, was betrayed. Churchill, who may also have come too late, became the sole hope of democracy, vested in English dictatorship.

The war, contrary to Hitler's assertions, was not made by the capitalists, who were the appeasers, but it is likely to be lost because of them. Without understanding, these super-tradesmen hypnotized themselves with commercial statistics and took no account of national characteristics, literature, or trends of thought. Able to read the financial columns of the papers to perfection, they were unable to understand the sky signs of international unrest, or the significance of tanks, and airplanes blowing in the wind.

How nearly is the United States going to follow England's footsteps? In 1934 England had more planes than Germany, but in 1935 there was a general election and the British public postponed rearmament. The public has been blamed for this, but the public knows only what it is told. Butter is a better platform than guns. Butter got in. Here lies the danger of the party system, of election platforms which must solicit votes as a traveling salesman solicits housewives to purchase his wares.

And who are the men Doctor Gerhard Westrick came to see in the United States? What promises did he give them in return for their support of his suggestion that America loan Germany five billions of gold, and lower the tariff barriers to allow subsidized German exports into the country? If they know nothing else, business men at least know business, and if the national disadvantages are apparent to them they must be counterbalanced by some personal equivalent.

*   *   *

At last the war became real. Hundreds of thousands were killed, millions were homeless. There were battles between the French and British navies. The French were divided into two peoples—free Frenchmen and unfree. England became an armed camp, and then a fortress. Invasion, unthinkable a few weeks before, was awaited. Property, class tradition, possessions ceased to exist as a united England awaited the onslaught. War aims hitherto nebulous, though described as the restoration of the status quo in Europe and the defeat of the Nazis, were clarified, almost too fully, into the defense of England. To save life and liberty, life and liberty were enclosed in the straitjacket of a willingly accepted totalitarianism. Those who were left when it was over would have have to regain them. At the moment they were in pawn.

Since then there have been great changes in public feeling. When Sir Kingsley Wood announced the increase in the income tax to the House of Commons there was an outcry that the increase was not large enough. In America isolated men are demanding that they pay more taxes, that they can afford them. This seems to indicate the change—from a belief in unlimited private possessions to one of limited private possessions, to the theory that the state is the people, and worthy of the people's support. The very wealthy are now to some extent ashamed of their wealth; they feel its burden, they are not sure that they are justified in having so much when others have so little, and they are careful not to flaunt it.

The Declaration of Independence—which would be classed, were it written today, as proletarian propaganda—is by degrees assuming form as its interpretation becomes more clear. Great numbers of men now feel these truths to be self evident: that all men are created equal; that they are endowed by their Creator with certain inalienable rights; that among these are life, liberty, and the pursuit of happiness. This alone, for those who accept it, is the answer to totalitarianism.

The spirit of sacrifice, to which men gave lip service, is becoming a reality. This is a period of emergency that can be met only by a willingness to acknowledge the fact, and to meet it with that characteristic of all free men—their readiness to sacrifice themselves and their fortunes for the common good. Freedom, to exist, must remain active. Passivity, neutrality in the face of evil, is not freedom. Nor is there any freedom of choice between good and evil, between high standards and low, between the desire to give and the desire to retain.

The United States of America has stopped looking backwards at the war debt, and begun to think of the British navy, of the vulnerability of the Panama Canal, of its miniature army, of a new navy that would take six years to build, of conscription and military rearmament that would take a year and a half, of the workshops and dockyards of continental Europe with which it might soon have to compete. It began to stop thinking of the war as a super ball game and to listen to its prophets. There was no lack of them, and they all, with minor variations, said the same thing. Dorothy Thompson, Raymond Gram Swing, Westbrook Pegler, Major George Fielding Eliot, H. V. Kaltenborn and Walter Winchell all pointed out the dangers of the future in terms of the present weakness; all were concerned with the corruption of the courts and municipal administrations, with the inefficiency of the army, the lack of co-ordination in business effort.

The common man in America, the man in the street, began to wake up. All was not quite as he thought it was. He began to question the democracy of his country, the courage of its youth, the wisdom of a vaunted efficiency that led nowhere. He began to see that if it was to remain his country he must do something about it. He questioned even the position of American womanhood, the theory of child worship, and a culture of gadgets. His life, which had been so simple, became complex. There was so much to think about. There were so many decisions to make. There was so much to rectify.

It occurred to him that perhaps England should be given "all help short of war." He saw isolation in its real significance. The isolation of standing alone, friendless and unarmed facing enemies flushed with victory. He saw some of the anomalies of his time, the combination of surpluses and starvation; the lapse in reason that quibbled at war losses while homicide and accidents went by unnoticed. He doubted the economic system that had ten million unemployed, where 15 percent of the population received relief, where 40 percent have an income of between 1000 and 2000 dollars per year, and another 40 percent an income of under 1000 dollars a year—where 70 percent of the riches are on the Eastern seaboard, and most of that in the hands of women, and where 49 people have incomes of a million or more dollars a year.

It did not add up, on analysis, to the prosperity he had been led to believe existed. It did not add up to the American way, or the American standard.

He thought about education. There seemed to be no reason

why the elements of law, of justice and individual rights and responsibilities should not be included in the ordinary educational curriculum. The understanding of the actual detailed operation and composition of the legislature was less important to the ordinary man than the part he should play as an individual citizen. He had moral rights and legal rights, and moral and legal responsibilities. But modern education, in all countries, has been deflected into academic channels, or has been used as an instrument for conditioning children to fit into a particular pattern, even where that pattern has lost all semblance of relation to the actualities of life.

* * *

The English public school, in its present form, set out to produce young gentlemen capable of being fitted into the machine of Empire government. Above all, they had to be forged in an interchangeable pattern, and originality was invariably sacrificed to an outworn tradition, with the result that great Englishmen from the public schools have been the exception rather than the rule. The great Englishmen, and there were great Englishmen in other days, were produced by the old public school before the Dr. Arnold of Rugby period, by tutors and the grand tour. The difference between the education and conditioning of the totalitarian states and England is one only of degree. There is as much snobbery in the National Socialist degrees of rank as in the English public school man's code of dress and sense of honor. That one is relatively good and the other bad does not change this. Neither is true education, neither consists of an objective search for knowledge. Both are a means to national ends and, because of this, produce reflex thinking that is biased and unsound. Produce, on the one hand, young Nazis fanatically inspired who are capable in good faith of the utmost brutality, and Chamberlains on the other who, because of their upbringing, are incapable of disbelieving a promise, or of coping with an unorthodox situation.

National Socialism is the result of those circumstances that forced it, as part of the German evolution, on the German people. English education is the product of an Empire tradition that required young rulers with a relatively fixed code of class honor and integrity. American education, while emphasizing the freedom and the greatness of the Republic, has failed to insist on a sense of individual responsibility, and has over-emphasized the necessity for economic success and a socially competitve form of life.

The lack of understanding between nations is not only due to dissimilarity of language, but to dissimilar forms of conditioned education, so that the nationals of one country cannot understand the desires or aspirations of another. As art is universal, so should knowledge, in the form of educational truth, be universal. Until all countries learn history objectively—learn to see it as cause and effect and not merely as a series of inexplicable victories, over-emphasized in their school books, and of equally inexplicable defeats that are glossed over—can there be any real understanding of international relations.

War is an effect, not a cause. Behind its psychological causes, the main causes of war are trade and mass migration. Only by pooling the raw products that are the actual cause of war, and by the free trade movements of products that are superfluous in one place to those places where they are wanting, can war be stopped. The League of Nations was an effort to achieve this, but it was sabotaged by national selfishness, disguised as patriotism, so that finally the only issues on which all countries could agree were a collective security that applied sanctions to the white-slave traffic and the illicit trade in narcotics.

Thus one of the finest conceptions the world has ever seen died slowly as its functions atrophied through lack of use. The League without America, its formulator, without mechanics for international law enforcement, and with England manipulating to turn it into an instrument for selfish purposes, failed.

Germany and Italy were always against any solution of diffi-

culties by negotiation. And the fear of war prevented the
League from acting decisively when the Japanese entered Man-
churia, when Italy attacked Abyssinia, or when Italian and
German troops were landed in Spain.

President Wilson's conception of 1918 finally died in the
arms of Mr. Chamberlain in 1938.

The modern disbelief in the Almighty seems to have resulted
in the substitution of a mythical someone or something in God's
place. In England and France the general belief was that someone or something would stop the war—Mr. Chamberlain, President Roosevelt, the three Scandinavian kings, Mussolini. There
was a pathetic faith in some unexplained circumstance that
never took place. Miracles, which were believed in while men
still worshiped God, were apparently still believed in when
man refused to believe in God on the assumption that such
belief was irrational.

God, had He been believed in, might have stopped the war.
Or He might not have stopped the war. But belief in God, and
the service of God, would have given the democracies a spiritual
faith that would have held them bound in unity. Strangely, the
politicians, like Mr. Chamberlain, who were religious, and did
believe in God, did not believe in the Devil. More strangely
still, it is possible that a new faith will come upon the world—
a new belief in God—inversely, by the fact that the Devil is
being forced upon us, forked tail, flames, sulphur, and all.

That America can remain unaffected by the cataclysm, the
war, the results of the war, and the revolutions that inevitably
will follow it, is impossible. That the defeat of Germany will
not result in a reign of terror inspired by the Europe the Germans have defeated, and ill-treated, is also impossible. Even the
gold that America holds in this war is as certain to lead the
country into participation in world affairs as the gold it lost
in the last. Either Europe will have to be financed with gold,
or Europe will go off gold completely. The game cannot go on
unless the chips are lent to the bankrupt players. All America

appears to be united in the idea of national defense and rearmament, but quibbles at the military dictatorship it may entail.
National defense is not something that can be relegated to
others. It is national. It must concern everyone and everyone
must suffer and participate unless there is to be such injustice
as will bring revolution. It will be found impossible in America,
as elsewhere, to have the democratic cake and eat it too.

* * *

The news is disquieting. Day after day in the press and the
magazines new scandals are exposed, new accusations made,
each more bewildering than the last. Lindbergh, the hero of
America, with his German decoration and homing-pigeon mind,
is accused of appeasement and of favoring the principles of
National Socialism; Henry Ford, of a tie-up with Germany
through Edsel Ford's directorship and sole agency of the I. B.
Farben Industrie, a chemical and explosive concern.

It is surprising to read that Henry Ford was happy to accept
a German decoration and that he gave employment to Fritz
Kuhn. That the ex-king of England was supposed to have been
offered the throne of England by Hitler. That Leopold of Belgium betrayed his people through the negotiations of his sister,
the daughter-in-law of the King of Italy, with Mussolini. That
a British admiral, late head of naval intelligence, was an inti-
mate of Hitler's and a moving force in the "Link," the English
Bund. That American labor is under the control of ex-convicts.
That there are nine million underfed school children in the
United States. That Assistant Attorney General Thurman Arnold
has been preparing a suit against the big oil companies which
will prove that the public is being overcharged millions of dollars a year on high-test gasoline alone, and that this suit is being
slowed up on account of the delay such a suit would cause in
the national defense program.

It is astonishing to learn that the country is being blackmailed
by big business and labor alike, while every conceivable kind of

red herring is being drawn across the track of rearmament by direct foreign agencies, and indirect agents who have been deluded into ultra-pacifism as an answer to totalitarian aggression and who claim, with Ford, that preparedness for defense is also preparedness for war. That naval and military secrets have been sold to Germany. That patents vital to war industry are partially under German control. That the seepage of German and Italian agents into South America has been far greater than was hitherto imagined. That the country is riddled with saboteurs and with *agents provocateurs*.

The main difficulty of democratic government seems to be that any direct action it attempts is described as fascist. Procrastination, discussion, trial by three or four courts have come to be regarded as the only democratic procedure. Anything active or final is fascist. Obstruction, argument, and appeal to higher authority from every legal decision have become synonymous with liberty.

The Associated Press reported in August that the convention of the C.I.O. United Automobile Workers of America adopted a resolution expressing "unalterable" opposition "to any form of compulsory military services at this time."

Anthony Nowakowski, 22 years old, of Detroit, who said he probably was the youngest delegate at the convention, spoke for the resolution and declared that "military regimentation smacks of fascism."

"Young people do not have to be forced into the army to defend our nation," he told the convention. "We will defend it voluntarily. If the young people are forced to become part of a military machine, they may later be used as a weapon of the imperialists in this country."

The Earl Browder and Harry Bridges controversies further illustrate the cleft stick of the democratic legislative system. Bridges asserts that "Democracy is not to be defended by imitating the arbitrary legislative devices of despotism."

While Browder, when asked about the bill that would enforce the registration of foreign controlled or directed organizations, stated that such a bill would undoubtedly constrict the activities of the Bund, but added, "Any incidental embarrassment this bill might give the Bund would be much more than offset by the victory that would be gained by the Nazi political philosophy."

Truths, half truths, or lies, these are things that have appeared in the press during the last few months. These are the things that disturb the man in the street, the things that he must reconcile within himself, the difficulties he must meet. He can think no more in terms of personal security, or in terms of life as he has known it till today. The situation, both public and personal, is beyond hedging. It is beyond everything but the knowledge of good and evil.

There is an immense criminal population at large, thousands of whom are known homicides. There are an incredible number of guns, rifles, and revolvers in the hands of men with criminal records, there are over ten thousand machine guns unaccounted for. There is a political tie-up with the various rackets that makes successful prosecutions all but impossible. These criminals and crooked politicians who can not be bought one way can surely be bought in another. There are rumors, more or less substantiated, of criminal organizations and rings that spread from coast to coast; there are men who held responsible civic positions in jail and others on the verge of jail. There is continual sabotage reported in the papers, much of it described as accidental with such vehemence as to suggest the contrary. There are papers published in foreign languages that deride all that democracy stands for. Propaganda leaflets are coming in through diplomatic channels to supplement others printed on secret presses for distribution throughout the country.

There are bunds, organizations, and fraternities of all kinds that are permitted, though they are known to be prejudicial to national order and perhaps even, when the time comes, to national existence. There is hatred fostered by various groups against Jews, against Catholics, against Negroes, against capital, against labor. There is a public mentality that likes cheer-leaders and drum-majorettes, that stands for immorality classed as amusement, that tolerates walkathons, children eating live gold-fish, organized sensationalism of any kind, and there are people who will, at the drop of a hat, organize vigilantes, purity campaigns and prohibition programs, and who would, in fact, at any time attack anything of which they did not approve in the name of the public weal, without reference to public opinion.

It comes as something of a shock to find that perhaps the Americans who pride themselves on their freedom and unconventionality are the least original, most conventional, and most easily led of all peoples. Continually moving from apartment to apartment, from state to state, from one job to another job, from one amusement to another amusement till their restlessness becomes almost an hysteria. They are stampeded by advertising into an orgy of competitive buying "on time," of living on time, even of traveling on time. Their culture, that deep-rooted American culture which created the United States, has become submerged under a welter of time-saving appliances. Considering themselves hard-boiled and cynical, they bolted like rabbits when Orson Welles announced that men from Mars had landed in New Jersey. Considering themselves smart business men, they fall for confidence rackets, gold bricks, and continental impostors. Considering themselves hardy, the maneuvers in Louisiana proved even the soldiers to be soft and unwilling to walk. The automobile has amputated the legs of America, has sent America road mad in its processions to the shore and to the country, in its desire for endless and meaningless rides on wheels. The motor car has replaced the American home for everything from love-making to murder. The fact that it is now mechanically possible for anyone with a car to go from New York City to California carries with it no spiritual necessity for such travel. Movement, by the destruction of space, has destroyed craftsmanship. Before America can go forward she is likely to have to go back.

The errors of an almost defeated Europe are there for all to see. The errors of a materialistic, selfish civilization that failed utterly on every count, a civilization whose apathy rivaled its cynicism, whose smugness destroyed its faith, whose riches betrayed its strength.

And with this example before her America seems to be making every false step that Europe made. Searching her boundaries for experts she discounts their opinions. Each man, instead of seeking service, is trying to force it on his neighbor with a "what's in it for me" instead of "what we must do to protect ourselves, our wives and children, from the threat of external invasion or internal collapse."

The choice between conscription and voluntary service is a choice between all the horses, or just the willing ones. All the men or just the bold, the adventurous, and the idealistic. A matter of sacrificing the best male stock in the country or merely, by conscription, a percentage of that stock.

By conscription, which is service, a nation can be made to feel itself a nation, made individually to feel its civic and national responsibility.

The future of the world is in the hands of youth, such youth, that is, as survives. And who can calculate the standard of their behavior? Who can tell what the results will be when whole nations have been shell-shocked, starved, and driven from their homes? When babies have seen their parents killed, when children have been transplanted, like trees, to foreign soil. When ruin and death have been accepted as normality, and blood has flowed more easily than water. Can hatreds thus born be stemmed by words? Who is to speak to them? Can broken minds be healed as simply as broken bodies? Who is to heal them? Can order emerge from chaos when the guns are silenced? Can those brought up to betrayal be trained to loyalty? Can the heroic dead be replaced by the heroic living? Can the effect of nocturnal alarms, of courage bolstered by despair, be dissipated and forgotten?

Can America, the last great democracy, survive without going back to the roots of the democracy, back to the ideals that made her great?

Chapter Six

The Dominion of Fear

PROPAGANDA HAD PREPARED EUROPE for war as vaccination prepares a child for smallpox.

It was a menace. It might come; it would come, but it had not come yet. "Peace in our time" was telescoped into peace today, was perverted into "make hay while the sun shines" into "make merry, for tomorrow we die," into a careless way of life, comparable only to that led when the Black Death was sweeping through Europe. It was a strange mixture of prayer, of dissipation, of preparedness and resignation. Prophets were heard on the street corners. They were shouted down. Who wanted to be reminded, since everyone knew? A moral miasma spread over the painted face of culture. What was the point of a morality based on fixed standards, since standards were no longer fixed, and were likely soon to disappear completely. Nature, the goddess of fructification, increased the natural urge of men for women, and women for men; forced it, as she forces flowers in a desert to bloom and bear seed, all in a week or two after rain, since the time is so short. A premonition of death was accompanied by a desire for compensatory reproduction. Children, perhaps the object of life, must be born into the totalitarian states as cannon fodder, into the democracies as the outward and visible sign of their lack of fear, as an overcompensation for the fear they felt.

Childless marriages represented the compromise between the natural instinct of reproduction and the civilized instinct for self-protection, the sexual act becoming symbolic and not functional. Money, since it had lost its value of implied security, became relatively valueless. Property was something taxable and no longer an asset. Life itself had become a bond that might be called in at any time.

For twenty years man, utterly unequipped to meet such metaphysical emergencies, had sat back and waited with an almost animal passivity for the end. Gaiety went with confidence. Children became cynical in self-defense. Music changed from sweetness to the nerve-tearing drum-jazz of the jungle, to the hopelessness of slave-born spirituals, to the nostalgia of the "blues." Ancient ballads were replaced by meaningless lyrics in a kind of musical amnesia. Painting swung to surrealism. Beauty, because it hurt too much, and now seemed improbable, was called banal. Literature became more realistic than Zola. Epstein replaced Rodin.

In the art of the last twenty years, the story of those years is written. For art, being the unconscious expression of the artists at any given period, expresses the unconscious mass mind of that period. The artist is no different from the man in the street. He is the man in the street keyed higher, driven harder, and forced against his will to express, in art, the unconscious public trend of his time.

Belief in war came to be accepted as a protection against war. If you said it would come—it wouldn't. Just as when you take an umbrella out with you it does not rain. So people remained convinced that this new folklore, this continued talking about the coming war, would keep it away.

Yet when it did come, they were not really surprised, they were not shocked, they thought how lucky it is we have been thinking about it for so long. Just as they might have said, when it rained after all, how lucky we brought our umbrellas.

Only the dreamers had said, "Behold, a flood is coming. Make haste and build an ark. Be quick, get ready, buy airplanes where you can, train men, build ships, conscript the wealth." These were the fools, the criers in the wilderness. They were Churchill, H. G. Wells, and old Lloyd George.

But what after all were they? Churchill was too clever, a jack of all trades, and half-American at that. Lloyd George, an old discredited Welsh lawyer; H. G. Wells, a novelist. They did not smoke pipes. They were not accompanied by Cairn terriers. They did not carry umbrellas. They were not associated with heavy industry, a matter of paramount importance for a member of the British cabinet, presumably because of the respectability of pig iron, or the impressive weight of metal in comparison to the nominal weight of the human brain.

The truth might have saved France, but France the Mother had got lost, mislaid as she wandered from chancellery to chancellery, and Britannia was tired, having carried her trident for so long. Politicians, in all democracies, had dropped the heavy burden of leadership and picked up the feeding bottle of domesticity.

War, even before it began, had become a factor in the personal lives of everyone. They would take a holiday in September if . . . they would buy a car or a house if . . . they would have another baby if . . .

The war, with the accompanying "if" and "when" was present, a silent spectator, a real element, in every thought and act. Yet they still considered war as inconceivable—like God. They used the name of God in their oaths, and sometimes in their prayers, but they did not believe in God—not seriously. It was as impossible to believe that London or Paris could be razed to the ground, even after Warsaw, as it was to think of Mr. Chamberlain being translated heavenwards in a fiery chariot. Such things might be talked about, but they did not really happen. Bombing joined the policeman as another bogey to frighten children into obedience.

Oddly, the fear of gas was more prevalent than the fear of high explosives, or incendiary bombs, although gas has not yet been used, and its use seems unlikely owing to its bulk, expense, and doubtful efficacy. Perhaps gas was more easily understood. Everyone knew about gas stoves and the danger of gas, whereas few could visualize the result of great fires or explosions. The issue of gas masks in England was less due to public demand for them than to the desire of the government to make a gesture which would prove to the people that something was really being done. They served the purpose of comforters. When an air raid came you were not helpless. You could put on your mask. Another example of the way the British government, of that time, underestimated the courage and determination of the British people.

It was Munich that let the cat out of the bag. Everyone knew that the bag was full of cats—black ones, white ones, spotted ones, but no one had seen them before. Appeasement was an effort to tie another string round the top of the bag. It did, but Hitler ripped open the bottom. The cats were loose, the Russian cat, the cat called Franco, the Balkan cat, the Japanese cat, the cat of the French fear of Germany, that of German fear of encirclement, the English cat of world dominion with France. All that was left was the dead cat of the League of Nations.

The words "democracy," "dictatorship," "communism," were shouted. Banners flew in every European breeze. There were no definitions, only slogans and cries. Because some Jews were rich, the anti-Semites attacked all capitalists. Because some working men were communists, governments based on the capitalistic system feared all working men. And within the great wheels of public feeling were the lesser wheels. Jews who were allied with capitalism were also, in some way, allied with the communists. And this, instead of destroying the earlier argument only made it, by its irrationality, much stronger. Accustomed by mass advertising the public, in its emotional moments, substitutes slogans for thought.

It was all very disturbing to the business interests. In the last war there had been profiteers. After it there were several thousand new millionaires in the United States alone, but in another war this would not happen. The people, the fighting men, had become wise to this form of prostitution. There would be revolution, and there might be revolution anyway. It was revolution once the war began its active phase.

There was plenty of cause for it, and more than anything else, a revolution must have a cause. It represents the efforts of men to adjust themselves by violence to conditions that have become intolerable. It is the turning of the proletarian worm when it is pressed beyond endurance. No leader can produce a revolution. The most he can do is to touch a spark to the explosive material of suppression, or kick an already smoldering pile into open flame. Malnutrition to the verge of starvation is at once the main factor conducive to revolution and, at the same time, the greatest motive-power for production in the hands of the exploiters of labor. The juggling of these two forces is the basis of capitalistic production.

The laboring man, the wage earner, with a year's salary saved in the bank, is in a position to negotiate with his employer. The union strike funds are based on this theory of economic, collective security. They are employed to tide over the wageless period of negotiations, but have never attained the size necessary for such purpose owing to the low rate of wages received, and the often criminal administration of such sums as have been collected.

But unquestionably a skilled tradesman without debts of any kind, and with enough money banked to carry him and his family for a year without acute discomfort, is something that few employers like to consider. The possibility of starvation is the big stick that the employer holds balanced over the head of the worker. But the balance must be kept continually adjusted.

Should nutrition fall below a certain level, efficiency is lost and dissatisfaction increased to the point of actual danger. Should starvation be continued, the savage temper of hunger is followed by the apathy of starvation. It is this fear that prompts the German appeals to America for food for the conquered countries. Germany fears first the revolt of hunger, and then the apathy of starvation with which no methods of brutality will be able to deal. The wheels in the workshops of Europe will spin slower and slower without food. Then they will stop.

But even with comparatively high wages, the labor situation has been controlled by the appeal of advertising, by high-pressure salesmen who encourage the purchase of non-essentials on time. Debt in the white-collar class corresponds to hunger in the laboring masses. Success, even the smallest, is based on economic independence, but the trend today is away from such small successes. The little business man—the little grocer, and butcher, and drugstore owner—is crowded out by the big concern. The international pattern of zones of influence is paralleled in business. The corporation, the chain, the affiliation, the subsidiary company, are replacing individual ownership. From the greatest oil well to the cheapest prostitute there is little now that has not been organized into some form of combine.

The captain of industry is a dictator; strike-breaking organizations are storm troopers. Individual breakers of contracts are on a par with national breakers of contracts, and the great events of world evolution are followed exactly by the little events of personal evolution. A new world, with a new code, is taking shape. And what is the good of combating the great international dictators unless the smaller national dictators are combated?

Millionaires will become extinct as mastodons, mammoths and saber-toothed tigers became extinct, but they may be replaced by power millionaires, by party officials who, without money, have all that money could buy, if it still existed.

Money is still thought of as something real when its reality exists only in its latent value. Five hundred dollars, as such, is useless unless it represents an automobile, a fur coat or food for six months.

Power, in a totalitarian state, is money. Money, in a pseudo-democracy, is power. Money, if the world is to go on, must be wrested from its trend of dynamic increase towards more power, and be harnessed to the contemplative and benevolent forces of truth in the form of medical science, research, the improvement of social conditions, and the inculcation of those ideals of beauty that are becoming lost.

Revolution is possible only if the armed forces of any nation get out of hand. The means of revolution consist of four factors: the will for revolution, the mass of men who will become revolutionaries, the arms which they must possess to execute their design, and a leader. These factors are all present in Europe today, and are likely to exist there for many years to come. Just as the threat of war has been present in all minds for several years, the possibility of revolution is present in all minds today. By some coincidence the necessary factors of time, place, and circumstance may come at any moment. And equally, by lack of the necessary coincidence, or time lag, may never come.

Nor need revolution take the accepted and historical form. Actually, a revolution has been going on slowly since 1914. Since the English income tax jumped to one-and-sixpence in the pound, since death duties began to kill the big estates and fortunes, since the New Deal began the devastating program that, in the long run, may prove to have saved democracy in the United States.

It is questionable if anyone can justify the present economic system. It is without justification on any count, even that of its working, because it barely works, and then only when adjusted and tinkered with from day to day, almost from hour to hour. Nor are those who feel the present civilization a failure necessarily communists, National Socialists or fascists. There are many others who have no name or slogan. They might be described as Christians, though they would say that they belonged to no established church. They might be described as liberal-socialists, but both liberals and socialists are dogs with bad names. Yet, without a party, without a war cry, without propaganda or a political machine they are, most probably, the bulk of any civilized population, men of good-will, who are ready to give up a little of what they have so that others shall have more. It is this vast force of latent good-will, of unexpressed Christianity, that the politicians are unwilling to acknowledge and unable to deal with.

It is this force that is now stirring slowly to drive the money-changers out of the temples of their sacred governments. They who are beginning to demand definitions instead of banners and show-girls. And it is they who will, in the end, when they are roused out of their lethargy, produce an order that may approximate the Bill of Rights.

What is the good of talking of justice when there is little justice? Of equality when there is no equality? Of fraternity when there is no love? Or virtue when virtue must be its own poor reward? Man cannot live by bread alone, yet many have no bread. Nor will the crumbs falling from the rich man's table long satisfy the destitute who are ill-content to scramble for the leftovers of justice and political representation. Revolutionary literature has been consistently destructive. Hypnotized by its desire for direct action, it has failed to see that revolution, of a certain kind, is evolution and that it comes of itself, by a kind of biological subdivision of idea, of creed, of ideal and hope.

Just as in every man there lies hidden a dictator, the animal side of that man who would seize what he wants by force and impose his will on others, there also lies an ascetic, that would renounce his possessions, his life even, for the general good. Hitler's strength has been his appeal to both these sides. To the animal and the ascetic. To the sadist and the masochist, to the eternal paradox of human behavior that is forever trying to pull man down to the level of the beast, and to raise him up to the right hand of God. This may, eventually, prove the undoing of Hitler and his like, for never have the ideals of mankind been so bitterly betrayed. The older people in Hitler's Reich have been tortured into submission, the children torn from their parents to be inoculated with the hydrophobia of his conception.

Fascism, National Socialism, democracy, communism, the New Deal, republicanism, liberalism, conservatism, socialism, anarchism, and Christianity, all began as idealistic religions.

It is actually impossible to disentangle religion from politics. A man's political creed and his religious code are inextricably tied together. The masses are persuaded to believe in parties because they contain ideals and are constructive, but in every case the desire for power on the part of minorities within the party has destroyed the fundamental ends of every political and religious organization.

There is much good in every system, in every religion. They all contain spiritual similarities. The fundamental conceptions of democracy and communism are not very different. Liberty, equality and fraternity should apply equally to either. There is little fundamental difference between Christianity and Mohammedanism; both believe equally in God and a godly life; both condemn evil. The Mohammedan believes in one God, the creator of all things, in Adam, Noah, Abraham, Moses, Jesus Christ, and Mahomet as prophets. He recognizes the resurrection of the dead and a final judgment of the sins committed in life. He does not drink wine or play games of chance. He believes in prayer and almsgiving.

Failure comes in practice rather than in precept. And in practice, the democratic government has much in common with that of National Socialist government. Power in both is held by small groups of men or families. France was said to be controlled by four hundred families. England was controlled, very largely, by a class that was socially distinct from the masses of England. And the same applies to the United States. Everywhere there are men, interests, and corporations on whom the mantle of an obsolete royalty has fallen. Since they control the law, they can do no wrong.

The duration of the war can be expressed by the equation: $1940 + (a - b) = x$ (a is resistance offered by the democratic principle, b the effectiveness of the principles of National Socialism).

These symbols include the democratic people within the Reich and the nations under the Reich's protection. And on the other side the fascists who are a part of the population of all democracies; for as there is a fifth column of Nazi fascists working within every democracy, so there is a fifth column of latent democratic feeling working within every dictatorship.

Slowly, with infinite pains, the common man is putting two and two together and sees four spelled in a new way, spelled as *disaster* to himself and his way of living. He has no source of information other than that which is printed, no aid to his thinking but the selection he practices for himself. The common man, the man in the street, the man with the telephone in his hand, or the pen, or the shovel, is the man who will have to fight for his rights if he wishes to keep them, the man who must think of himself as the common man in its true connotation, meaning good, ordinary. The word common is the bond of humanity that joins all men together in such word combinations as common-law . . . House of Commons . . . common land . . . common good. Common has nothing to do with vulgarity, though vulgar itself once had the same meaning.

In spite of the United States treaty with Germany of 1920, which made the shipment of arms illegal, American corporations sold one and a half million dollars' worth of airplane engines to Germany in 1934 and even advised the Nazi government which type of engine they considered best for military purposes. Vital patents were leased to Germany on a royalty basis. This is business, just as the removal of the fluorescent bulb from the exhibit in the New York World's Fair, at the request of the utility companies, was business, because it con-

sumed only one-third of the usual amount of power. It is said
that the utility companies have also forbidden promotion,
through advertisement, of this new kind of bulb in the magazines. More business, more public service!

It can no doubt be shown to be undemocratic to wish to get
more and better light for less money, as it is undemocratic to
fight for liberty since by fighting for it, it becomes endangered,
while by not fighting, it will only be lost. No doubt the companies that sell eyeglasses are equally against fluorescent light.
So do the wheels within the wheels of democracy and business
turn, powered by the myths of liberty and public service. Illusion is substituted for truth, and paradox justified by advertising.

It is impossible to gauge the exact strength of the forces
operating in Germany: the force of Hitler, the force of the
Prussian Junkers represented by the army, the force of Himm-
ler's secret police, the force of any underground movement that
may exist, the Black Front, or any other, the latent force of
jealousy in high places. Who knows the feelings of the two
million Germans who have, directly or indirectly, suffered from
the Gestapo; the feelings of mothers, wives, and sweethearts of
the dead soldiers; who understands the hatred of the populations of the conquered countries? There remain finally the
neuroses of Hitler himself, which will not become apparent
until his first reverse.

Hitler made the army, but the army also made Hitler. The
aristocratic Junkers can, in their hearts, have little respect for
the Austrian corporal. The German army represents the most
powerful factor since it is divorced from everything except its
own destructive purpose. The soldier mind has reached its highest development in the forests and marshes of Prussia, in the
closely knit officer caste that marries only within itself, a class
of nobles and lesser nobility that in its solidarity is unafraid of
Hitler. It now controls Germany and all continental Europe by
its trained and disciplined millions. Hitler is at once the guiding
star, the figurehead, and the master; but he could easily, by his

own revived German mythology, become the scapegoat and the sacrifice to those gods that he has raised.

The worship of Hitler, which is a national asset, could still function if he were dead, if he were killed at the front, a martyr to the cause of German living-room. His death would change things but would not end them. Only the breaking of the Prussian arrogance, of the Prussian dream, and the crushing of the new German youth spirit can bring the possibility of lasting peace to Europe.

* * *

For years, secular education, which has followed closely in the footsteps of the old religious education, has failed in its definitions. Failed because definition and the scientific objective approach are pagan and serve no useful purpose in the religious scheme which consists in the collection of souls for the God it considers its own particular property.

The words heretic, unbeliever, Mohammedan, Buddhist are bracketed together. All are damned. They were never defined, classified, nor were their religions analyzed. Nor were adjectives considered in relation to nationalities or creeds. Good or bad were never dealt with in the fullness of their application. A good Hindu is obviously more worthy of respect than a bad Christian; by virtue of his goodness, his religion becomes a personal matter and utterly irrelevant. Inversely, a bad Nazi, from the Nazi point of view, approximates a good liberal, their ideological resemblances being greater than their ideological differences.

These artificial barriers of race, creed, color, and religion are now being seen for what they are, instruments used to incite one nation or creed against another, both externally and internally, so that the seething pot of artificiality and conditioned dislike boils the soup of the politicians.

The human race is of a single genus. Biologically any race can produce offspring with a member of any other race, and these children can breed again; they are fertile and not hybrids. There are no human mules. A black baby has no objection to a white baby, nor has the white any particular feeling of superiority. These feelings are induced by later conditioning. The interbreeding of races need neither be encouraged nor discouraged, since like inevitably tends towards like and tends to produce like. Exceptions are negligible and miscegenation, the result either of force employed in subjugating the colored female, or of free choice, in which case it is a coming together of the lowest strata of white and black, is of little real importance. Few respectable colored women, whether they come from Harlem or Natal, will willingly have anything to do with a white man. Nor will many respectable white men deliberately seek intercourse with a woman of color. By and large, mankind tends to stay with its own kind and in its own social level within that kind.

* * *

Pure, objective thought would cause the greatest bloodless revolution the world has ever seen. Business would break down completely in a world of philosophers who believed only in doing good, in looking for beauty, in the ultimate simplicities of family life, and who held that all art, all pleasure, should be public property, the personal possession of no single man, but the public and shared possession of all men. The truth must be sought in the old Anglo-Saxon simplicity of our tongue, in the English of the New Testament that permits no liberties with meanings. It is the liberties that have been taken with the spoken and the written word that have destroyed the liberties they describe, just as the perpetual repetition of prayers has removed their dignity.

It is still premature to describe this as an ideological war. That is what it will be—what it will become when ideologies are adequately defined, and the working out of their vastly different theories resemble each other a little less. National

Socialism, which began as the enemy of Bolshevism, has proved to be so little different from it that their merging has affected no change whatever in the lives of the people living under those regimes.

War is further complicated by the fact that combatants are forced to copy each other. Savages, in order to fight civilized troops armed with rifles, have to acquire rifles, and by using the rifles they become at least partly civilized; while by fighting the savages, and owing to the act of battle, the civilized troops become, in part at least, savage. Thus in order to fight National Socialism in its present form of dictatorship, which is not necessarily its final form, the democracy of England has had to assume the form of dictatorship with its accessories of repression, propaganda, and nationalization of everything that can be nationalized.

The war so far has been only nominally due to ideologies. It has actually been due to national competition for raw products in the minds of those who made it, and what they can get out of it in terms of goods, personal happiness and security, in the minds of those who fight it. Now in England they look no further than the retention of their homes. The fall of France, and the leap from passivity into activity, have left no time for analysis. That will come.

The anomaly is that the statesmen have been driven by the national demands for a politico-religious creed to take verbal stands which they are, in practice, unable to support and which they do not really understand. Every government exhausts itself in efforts to whitewash the sepulchre of its platform, and justify an ambivalence induced by the internal dissension of the factions within it.

The war party and the peace party exist everywhere now, though they are not vocal in the countries actually engaged. There are the appeasers, the dickerers, the pacifists, the cowards, and the traitors on the one side, and the belligerents, the halfway belligerents, and the fight-at-homers on the other. Yet even these two parties apparently so divergent are one in their ends.

Both want peace. Both insist on peace. The only difference between them is in their means of approach. Yet both want war,
for appeasement is a form of war. It is the surrender to aggression without fighting, it gives the enemy what they require
without the necessity of combat. It is war as the war of nerves is
war. It is the victory of the war of nerves. It is defeat by intimidation alone.

Even business is divided, the heavy industries being more or
less inclined to war or, better still, to near-war that will bring
them contracts, while the banks, insurance companies and building societies are for peace at any price. Here again is a vital
division of interest, since heavy industry is real and banking, in
all its diversities and ramifications, only a myth, a clumsy device for handling the products of industry. But these two
parties, the war and peace parties, are there all the time in war
or peace. They are the liberal and reactionary parties, they are
the passive and the active elements in every government, in
every family, within the heart of every man. They are the positive and negative forces whose tension balances all action.

It is fear that will drive big interests to war and fear that
will drive the man in the street to war. Fear has always been
the final governing factor of existence; fear of penury, of old
age, of death, of loss of face. Abstract fear is the price we pay
for our humanity. No animal is afraid except in the face of
danger. What is known as worry is the abstract fear of some unknown and anticipated circumstance. War propaganda and commercial advertising are both based on fear. Yet fear, under certain and not impossible forms of government, could be removed
almost entirely. Without the threat of fear, and with the happiness that the removal of the threat would bring, the dangers of
national and international competitive life would largely disappear.

The machine which has given man more leisure has also
removed him from his place on the earth, setting him up in high
places, in great cities, where he sees no earth, only pavements

and concrete, where his feet are never on the soil. The machine has bewildered him with strange sights and sounds, with thoughts that have no real place in him, and wants that are not real wants. Man has paid too high a price for his machines, as he pays too high a price for all things, even for life, in his assumption that he is entitled to happiness. Who speaks of happiness that is happy, save to say, "I was happy then," to speak of it in retrospect? The state of happiness being like that of death, a state of unawareness, a state of not being, of being lost in the beauty of the hour, be that hour an instant or a year.

The cross of man is his life that he bears easily in youth, with some glory upon occasion, but which at the end he is ready to lay down, its weight too great for the weakened spark that is in him.

Man is tied by a dual chord. The ascetic and the libertine achieve the same ends by different means. The destruction of their bodies in their necessity for visions. The spirit to be free must be disembodied and separate. This has been known for thousands of years. It was better known in ancient China, in Greece, in Egypt than it is in the West today. It is as though man carried two torches, one in his right hand and one in his left, one in his loins, and one in his brain. The acts of his life are the result of the tension between the forces that govern him. He is what he must be. That which happens is that which must happen. There can be no effect without cause and the effects become new causes.

The duty of man today is to cast out fear from his own heart, and from that of his fellows. Fear of death which is only change has been engendered by the church for its own purpose. Fear of pain is now partly under control owing to the advances of medical science. Fear of starvation is one that no man should suffer in a world over-full of all necessities. Fear of personal unhappiness, that can, in part at least, be eliminated by the separation of economic factors from marriage.

There remains fear of snobbish competition, due to the unequal distribution of wealth. Fear of words which may not be spoken. Fear of ignorance. Above all the fear of God, that rises out of an atavistic fear of devils, for which must be substituted a belief in the new God, the God of Humanity, of whose existence Jesus Christ and every good man before and after Him has given ample proof. "There is no fear in love; but perfect love casteth out fear. Because fear hath torment, he that feareth is not made perfect in love."

Chapter Seven

Radio Is King

PROPAGANDA IS MORAL SABOTAGE, the means of undermining faith by false news, false rumor, and an occasional truth continually reiterated. It is based, like modern advertising, on the psychology of fear, sex, love of gain, and envy. It is geared to strike, by the variation of its notes, all classes. All are equally susceptible to its appeal. For the masses, direct propaganda; for the educated, indirect.

Why fight for Poland? Why indeed? *Wars are engineered by capitalists and Jews.* Recollections of war profiteers and armament manufacturers are exhumed. *The English will fight to the last Frenchman.* The old racial hatred between England and France is revived. *The English have come. They are behind the lines making love to your wives.* The sex angle. *The army is rotten. The statesmen are traitors and ineffectual.* Bringing doubt into national leadership. *You have been betrayed,* turns a strategic retreat into a rout.

A more complex form of propaganda is the psychology of disappointment, as used in Poland. Talking Polish over a well-known radio station, the Germans broadcast the arrival of the British army and of hundreds of British planes, and then later denied the report, saying that it was a mistake, that the British had sent nothing and were going to give no help. Still more subtle is the apparently irrelevant: an exact German report over the radio of the relief of a regiment in the Maginot line, with the number and description of the battalion that has just come in, even to the names of the officers; the menu of an official dinner in Paris while the dinner is in progress; the telephone message to the British Broadcasting Corporation who had just completed a secret move, asking them if they were comfortable in their new quarters.

Indirect propaganda of the highest class is coming from Germany. A report is received in New York that an American destroyer has been torpedoed in the Atlantic. If this were true it would be likely to bring America into the war. But who would want America in the war? England. Certainly not Germany. Therefore, when the report turns out to be false it is classed as English propaganda. At first it might be assumed that this serves no useful purpose. It does not bring America into the war. But what it does do is build up further resistance against any possible commitment that may drag the United States into the war, together with a dislike and distrust of British methods. It serves as another of those wedges that the German propaganda machine drives between nations who are friendly and whose interests are parallel.

The sinking of the *Athenia* was attributed to Winston Churchill. There are still people who believe that he was responsible. They are not necessarily intelligent people, but they are people. They have votes. They influence senators and congressmen.

The warning that the British were going to sink the *Iroquois* would have covered Germany if the *Iroquois* had been sunk; and some people would have believed the story.

Simplest of all is the direct threat, the straight appeal to fear, the story of what will happen to those who have the audacity to resist. Horror is piled upon horror, and to counterbalance this comes the reverse side of terror, a sympathetic regard for those about to die. Advice to mothers on how to save their babies in an air raid. And questions: "Have you enough water if the mains are destroyed? Many died of typhus in Poland owing to lack of good water." "Have you a reserve of food? Is it sufficient?"

Then comes insistence on latent hatreds and old quarrels. The British people are told the upper classes have evacuated their children and that the poor children will be left to suffer; that the Jews are responsible for the war; that the government is responsible for it. They are asked why they fight for a capitalist government. "What have you to gain? You are a brave enemy, we respect you, but why go on?"

Radio propaganda runs the scale of human emotions, comforts, frightens, creates hatreds and schisms, and endlessly attacks the morale on which resistance is based. By continued reiteration, by alternating threat with promise, objective opinion is warped, biased, and people are frightened into those lines of thought that the propagandists wish them to hold.

The great power of modern propaganda is due to the conditioning of the public mind by the advertisement of commercial products. Skepticism, so apparent in everything else, never enters into the consideration of advertisements. Everything that is said about a blended whisky, a fancy soap, or a new make of refrigerator is believed.

Cynicism and skepticism are reserved for those things which should be accepted without question, virtue, honor, love, and patriotism. Any national magazine will illustrate the resemblance between war propaganda and commercial advertising.

The magazine is enclosed between covers designed to attract the eye of the passerby. The stories are so arranged that to read any of them the whole magazine must be looked through. It is obvious that a magazine containing advertisements alone would not sell. It is equally obvious that a fiction magazine without advertisements cannot pay. Big business supports the fictional material which is the bait.

I have a magazine at my side. A girl, mostly leg, swings on the cover. What follows?

A linoleum floor that looks like a million dollars. It is not a million dollars . . . it is just linoleum, but it looks better than it actually is. Pink tooth brush . . . appeals to fear: one man in five has pyorrhea. A book on flower arrangement if you buy a carton of a soft drink. It has 48 color plates. Something for nothing. Halitosis. This is very insidious since no one knows whether he has it or not. Fear value with sexual and business strings. Silk stockings ably advertised by Hollywood legs ending in frillies . . . sex, garnished with lace. Beauty soap for brides . . . sexual equation and marriage. Beauty lotion illustrated with couple kissing . . . sex. Life insurance . . . caption refers to birth of baby. Sentimental . . . sex and fear. Diamonds with strange appeal to mothers to wear diamonds so that their children will remember them by the jewels they wore . . . sex, vanity, and snob. Cigarettes that give five more per pack . . . something for nothing. An impossibility but a good selling line. Lipstick that never dries . . . wet lips . . . sex. Toilet paper for babies . . . sentimental vulgarity appeal. Underarm perspiration . . . sex and doubtful appeal to economy. Perspiration carried further into the realm of clothes. Auto sales by appeal to woman's judgment . . . snob and sex. Facial cocktail . . . sex and snob . . . debutante value. Cold cream . . . sex. Face power . . . sex caption. Boots, scientific . . . fear. Washing powder . . . snob value . . . if you do your own laundry. Canned fruit . . . a health habit . . . fear. Advertisement for lubricating fuel . . . illustration: small girl going to rest room . . . irrevelant, vulgar, sentimental, sexual. Refrigerator . . . snob. Bath room . . . snob. Laxative for children . . . fear. Sheets . . . snob. Body odor . . . snob, according to caption. Menstruation . . . fear. Another deodorant. Soap. A hand smoother . . . sex . . . Soap, hygienic . . . fear.

*   *   *

The radio, the whisperer of false news, and the newsreel type of film are the best means of war propaganda since their appeal is directly emotional, through the ears and eyes. Printed forms of direct propaganda, such as the leaflet, fail to some extent because they are printed, and deliberate consideration can be given to the printed word. But inverted propaganda in the press is of greater value since it usually has a partly truthful basis and its purpose is not so clear.

Even the nursery-tale form, Little Red Riding Hood, and the story of the boy who cried "Wolf," come in. Nursery rhymes and fairy stories are based on ancient myths that fulfill a hidden function in the minds of men, rooting them into their ancestral pasts. The cry of "Wolf" loses its importance by re-iteration, and the wolf, in the form of invasion, is facilitated.

The part of propaganda in war is the intellectual softening process that precedes the actual blow. Counter-propaganda is an effort to destroy the effect of propaganda and carry the war of words into the camp of the enemy.

But there are other forms of propaganda. There are the verbal campaigns of enemy agents and traitors. There were actually in France, in the early days of the war, weepers—women draped with crepe who went about in public places crying. There were agents who slipped in with the refugees. They were disguised as priests, peasants, and nuns. Many of them were women. They mixed with refugees, disseminated false war news, and telephoned to villages ahead causing unnecessary panic in localities that were not in danger. They set farms and hayricks on fire. There were others who, supplied with counterfeit notes made in Germany, distributed them in an effort to destroy confidence in the currency.

The psychological value of words has been gravely underestimated: Blitzkrieg. Blood bath. Panzer. Total war. Perfume of Battle (stink of decomposing bodies). Blue Devil. These words carry mental associations. They are the modern counterpart of the Red Indian war-whoops and ring continually in the ears of those who read and hear them.

In Norway, England, and France newspapers subsidized by Germany emphasized the terrors of bombing, published articles written by eye-witnesses from Poland, even stressed air raid precautions as a further means of sapping the morale of urban populations, and suggested indirectly the uselessness of resistance in the face of such odds. Peace at any price they said would be both wise and honorable. Even those who denied this still served their purpose by bringing it to the minds of those who heard them. The denial of a lie can cause it to be carried into centers where it will be believed. Just as the suggestion of a traitor will serve the purpose of a traitor by causing lack of confidence. The uncertainty of suggestion is at times more valuable than certainty. A traitor can be caught and shot—he has been eliminated; but the thought that there is a traitor among them, makes each man look distrustfully at his neighbor. This was the object of dropping parachutes without parachutists in England. The parachutes were found and much trouble was caused by the search for the non-existent men.

Propaganda achieved great success among the workers in France by making them defeatists, by making them feel that they were caught in a machine and doomed to fight a bourgeois war.

Leaders have had to adjust themselves to new public feelings, to turn from a desire for war to appeasement, while others, who were pacifists, had to state that now peace could be achieved only by war.

In Norway, on the night before the invasion, a war film was shown to members of the government at the German Embassy. It showed with great detail what happened to those who had resisted the Germans in Poland. Intimidation by act and word, the instruments of the modern gangster and strong-arm squad, were equally the tools of Alva when he invaded Holland. At

Utrecht on July 15, 1573, he issued a manifesto to the people which contained the following passage:

"But if ye disregard these offers of mercy, receiving them with closed ears as hitherto, then we warn you that there is no rigor, nor cruelty, however great, which you are not to expect by laying waste, starvation, and the sword, in such manner that nowhere shall remain a relic of that which at present exists, but His Majesty will strip bare and utterly depopulate the land, and cause it to be inhabited again by strangers; since otherwise His Majesty could not believe that the will of God and His Majesty had been accomplished."

These are the same trumpets that blew as the Israelites circled the walls of Jericho.

Nor is propaganda all external. Student bodies within the Reich and in Italy were used to excite public feeling with their cries for Sudetenland, for Austria, for Tunis, for Corsica. The consciences of the totalitarian countries have to be taken into account. Inflammation must be justified if the heat is to be kept up to fever pitch. The old defeats of Adowa and Caporetto achieved this end in Italy, while in Germany the ignominy of Versailles was kept continually before the people.

These were national dishonors that had to be wiped out. They could not be forgotten. The old dead could not be allowed to bury the old dead but must lie under a mausoleum of new young corpses. It was this continual harking back to Versailles, and the continual cry of "Caporetto" that made Hitler and Mussolini possible by their appeal to these disgraceful memories.

Whole newspapers were bought in foreign countries by Germany long before the war, and journalists and editors were suborned. They were used to attack the government and to stir up trouble between different political and religious factions.

The purpose of propaganda is to keep the emotions of the many under the control of the brains of the few by every psychological device. Against the highly organized propaganda machine

of Goebbels, the English pitted conventional civil servants and
politicians and the French a great writer, Jean Giradoux, whose
beautiful and delicate prose was artistically charming but was as
noticeable as a fragrant flower in the field trampled by the German bull. Irony, beauty, and fantasy are not the weapons
needed to combat German propaganda.

*   *   *

Another field in which propaganda has entered is the family,
when the disintegration of the accepted system has become apparent—divorce, the changed economic position of women, the
reversal of the role of duty between parents and children.

Within the homes of Europe and America there exists a leftist and a rightist movement, a modern or reactionary division
of opinion that is an integral part of the world struggle for
adjustment. On the one side there is a feeling that morals are a
personal matter of ethics mutually agreed upon by those concerned; a belief in contraception; a continued attack on the
divorce laws, demanding further latitude; the feeling that ille-
gitimacy should carry no stigma; that venereal disease should be
met boldly by cures and prophylactic measures; and that parents owe responsibility to children who did not ask to be born.

On the other side is the reactionary movement, backed by
business interests and the church, that would have no divorce,
no contraception; that tolerates extra-marital relations on the
part of the man; that considers venereal disease the price of sin;
that believes children owe an unlimited debt to their parents for
the care given them in youth; that states a woman's place is
in the kitchen and in the bed; that denies even the most approximate sexual equality; and that will permit women no work
except domestic tasks.

The totalitarian countries are immensely concerned with the
home, as the recent legislation of the Pétain government shows
by substituting family, work, and patriotism for liberty, equality, and fraternity; by its revision of the scale of wages in favor

of large famiiles; by the abolition of divorce, which must carry with it a great increase in prostitution as a counterpoise, and by the denial of free expression in literature or art. This government refuses to acknowledge the obscene, the vulgar, and the pornographic side of life, which remains the only outlet for atavistic urges that still exist in man.

As Prohibition in the United States produced such an orgy of disorder, of immorality and vice, so will the suppression of other natural, though in no way admirable, liberties produce brutality and sadism within the permitted zone of the home. Even the Roman Catholic Church allowed certain liberties, such as Mardi-Gras and Mi-Carême, whose purpose corresponded to the Roman Saturnalia, knowing in its immense psychological wisdom the necessity for such an outlet.

When confronted by a situation primitive man, or an animal, has a choice. He can fight or run. But civilized man is without option. He is forced to inaction, forced to remain where he is by his work and prevented from using violence by the law. Thus nervous tensions and neuroses arise from the continual conflict of his instincts with his necessities.

Sex within or outside of marriage remains the greatest creative force in the world. It remains the source of life itself, since apart from the sex-act there is no means of creating life. As the power of the church was broken by the discoveries of Charles Darwin, so was the power of the old traditional morality destroyed by the knowledge of contraceptives, and the popularization of the motor car, a lounge on wheels that has eliminated time, place, and supervision.

That the professional classes are having few or no children is due less to their evasion of parenthood and the sacrifices entailed by it, than to the uncertain conditions of the world and society. The accusation of selfishness against those who refuse to have children seems hard to justify as they can scarcely be selfish towards a non-existent child. On the contrary, it is those who have children without considering their future who are selfish. As soon as conditions become favorable the children will come—inevitably. It is apparently forgotten how much easier it is to have children than not to have them. Control implies at least some thought, and a falling birth rate represents the unconscious revolt of a nation against its circumstance and government. If there be light there will be children to enjoy it.

Modern man has revolted against the burden thrust upon him by nature, has revolted equally against the burden that the law has forced upon him. He remains aware of the risk he runs in his relations even under the best conditions, but he demands that his chances for happiness shall be increased to the optimum rather than reduced to the minimum. He believes that marriage was made for man and not man for marriage.

In 1914 it was considered remarkable that there should be such a percentage of married men among the first volunteers in England. On reflection, the only remarkable fact is the outstanding tragedy that could produce such a reaction.

Neither rewards for breeding nor penalties for childlessness will produce children. Children are produced by affection between a man and woman who live in an atmosphere of security which gives them reason to believe that they can rear their young. In this, man is no different from any other animal. Where conditions are favorable he will breed up to the limit of subsistence; where conditions are unfavorable he will cease to breed. It is even biologically possible that the hopelessness of conditions in Europe will produce much impotence and infertility. Shock, malnutrition, air-raid alarms, and above all doubt for the future, and the enforced absence of men at the front will all play their part in a falling birth rate. Infant mortality will be largely increased by poor lactation on the part of the mothers, lack of prepared infant foods and milk, and often by deliberate infanticide.

Propaganda cannot force women to produce cannon-fodder, nor men to act as stallions for their sons. Were they willing, the forces in their unconscious would undo their political fornications. Increase, and the right to increase, is the power that God has given to man, in trust, for the generations that will follow. Creation, which is miraculous and God-given, cannot be tampered with by earthly dictators, nor can it be hoped for in a world where the desperate millions are ready to lie down and die rather than go on.

Aldous Huxley's "Brave New World" of conditioned workers will be possible when children can be synthetically produced in test tubes and do not spring from the wombs of living women or the loins of men. In the welter of dialectics, of class and race war, and competitive armament, the fundamental humanities have been forgotten and the words of Jesus Christ, who said, "Suffer the little children to come unto me," are drowned by the drumfire of the cannons. The world faces a new form of asceticism—the asceticism of despair.

Propaganda despite its ultra-modernism has an ancient, almost pre-historic flavor. Its appeal is to what are assumed to be the lowest instincts in man, at any rate, his most primitive instincts. There is a kind of magic in the words that come over the air, that ring from loud-speakers in the field and the mahogany radios in the homes. There is a combination of African Voodoo and medieval sorcery in the continuous interchange of wishful evil; there is a harking back to the evil eye, to the little waxen figure stuffed with pins, and the magic potion.

On the invisible sound waves of the heavens come Valkyries, mounted on white stallions, their long corn-hair flying and spears in their hands. On the breeze come the marches of Valhalla, come the spirits of the dead horn-helmeted warriors who raped the primitive innocence of Europe, raising her garment from Norway to the great Atlantic. Over the air comes the thunder of Thor hammering, the spirit of Odin, the wild-wood worship of robed Druids with their golden sickles and their sacred symbolism of mistletoe and oak.

Over the air comes an atavistic folklore of blood, of iron, of human sacrifice, of human hearts held bleeding to the rising sun, subtly dressed with modern marches, with soldiers' songs, with news from home, with praise and hate—all, from the first note of music to the final paragraph of prose, calculated for its emotional appeal.

War being ancient, it is the ancient appeals that come into their own—appeals to brutality in man, to motherhood in women; appeals to the unbalanced emotions, hatreds, passions; appeals through long-dead gods whose worship lies dormant within the breasts of men. The complexity of the Virgin Birth, of a Christ hanging, while He bled on a wooden cross, are crushed beneath the visible symbols of war, the rhythmic tramp of boots, the scream of diving aircraft, the thunder of guns, the clear call of the trumpet in the dawn. The scent of the cabbage rose in the cottage garden is soon forgotten in the intoxicating perfume of death that fills a summer battlefield.

The master of Germany has brought up his young men to fight, brought them up warriors and ruthless; by their very hardihood they will be condemned, by the sword their master forged they will perish, blown like chaff on the whirlwind they have raised. The sword can gain nothing unsupported by the plow, nor can young men wedded to such war be torn from their brides. The battalions must march on from conquest to further conquest, must march unreasoningly, as lemmings march, as locusts march, until, when all is destroyed, they turn inwards upon themselves.

These are the aims of propaganda in war: to stir up hatred, to break the objectivity of the civilized man into its latent, subjective, and tribal parts; to stir troops to valor, and reduce the courage of the enemy by terror.

*　　*　　*

Another method of propaganda is the undermining of authority by ridicule. Children are encouraged to play tricks on the police force, to break windows, to hang out Nazi flags, to chalk swastikas on walls and pavements. But the final object of all war propaganda is to divide nation from nation so that they may be destroyed separately, and to divide nations against themselves, within their own boundaries, so that they are unable to organize a full resistance. The simplicity of this device, and the fact that it has been employed so often, has been ignored.

The unrest of the United States today over the elections testifies to the existence of the wedges already driven into national solidarity by enemy agents who understand the intricacies of American political hatreds. There will be continued dissensions between colors and creeds, continual differentiations between sections of the American public. There will be anti-Semitic, anti-Negro, anti-capitalist, and anti-labor movements. There will be the employment of force by the legitimate government through the police and the National Guard. There will also be the employment of force by illegitimate methods, strike-breakers and gangsters will be hired with German and Italian money to create disturbances. Even an ineffective disturbance serves its purpose in distracting public opinion from the only important issue, which is the war in Europe, the possibility of war in the Far East, and the necessity of immediate rearmament.

There are interests in America that would prefer to do business with Hitler. They already regard him as the victor. But there exists in America a vast distrust of big business, which the recent charges against it by the Assistant Attorney General have done nothing to alleviate. The oil combines and the tobacco industry are examples of highway and parlor robbery made by the big combines on the little man who likes to ride in his automobile and smoke his cigarette when he is finished with his work. This distrust is similar to that which existed in England and France until the war forced complete cooperation of all classes in the one country and destroyed the other.

The man in the street did not understand how it was possible that even after the war had begun France was trading coke from Lorraine for iron ore from the Ruhr. Coal and coke combined make steel, which after processing was used to kill Germans and Frenchmen. Yet there were Frenchmen and Germans who profited by this traffic. Many do not understand why the trade in scrap iron between the United States and Japan was allowed to go on for so long when Japan has been acknowledged to be threatening America's interests.

The common man can make nothing of the functioning of big business or high finance. The relationship between parent and subsidiary company remains a mystery to him. But he now sees that labor and capital are each parts of production, and that the one is helpless without the other. He wishes to participate in management, to work on a share basis, to invest savings in the concern he works for. He has learned that a great British armament manufacturing company controls a similar plant in Japan and has a subsidiary company manufacturing the best and most expensive artificial limbs. The relation between armaments and artificial limbs is very simple.

*　　*　　*

The grave danger of the democratic party system lies in the way that the various parties can be brought to combine in their dislike of each other. All groups lose their democratic principles when it comes to dealing with other groups. All are willing to use totalitarian methods of repression in the name of liberty. Tortuous involved thinking is followed by emotional action; private dislikes are turned, by the alchemy of the stressful moment, into political disasters. That Miss America, and Miss Bathing Beauty of forty-eight states, should show her curves in the cause of voluntary enlistment appears to epitomize the failure of something—if only of good taste. But perhaps, as George Washington wrote from Valley Forge, "A great and lasting war can never be supported on the principle of patriotism alone. It must be aided by a prospect of interest or some reward. . . ."

Propaganda like everything else can reach a saturation point and can even, by the exhaustion of its methods, build up a resistance against itself, as a human being, poisoned, will in time produce within his blood stream an immunizing serum. The continual references to Herr Hitler as Lucifer, as the Anti-Christ, have tended to make people believe that there must be something to be said on his side! Just as the continued persecution of the Jews for two thousand years has made people believe that there may be something to be said for such persecution; that a whole people could not have been persecuted so much without cause.

If a man hits a woman over the head with a hammer it is considered a terrible crime. If he poisons her, and then pulverizes her with a hammer, and then dismembers her body, inserts it in a trunk, and ships it to her mother, the situation is changed. He must have disliked her. There must be some reason for his dislike. By exaggeration, his crime is in some way justified.

People are annoyed with the Jews for being so persecuted. They ought to stop themselves from being persecuted and continuously demanding sympathy. Humanity has only just so much sympathy and when the supply is exhausted, humanity becomes irritated. The value of anti-Semitism to the Nazi ideology is said to be the fact that anyone who has any anti-Semitic feeling cannot be entirely anti-Nazi. Even those who state that they are not anti-Semitic may easily become so. Their statement is sometimes an effort to convince themselves. The only really non-anti-Semitic people are those to whom the question never occurs, who are unaware of the problem, who do not know whether their friends are Jews or not. It is curious that the smallest personal slight or business "smartness" is resented from a Jew. People say "damn little Jew" where they would never say "damn Scotsman" or "Irishman" or "Englishman" or "American," if such nationals did exactly what the Jew had done.

Nazi propaganda has the advantage of elasticity. It changes its spots to suit the country or class where it operates, assuming the necessary protective coloration. In the West of Europe it appealed to the upper classes as an antidote to Bolshevism; in the Southeast it appeared to be a revolutionary movement to throw off the yoke of the great landowners. In London and New York, great Jewish centers, it is anti-Semitic. In Boston and Glasgow it is anti-Catholic. In the Southern States it is anti-Negro and anti-Yankee. The form changes, but not the spirit, which remains constant and is simply the setting of one faction against another. An anti-Jewish campaign is useless where there are few Jews; an anti-Negro campaign useless where there are no Negroes.

Atrocities, as such, have gone out. They exist as they never did before but as propaganda they are obsolete. They are too obvious in their direct emotional appeal to a world that has hardened its heart against them. Today anything is propaganda, the truth as much as a lie. Anything but the most objective generalization must influence opinion one way or the other. But the efficacy of the German methods has certainly been justified by its results in what is now all but an Anglo-French war.

Both the Allied forces and Germany, in the earlier days of the war, tried by propaganda to cover the war in their own countries with a blanket of unreality. German soldiers were captured who thought they were on maneuvers. The French and British were led to believe that success was certain and that it was only a matter of time. From the threat of war, to which all Europe was accustomed, a period of new conditioning to actual war had to be arranged to prevent a breakdown of morale among people too suddenly confronted with the fact instead of the specter. This was rendered easier by the psychological refusal of the man in the street to recognize hostilities till his unconscious was ready, a form of willful forgetting, of amnesia and wishful thinking self-engendered in self-protection. That there was no activity either at the front or behind the lines made this period like the slow awakening from a nightmare. Something terrible had happened. What was it? Oh, the war? But the war had not happened. There was no bloodshed, no bombing. Was it real? Was it a dream? Was life really coming to an end? Since it had not really started could it not be stopped? Could the appeasers not appease again?

The troops that went, went silently, without bands, without cheers, without panoply, without songs. There was no Tipperary, no Mademoiselle from Armentières, no Madelon. It was all cold,—as cold as an icy hell in the hearts of men.

Chapter Eight

Total War

TOTAL WAR IS A MEANS to an end. It is the ruthless and logical application of the imagination upon the mechanical possibilities of destruction.

It is the organization of a whole people into a single engine of war. Its limits are only the limitations of that engine. There are neither ethical, humanitarian, nor social considerations. Everything but success is irrelevant. One man, one people. One aim . . . world dominion.

What we consider the destruction of the world is to Germany its reconstruction. There is nothing new about the German desire for world dominion. Before the last war they had by peaceful penetration obtained enormous power in Latin America. Before the last war they had plans for an African Dominion and a Mittel Europa Empire, a pan-Germanic association that would have stretched from the North to the Black and Mediterranean Seas.

The Germans have always been a military people. It was so in the dawn of the historical period, in the Holy Roman Empire and after. For centuries the Germans have fought as mercenaries in every army of the world. They have an affinity for war. Of all the countries in Europe, Prussia and Russia are the only two never conquered by Roman legions or affected by Roman civilization.

Total war is cerebral and scientific. The engineers construct weapons, the chemists search for new gases and explosives, the psychologists search for the most efficient means of terrifying a civil population, and the resources of the police are organized to hold a conquered population in subjection. Nothing is left to chance. By the use of high explosives dropped from the air, canyons are blown through the strongest fortifications. By the application of cavalry tactics to the air force and tanks, enemy concentrations are broken up and lines of communication destroyed. By the bombing of cities millions of civilians are flung onto the roads which the enemy need for their maneuvers. By intimidation, populations are kept in order by a minimum of troops. By the development, over years, of an underground system of spies and traitors, difficulties are made at points hundreds of miles behind the fighting lines. By the employment of parachute troops, some of them women, some of them disguised as civilians, as priests, as housewives, and even as soldiers of the opposing forces, such confusion can be created as can destroy the morale of a nation. By concentrated bombing, factories and power stations can be rendered ineffective and the troops in the field left without supplies.

It is the simplicity of this conception that gives total war its horror. Not total war, but the knowledge that the human mind can so quickly and so easily revert to savagery. It is a technique of frightfulness. There were glimpses of it in the last war, mere suggestions, buds, as it were, of the now ripe fruit. It is not astonishing that it should have grown in the German forests. It is only astonishing that those who knew the Germans refused to believe them capable of such things. It was said they were a sentimental, song-loving people. Yet the brutal swashbuckling of the Prussian officer is a part of the German culture. The saber-slashed face of the German student is considered admirable among his countrymen. The women like it. It has come to be regarded as a secondary sexual characteristic, like the red comb of the cock.

There is no denying the German culture; their music, their literature. But it has always been accompanied by the rattle of their beer steins, the clinking of swan-necked spurs, and the rattle of long saber scabbards against the pavements.

Thousands dead, millions homeless and destitute on the roads of Europe; cities razed to the ground; whole countries devastated, burned, and despoiled. That is Europe today; the Europe that total war has made. But the mills of the gods grind slowly, and the immense, tireless forces of nature are working. Dying women and children seek water. They die by the rivers and by the wells. Dead men rot. The very defecations of the fighting and fleeing millions run into hundreds of tons daily spread over a small section of the earth. Who will get in the hay harvest for the beasts? Who will reap the corn even if it has been sown? Famine and pestilence stand waiting. Science which has hitherto been used to defeat them is now their servant. Science is preparing their way. Whole nations are shellshocked into apathy and starved into weakness. Every sanitary service is dislocated by the horrors and exigencies of war. The fields lie fallow for lack of workers. The water courses are polluted by excrement and blood.

Five million refugees have clogged the roads of France; thousands are dying each day of wounds, fright, and hunger. A hundred thousand dead are buried under the ruins of Rotterdam, whose destruction took seven and a half minutes from the first bomb to the last. The barbarians, the brown and black-shirted legions, have marched across Europe. With destruction the German legions have sown famine. With death they have sown pestilence. The Stukas may soon have to dive upon the microbes and the tanks throw their flames upon the bacilli that their destruction has brought into being.

•   •   •

There is no analogy between Adolf Hitler and Napoleon Bonaparte. Napoleon was a soldier, perhaps the finest the world has ever seen. He had no new weapons, no Stukas or Panzer divisions. He was a young officer of artillery. He rose to power by leading the ragged troops of the revolution to victory against enemies that were vastly better equipped. He won his battles against great odds by his genius alone. By degrees he built up his Grand Army. There never were such troops as his at their best. There never was such panoply, such military display. There never were such veterans. Hitler's troops who have run through Europe in their amored cars are not veterans. There is no bear-skinned old guard in Germany, men of forty and fifty with years of fighting behind them. No young guard. No Polish Lancers, no Cuirassiers with horse-tail plumes, no Imperial Eagles, no Marshals like Murat or Ney.

Hitler has a force of young men held by fanaticism who are trained like dogs to perform the duties of motorized murder. He has a general staff remarkable for the German ruthlessness with which it prosecutes his designs. But there is no elasticity there. He is no genius who can turn disaster into victory as Napoleon did. Hitler's power is the power of his voice over the radio. He is not the Napoleon who sat his white horse at Marengo and watched the smoke of battle. He is the corporal but he is not the "Little Corporal"—the stuff of which Emperors are made.

As Hitler's army is mechanized, so is the Nazi machine. It is so constructed that if it is not going full speed ahead it slips into reverse. It is still too early to prophesy, but it seems possible that the zenith of Hitler's power has been reached; that he is now poised on the wings of his air force as a ball is poised hovering on a jet of water in a shooting gallery before it falls. If his air force fails to destroy the morale of England, fails to stop food and war material from coming into the British harbors, his course is run.

There is no precedent for disaster in England. The battle

will be fought to the end; in the air, on the sea, on the beaches, and in the towns. It will be fought across all England if it must be, and then it will be continued from overseas. Everything is already lost in England. Everything is lost but England, and that will stand.

Europe will starve. First all Europe outside the Reich, and then Germany. Hitler's conquests will prove empty of everything but corpses. The riches of those lands will lie rotting, the machinery rusting. Men can be forced to work but they cannot be made to work well. In addition to intentional sabotage there will be unintentional sabotage, the product of hunger, hatred, and despair. Production capacity remains dependent on labor. There will be no revolution against Hitler. There will be a revolution against life under the conditions he has enforced. That revolution has begun. It is covered by the silence of Europe, the blanket of despair which National Socialism has flung over a continent. Starvation is near for millions. Influenza and typhus and dysentery have broken out, and those who might in better times have recovered, will lie down and die. It will be simpler for them than living.

There is no lost cause unless it be first lost in the hearts of men. It has been said that the last war was fought to no purpose. This is not so. Democracy went on. A new world was nearly born of the League. New ideals came into being, new angers rose out of the disillusionment, new demands were made upon life. Materialism was given the rope to hang itself. The lives lost in the last war were not thrown away. But the war was not great enough. The issues were not clear enough. Humanity, weighed down and exhausted by the struggle, was ready for peace, but had no energy for reconstruction. The men who should have ruled England were dead and the country was left in the hands of those who had made the war. The fire that had flamed up so fast in 1914 died down too fast in 1918.

This time everything is different. Men took up their arms reluctantly. The flame of their anger has risen slowly. This time they will make an end. This time, before the war is really begun, they are talking of the new England they will make.

A peace must be just or terrible. Versailles was neither. It was unjust and not terrible. It was nothing like the peace that Hitler, in the event of his victory, would impose upon the democracies. He, who has railed at the indignity of Versailles, has stated this. The free men of the world would not merely be defeated. They would be crushed and utterly broken. This is a war of extermination. The idea of freedom must be exterminated, and to achieve this all who believe in freedom must die. There are no appeasements, no half-way measures.

History is repeating itself in the French debacle, in the ill-ease of the man in the street about war aims, about fighting while others grow rich, about the prostitution of youth, about the treatment of ex-soldiers, those old-young men who came back to a world that had no place for them, who, drawn together by the dangerous bond of their suffering, knew themselves to be bought off by gratuities, doles, and pensions. Those who had fought were not allowed to rule. The phrase "a home for heroes" became no more than an uninteresting alliteration.

The army does strange things to men; it forces them into a pattern. Self-reliant in their military activities, soldiers become economically and spiritually helpless. They must be led, fed, and clothed like children. They become punch-drunk with death. Called from their homes to arms, they base their lives on the power of arms. Men will weep when parted from the guns they have carried in war. The rifle gave them significance. It was power. Their disciplined battalions were power.

Life is simplified in the army, ideals are translated into the simple essentials of fighting, staying alive if possible, and obtaining food, rest, and women. Meeting death so often, having so many friends among the dead, soldiers fear a return to civil life where they will be without companions.

The statesmen are well aware of this. Post-war conditions remain one of their preoccupations. Military dictatorships are likely to follow the war. De Gaulle in France, Churchill in England, other men in other places. A dictatorship like Napoleon's is safe. A man knows where he is, serving in peace under the generals he served in war and if the men of a nation take up arms under compulsion, who can compel them to put down their arms if they are dissatisfied?

While Germany was saving corks the citizens of the United States were throwing automobiles away. So rich has this country been that its citizens can afford to do this. So prosperous has it been that its policy was to encourage wastefulness instead of thrift. Consumption is increased by wastefulness. It is harder in America than anywhere else in the world to get anything repaired. Americans do not have things repaired. They buy new things. Even their land they have not conserved, but have used recklessly and moved on to new land. This is the pioneer spirit but the pioneers, the great armies that moved westward in face of incredible odds, were strong men. That they survived those odds is the proof of it.

The pioneer must return. Again men must set their hands to the plow with rifles strapped to their backs and their Bibles in their pockets. The women must help them. It is the women with their incredible demands on the pocketbooks of men who have forced this parody of civilization on a people whose exploits were the admiration of the world.

If it has been possible by advertising to frighten the nation of its own smell, the smell of its breath and its body, it should be possible to frighten it into the consciousness of its more vital necessities—the defense of its liberties and the reorganization of its spirit.

America has accused Europe of decadence. Let the decadence of Europe be an example.

The resources of this country are only scratched. Only the best has been used, the second best, the third best, and the bad remain. It is no use looking back and wishing that things were not as they are. It is no use assuming that they will, of their own accord, become better. We who are alive today have seen the best we shall ever see. Things will become progressively worse. Only one thing stands, the fundamental spirit of America. If the money goes, if the standard of living goes, the Constitution and its implications in the minds of those who made it continues.

The declared, the undeclared wars, and the terrors of today are more than they appear to be. They are in fact not at all what they appear to be, they are symptoms; the outward and visible signs of an inward and world-wide spiritual unrest. They could not have been cured from the outside by treaties, by palliatives or by slogans. There is everywhere a vast and increasing unrest. Under superficial order humanity is twitching with anger, as the muscles twitch under the skin of a beast. Disintegration, disorganization, and lack of security are increasing. The immediate future looks even darker than the immediate past. Less and less are people content with life. Nor are they ready to wait for happiness in the next world. More and more, people want something now. And how little they want—only the right to live. They have suddenly become aware that life is good, that people are good, that there is enough for all, but that by some unknown trick, some mismanagement, some lag, some disorganization, or error, they are not getting their due. Having been brought up in the belief of a purely material world, they find themselves betrayed by it. They have been fooled long enough. The history of mankind is no more than the history of man's spiritual development: from devils to polytheism, from polytheism to monotheism; from there to materialism and from materialism to the conception, newly conceived, that God and man are one, that above everything it is humanity that matters to humanity; to a belief, not in the New Testament as interpreted by the Church, but in the words of Jesus Christ.

This struggle is a war, a revolution of the imagination. The figures that emerge are the men of imagination. Hitler the painter, Churchill the author, the adventurer, the soldier-sailor jack-of-all-trades. New generals arise who suffered the obscurity of their unorthodox dreams in the past period of orthodoxy. Brains, unrestricted by precedent are in action . . . de Gaulle of France . . . Dill of England.

The novelists are justified. The war is waged on a Jules Verne basis. It is the *War of the Worlds* that Wells wrote. Huxley's *Brave New World* was a satire from which the National Socialists of Germany seem to have drawn many lessons. Until a thing happens it is fiction. Lister's discoveries, and those of Pasteur, were laughed at as fictions until they were proven. It is by fictions, by ideas, that men progress and live. The novelist looks back into the past and sees it living, catches up with it as it flies, indestructible, on the waves of light. He looks forward into the future and sees the straws in the wind. He is the man who rides his unconscious as a man rides a horse, and trusts it. He has faith and sees something of the vast pattern in which the importance of today is lost in the immensity of yesterday and the infinite tomorrow. Sinclair Lewis wrote *It Can't Happen Here.* Because it was a novel its revelations have been forgotten. Wells wrote the *Holy Terror* and it was lost in a sea of journalistic literature, just as when he wrote the *World of William Clissold,* already sensing something of man's illease and gave it to the world, it was read and promptly forgotten.

It is possible for the United States to be attacked through the Hudson Bay and Canada from Greenland bases; possible for it to be attacked through Alaska from the USSR; possible in the event of a German victory, and with the Allied fleets in German hands, for it to be blackmailed into almost anything.

There is no question of active American aid or participation in the European struggle; if the Americans even wish to participate in it, in its most critical hour, there is no time. All that stands between America and a world dominated by totalitarian dictators is the flesh and blood of some millions of English men, women, and children. That and that alone, flesh and blood, and how long it will stand against steel, is where the issue lies. America must save herself, and with herself, should Europe fall, save those principles of democracy that make life worth living. Once again the ostrich must give place to the eagle. Once again man, who thinks subjectively of his business, his home, and his family must think more widely—not only of his sons who may be called upon to pay the price, but of his grandsons and his great-grandsons who may reap the reward of the price that is paid today.

Few, even now, seem to understand the philospohy of National Socialism. For two thousand years man has fought to raise himself. Despite his base desires he has succeeded. Now those desires are being given prior right. The sadist and the beast are being encouraged; the ruthless man, and the man without mercy, praised; honor and gentleness are decried.

We cannot even assume that, over a long period, things will right themselves. This is wishful thinking. There is no reason why a nation cannot be reduced to complete subservience by the killing or elimination of its intellectuals. The death of these people is mechanically possible, requiring only arms, ammunition, those who would use them, and some arrangement for the disposal of the bodies. In any country this would leave a leaderless and comparatively helpless working class who could be used in chain gangs for reconstruction purposes. The children, taken away and conditioned by false history can become, by utter isolation from the rest of the world, exact copies of their teachers . . . a *brave new world* indeed. There is nothing impossible in this, nothing even particularly alarming once it is conceived as a possibility to which men must be prepared to subscribe or to resist.

Clausewitz, the German general, defined war as a political act, the extension of state policy by means of violence. A threat of violence is violence by implication. This war was begun in 1933 when Germany left the League of Nations, and it has continued by means of threats, kidnapings, and ransoms. It has passed through the phase referred to as "the war of nerves," and the stalemate of the "passive Maginot defense principle," before bursting into the conflagration that destroyed the Low Countries and France.

The rapidity with which results were obtained is extraordinary and without precedent, as are the relatively small number of military casualties and the immense displacement of civil populations. With this displacement and the destruction of property that caused it, comes the impossibility of restoring the status quo based on law, order, and the normal processes of inheritance and transfer of property. With it has come an enormous section of people, perhaps ten millions of them, who are homeless and detached from those anchors of family and property that are necessary for an ordered existence as we know it.

Another astonishing thing is that in all the democratic belligerent and neutral countries there was a section of the upper class that politically, and within the frames of their respective constitutions, believed in the ideals of Germany. There were fascists in England. There was the *Croix de Feu* in France, there were societies and organizations loosely or closely affiliated to the German National Socialists in Czecho-Slovakia, in Poland, in Holland, in Belgium, in Norway. There are such parties and organizations in the United States, in Canada, and the republics of South America. These parties, which still have immunity, owe it to the cleverly devised argument that the curtailment of free speech, even if such speech be directed against civil liberties, is a breach of those liberties. So is democracy caught in the cleft stick of its own ideology.

The move of the French government at the beginning of the war to imprison not only communists but all who had left wing tendencies and to allow the pro-Nazi rightists to function freely, characterizes the attitude of the ruling classes in the democracies. It is comparable to their attitude in the Spanish Civil War and the Italian war in Ethiopia. A war that could have been stopped at any time had sanctions been enforced or the Suez Canal closed.

The ultimate appeal of the reactionary to people of the middle class is that only fascism can save them from proletarianism. Proletarianism has been damned but never defined. It seems that it might mean an approximate equality among men.

It must be remembered that modern war, and the complex instruments of modern war, are particularly suited to the middle class. If only partially educated it is, as a class, educated well enough to use weapons that require knowledge of mathematics, map reading, and mechanics. The small, highly skilled, high-powered striking forces of today are manned by boys of more than average education.

As a result of skillful propaganda anyone with liberal or mildly socialist views is called a red. In Spain Freemasons, Protestants, Jews, and Basque nationalists were Reds. To own a copy of Ramsay MacDonald's *Socialism* or to suggest that education should be in the hands of the state and not the church made a man a red. While everywhere free thought, if it were tinged with any unorthodox views, was Bolshevism. Much contempt has been poured upon the intellectuals for their "parlor pink" views. Yet pale pink seems to be about the best political complexion. It is at least healthy and ready to consider change. It is an improvement on the communist red or the apoplectic purple of the reactionary.

The significance of the Spanish war lies in the fact that it was the first battle of the present revolution and it seems likely that England was entirely responsible for the anomaly of non-intervention, while intervention was actively going on. England apparently believed the lies told by the German and Italian members of the non-intervention committee who claimed they had not intervened and had no intention of intervening. Even the irrefutable proofs proffered by the Spanish government were disregarded. It is, however, hard to believe that the intelligence departments of the British and French, apart from the representatives of those governments who were in Spain, were not fully informed of what was taking place.

By propaganda, the totalitarian states persuaded the English conservatives and the Roman Catholics throughout the world that such interference as there was in Spain was the only way of saving the Spaniards from themselves and from the communistic state that they proposed to set up. This is interesting, since in the New Parliament there were only 15 communists out of a total of 473. It is even more interesting, objectively, in that it shows the social solidarity of the forces of reaction which can and will, in the event of some country turning socialist, step in, and by direct action, check the government of the people by the people and thus eradicate what is assumed to be the ideal of democracy.

The British method of applying pressure on France was simple. Notice was given that if she precipitated war in Europe by supplying arms to the legitimate government of Spain, England would consider herself released from the Locarno Pact and France would have to fight alone. It would be interesting to know who brought sufficient pressure on British policy to make this possible.

There is little doubt that the Germans have always abused their diplomatic privileges. They did it during the last war. They have done it consistently ever since, both in Europe and America. Even today new posts have been created in New Orleans, though trade is practically non-existent, and the consular services are mainly concerned with trade and incidents arising out of the presence of German nationals as sailors in foreign ports. In Dublin the German consulate has added sixty members to its staff in the last few months.

Spain was a training ground for men and a practice ground for testing out material. Though the Germans had no more than ten or twelve thousand men there at one time, they were continually changed, so that probably 100,000 German technicians, officers, non-commissioned officers, and pilots had war experience in that country. Germany did not send ordinary private soldiers adventuring abroad; only picked men were sent. The German tanks tested there proved inadequate because their armor was too light. This defect was so well remedied that later when the tanks went into action against the English and French, the Allied anti-tank guns were useless against them. High explosives, dive-bombing, propaganda, and fifth columnists were all tested and perfected in Spain, and the Italians added their Spanish experience to that of Abyssinia.

A positive force cannot exist without a negative to counterbalance it, and inversely the negative policies of Great Britain have helped to produce positive policies in the dictatorships. An ever-recurrent phase of contemporary diplomacy has been the alternating movements of the German Reich, Italy, and Japan. With every withdrawal on the one side there has been a step forward on the other. The surrender of Minorca to Franco was followed by the landing of Japanese troops in Hainan. The capture of Canton followed the Munich paper-chase; the closing of the Indo-Chinese road to China followed the defeat of France; and the closing of the Burma Road preceded the opening phases of the Battle of England.

By threat, by counter-threat, by move and counter-move, by international blackmail are such things achieved today, to the complete bewilderment of diplomatists who cannot adjust themselves to power politics where the power is openly paraded instead of being disguised by polite nothings at ambassadorial functions.

There is no point today, except in extreme cases, of open annexation. A zone of influence, backed by a secret police and the pressure of totalitarian trade, produces the effect of colonial expansion without risk, or the expense of actual, direct administration. Sweden belongs to Germany. So does Switzerland. Completely enveloped, how can they move without German permission? They are confined within the boundaries of their countries as a private citizen could be confined to his house if it were surrounded by armed guards.

*   *   *

Hitler's voice . . . Churchill's voice . . . the voice of Duff Cooper . . . of Roosevelt . . . of Lord Haw-Haw . . . of Renaud . . . of King George. . . . The voices of American reporters in the capitals of Europe. The voices of news analysts: of Raymond Gram Swing, of Elmer Davis, of Major George Fielding Eliot . . . the pathetic bleating of the politicians . . . the heart-rending cries of a broken France. . . . When has the mind of the man in the street, or the soldier at the war, or the woman at the fireside, been attacked by such a superfluity of information, of propaganda, such a continual barrage of threat, of appeal, of real and false news, of real and false ideas? How is it possible for anyone to make up his mind, to think, or to see clearly under such conditions? The intelligent become bewildered; the less intelligent give up. And all, whether they wish it or not, select from the mass of information they receive those facts or fictions best suited to their temperament or economic position.

The actual truth is known by no one. Something approximating to the truth is known in Washington, in the Wilhelmstrasse, at 10 Downing Street; but even in these places there are vast gaps that must be bridged by guesswork, by such statistics as are available and by the very fallible opinion of experts.

The fact remains that we know nothing, that we are swayed, conditioned, and coerced by what we hear, see, and read. The human mind which at best can put two and two together with some accuracy, is now engaged in astronomical calculations of cause, effect, and probability. Actually in all countries men are being led and driven; tempted, and forced towards conclusions that are already foregone. Conditioned by years of advertising, by the radio and the magazine and the newspaper, we still retain the illusion of free will and thought, and are unaware that our conversations, as well as our purchases, are based, in a varying degree, on our power of sales resistance. And even this resistance is a danger. Everything is not propaganda. Twenty-five years of terror, of horror have produced a hard-boiled attitude to horror; a feeling that, provided nothing happens to us personally, nothing matters. The sacrifices of the last war have been termed useless, but had the post-war sacrifices been in any way commensurate with them, democracy might have been saved for good.

Man, driven into himself, has developed a cynicism from which he is at last emerging. Life cannot be based on cynicism, which remains, oddly, an animal characteristic. Animals are unperturbed by the sufferings of other beasts and are concerned only with their own nutrition and sexual activities. Man desires order, desires God; desires, despite himself, a life which is useful to others. His pride and self-respect demand it. Man believes in God. From the orthodox Christian believer in the Bible as it stands to the atheist who believes in a system—a nebulous ethic of good and evil, which is in essence God, or the emanation of that power which, because we cannot understand it, we call divine—man believes in some kind of God.

Chapter Nine

Oh Israel...

THERE MAY HAVE BEEN SOME JUSTIFICATION for the German dislike of the Jews who crept into power in the Weimar republic. With their racial gift for finance, with relations and affiliations abroad, many of them had taken undue advantage of a defenseless currency. But they had done no more than war profiteers in England, France, and the United States had done, or have continued to do, whenever the opportunity offers, as it does today.

There can be no excuse for injustice, for brutality, for blackmail, for the tremendous forced exodus of thousands and for the employment of Jews in chain-gang labor battalions; none for banishment of German Jewish soldiers who had fought for their country; none for the rape and torture of sweated Jewish seamstresses, furriers, and tailors; none for the treatment received by the men of science, the writers, the musicians, composers, painters, actors, and doctors; none for scientific persecution on the entirely unscientific basis of pigmentation, or for an Aryan dream whose every premise is founded on ethnological error.

Eventually, Germany will regret the loss of her Jews and will see that in casting them off she followed in the path of Isabella's Spain, for Spain's failure to uphold her position among the great nations of the world is due in great part to the expulsion of the Jews who were her men of business, and the Moors who were her agriculturalists and men of science. There is a parallel between the vehemence with which the Roman Catholic Church of Spain proselytized the New and Old Worlds with fire and sword, and the manner in which National Socialists and communists preach, armed with rubber truncheons.

From the beginning of our civilization the trade routes of the world have been opened and followed by the Jews. The Phoenicians developed the tin mines of Cornwall, were responsible for the spice trade of the East, the China trade, and the vast caravans that penetrated central Africa in search of gold, ivory, ostrich plumes, gums, and slaves. The Jews, by their racial affiliations, now condemned, were able to stabilize trade, negotiate loans on goods, and establish international credit, despite the international disorder of the times. From the itinerant trader with his pack on his back, to the great bankers such as the Rothschilds, the Jew has served a purpose. That business has today over-reached itself does not detract from these achievements. The probable reorganization of trade and economics, on a new basis, will almost certainly be achieved in part by Jews, since they alone have the necessary financial gifts.

Jewish literature remains the greatest in the world. Every Sunday it is read to the millions of Christians who go to church. The Christian God is a Jewish God. The Christian Christ was born a Jewish child. There are great Jewish writers, composers, sculptors, artists; and the Jews are among the only really pure racial stocks, with traditions that have been handed on from father to son, from rabbi to rabbi, for thousands of years. The laws of Moses are still the Law. The integrity of the Jew approximates that of the Gentile. The charge of usury is equally applicable to all races, and the dislike of Jews is a residual, hereditary dislike, dating from the times when they were confined in ghettos, denied human rights by the church, and exploited by the nobles. Their solidarity has to a great extent been forced upon them by repression, and their social offensiveness, among the lower class of successful Jews, is no more than an effort to over-compensate.

Hitler's dislike of a race within a race, which might find some supporters, could have been met by a reversal of his marriage laws. Had he made it illegal for a Jew to marry a Jewess, the Jews who clung to their religion would have left Germany, and the others, who were willing or wishful to marry out of their race, would in the course of a generation or two have become absorbed within it.

But to Hitler the Jews represented a number of factors. Unquestionably at first he attributed the first world war and Germany's defeat to the manipulations of Jewish finance. But he went much further than this. He needed a scapegoat, and he found a helpless one in the Jews. The rancor of the German people could be turned against the Jews. Thus they got practice in the legal brutality which, in a civilized country, is not a natural gift, but has to be induced by education. In addition, the Jews were rich. Their goods could be confiscated. More, they had in England, France, and America rich relations who could be blackmailed for the gold in which the Reich was so lacking.

The docility of the Jews is a remarkable racial characteristic which served Hitler's turn. Even now there has been little Jewish reaction against National Socialism, though according to Hitler's latest decrees, the Jews are to be expelled from all Europe to live somewhere in the tropics, to live or die as best they may. Yet the Jews remain an integral part of the social structure. They, and their blood, are necessary to it, as a leaven, as the bond between production and distribution. Their culture and learning cannot be divorced from western culture and learning, for, stretched to its limit, the Semitic culture embraces the Prophet Mahomet, includes the Koran, and cannot be separated from the Moorish arts and sciences that reached western Europe through Spain. Astronomy, algebra, civil engineering in the West, all have their roots in the Semitic culture destroyed by the Holy Roman Empire that supplies Adolf Hitler with his historic precedent.

The Jewish problem is not new. Persecutions, massacres, and pogroms have followed each other through the centuries. Hatred has been fomented by scandals. Disraeli was attacked as a Jew. The Dreyfus case of espionage in France was an anti-Jewish fabrication, and the espousal of Dreyfus' cause cost Emile Zola his fortune, and almost his life. From Shylock to Svengali, Jews have been used in literature as symbols of vicious exploitation in an attempt to justify their persecution. Yet the practicing Jew, still worshiping the jealous God of Israel, is a man of his word. The Jewish God has not the moral elasticity of the Christian Deity. His bargains are hard and inexorable. His law is terrible but it is just.

The Talmud brooks no sophistry. It has not been annotated or explained. It has not been manipulated to fit the form of modern business ethics. It endures, word for word, graven on tablets of everlasting stone. The good Jew is good as the good Christian is good, or the good Mohammedan, the good Hindu, the good Buddhist. The city of abstract virtue has many mansions; it contains the sum of all virtue, gentleness, lack of envy, and the refusal to bear false witness.

The international Jewish question is one of the many new facets of this war, another head to the Hydra of the new fanaticism and inter-racial hatred that are being intentionally fomented by National Socialist ideologies. Today Jews in Europe are classed as vermin, not even as game, to be destroyed without license. They are deprived of rights, of justice, of government office, of service in the armed forces, of medical or other assistance, of free movement, of travel, and of the use of public buildings; forbidden to live among other people, to enter any but specially selected shops and streets, to sit on any but certain designated seats.

They are deprived of everything but their right to die, in which right they are encouraged. The Jew according to Hitler must be *Ausgerottet,* exterminated, by means of the concentration camp, by forced labor on starvation diet, and direct incitation to suicide. It will never be known how many Jews took this, the easiest way out, but in the first months of Hitler's rule of Austria more than seven thousand put an end to their own lives. These, of necessity, will have been among the best, the most cultured and intellectual, who preferred actual death to the spiritual death of life rendered intolerable by indignity and oppression. The taking of his own life remains a right that no power can wrest from man, a crime that remains unproven since the issue is between that man and the power that created him.

Political execution is relatively simple to accept. There are few men who could not take their stand against a wall, or ride with arrogance on a tumbril through streets lined with *sans culottes.* But for men and women of family, respectable citizens, to be forced to crawl on their hands and knees, to be compelled to clean up human excrement with their hands, to be starved, tortured, beaten in the presence of their wives, to witness the rape of their daughters, is more than they can endure.

And these are the lesser horrors. The full story of the sadistic perversions of the uniformed men and boys in the employ of the Reich has yet to be told. Along with the Jews, suffered the communists, the liberals, the free thinkers, the thinkers of any kind. National Socialism is the enemy of thought, for thought would destroy it. Purely emotional, on the lowest emotional scale, it strikes at all ethical principles, and endeavors to substitute in their place animal courage and animal obedience, treating its people as wild beasts are treated in a circus, with whips, rifle shots, hot irons, and rewards of meat.

No man need fear death since inevitably he must suffer it. What he must fear is the breaking of his spirit by brutality. Too much importance is placed on human life and too little on life while it is being lived. Too much respect is paid to corpses, too little to human beings. When the spirit has departed from the body, it is a body, no more than that; a thing empty of life that will decompose, be broken up into its elements, and reabsorbed by the earth from which it sprang. Its spirit has gone on, and it was the spirit that made the substance. It was the spirit that held the substance together. No wreath on the casket can replace the kind word that was left unspoken. No amount of standing, hat in hand, as the bier passes, can take back a slander on the living man. The dead are well able to bury their dead. Our concern is with those who are living, who share the miracle of life with us who also live.

All culture is now fugitive. All knowledge is in flight with the Jews as they bear the Holy Tabernacle of learning on their shoulders from land to land, looking back at their homes as they press forward into the void of unlicensed existence, surging away from the horde that would crush them out, homeless, without passport or citizenship, without money, or more than temporary rights.

What is the flight from Egypt compared to this, where men of all races are in flight, where millions tramp the roads, going and coming in search of asylum, or picking over the ruins of their houses, standing bowed beneath their broken fig trees, their flocks and herds slaughtered or dispersed? What was the slaying of the first-born by Herod compared to this indiscriminate slaying of children, to this separation of small children from their parents? To what has the world listened that is comparable to the wailing of their small voices or to the lament of stricken mothers, walking dazed, with dead children clasped at their breasts? For it is thus that it must be seen, not as a war, in which there might be some glory, but as an end of a state of things, as a socio-geological period, in which the vegetation of an ancient culture is blighted by the ice of mechanized force, buried beneath it and frozen.

*   *   *

In Europe, England alone remains, and on the fate of England hangs the future of America by the thin thread of her help to England. America is tied to England less by a common culture, less by a common language, than by the umbilical cord of the ocean, the vast waterway that at once divides and joins them, the mother to the child. The mother now ancient, the child vigorous and strong, but perhaps over-confident in her youth and beauty.

All too slowly, the straws rise on the winds of controversy. All too slowly the chaff is becoming separate from the wheat. The pattern still remains unformed, changing from hour to hour with the circumstance of that hour; but the Quislings, the vast progeny of the Iscariot, begin to claim their shameful silver. Already the night gleams with the phosphorescence of their corruption. Daily, new events take their places in the panorama of failing democracy, fitting into it with terrible precision.

The industrial giant of the automobile industry is seen to have feet of Nazi clay. The hero of the skies betrays with fascist appeasement the ether that made him great. Senators, blinded by foreign might, see ahead nothing of importance but the election, which has bound the United States in what may prove to be its winding sheet.

Colonel Charles Lindbergh is questioned about the economic side of his fifteen-minute broadcasts over the networks. It is suggested that there are interests behind him. It is insisted that there are great forces in industry and politics who believe that the lamb of America can lie down with the wolf of National Socialism. It is felt that there is in the western hemisphere a Cliveden Set that is plotting another American Munich and using Colonel Lindbergh to pave the way.

To some men and interests, the failure of England is a foregone conclusion. They can scarcely wait for the autopsy, and using the mask of patriotism to cover their self-interest, plead for cooperation with a victorious Germany in order to maintain the "supremacy of our western civilization and the right of our commerce to proceed unmolested throughout the world." It is they who balked at the President's demands for power to mobilize and use the National Guard, they who imagine war can be confined by academic lines drawn through the ever moving waves of the ocean, who are ready to limit the Monroe Doctrine on which, in the beginning, they placed so much importance, to the nose of Brazil in the South and some equally fictitious point in the North.

The desire to fight only upon American soil is a sure consolation for the dictators, since it is a euphemism for not fighting at all, an appeal to the appeasers. Money voted and appropriated is not war. It is not even preparation for war. It is money that is going directly from the taxpayers' pocketbooks into the hands of industry that will circumvent its war-profit taxation and make peace with the enemy in an effort to retain its gains.

It is the enemy who will decide when and where war will be fought. Few can believe that it will not come. The only initiative left for the United States is that of preparation.

The attack on Finland produced a sentimental crisis; the defeat of Flanders, a further crisis; the fall of France, coupled with the possible loss of the French fleet and destruction of the British navy, a panic. But now things have changed. It is hoped that England can stand, and hold off Germany. If she does, as is considered possible by those who know the British temperament, no suggestion is offered for the next move. There is only a wishful thought that, by delay, something will happen which will leave America and the American way of life unimpaired. As England was said to have been ready "to fight to the last Frenchman," so is America today ready to fight to the last Englishman, and hoping, by some miracle, to get possession of the British fleet if England is defeated.

The feeling for Finland was largely due to the fact that it has continued to pay its debt. The apathy concerning England and France was due to their default. The crash of '29 has been attributed to this failure, but if that was the cause, then the unprecedented prosperity that preceded '29 must also be due to it; as must, logically, since so much importance is placed on gold, the present boom of the United States, which holds nearly all the gold in the world buried in its vaults.

In final values of bullion, of labor and material, the future war preparedness expenditure of the United States, with an army of two million fully equipped men, fifty thousand aircraft, and a two-ocean navy, will cost the country more than the Allies' default, and this cost is only rendered necessary because of the defeat of France and the plight of Great Britain. For over a hundred years America has saved money, has grown great because of the defense afforded to it by a friendly England, by the British navy that patrolled the seas.

There is no end to the hatreds that will be engendered by the war. With some slight cause, some fragment of truth behind them, they will be exploited to the full by enemy agents. The French think that the British war effort was insufficient, and are now all but at war with England. There are Frenchmen today who state openly that the sooner England is defeated, the better it will be for France. French honor is in pawn to French starvation. The English think that the French did not fight, that they should have completed their line of defense from the Channel to the Mediterranean, that they allowed themselves to be betrayed.

Both the English and French feel that they were betrayed by Belgium, and that America should have come to their aid. The old bitter jokes against America have been revived. There is the story of the English barmaid who answered a complaint some doughboys made about the beer in 1917 with: "Of course it's flat, it's been waiting for you three years." And a new one: "We will go down fighting and leave the two yellow races to settle things between themselves."

Misunderstanding will be piled on misunderstanding, will be amplified by books, articles, and cartoons. Hatreds born quickly, in moments of anxiety, will smolder for long years after their cause has been forgotten. Only by thought, by writing, by speech, by explanations, by truth unwhitewashed and without self-justification, can international understanding and confidence be regained.

Today is only the beginning. Nothing has happened yet. If England holds out, and no one knows the strength of England, events will begin to move. The elections in America will be the focal point in the western hemisphere. The Balkans and Africa are other spheres. Hitler will be driven to force all issues. Cries for assistance will come from a deliberately starved Europe. Rescue ships, if they are sent, will be seized by the British, or sunk by the Germans, who will say that any child that dies of malnutrition in the Europe they have conquered has been murdered by "perfidious Albion." Anti-British feeling will be stirred up in Europe against the country that is blockading them, and though the hearts of men in the conquered countries will know that only by British victory can they regain their freedom, their empty bellies will cry out against their hearts. Shiploads of children will be sunk, peace offensives begun and terminated, threat will be followed by act, the bombing of civil populations will precede the bombing of further civil populations, and no man in all the world will know where he stands.

* * *

There is at least as much original virtue in man as there is original sin. By dwelling on sin we have given it undue importance, particularly with reference to sexual irregularity, which is so strongly condemned by the established churches because it weakens their economic hold on the community. Great incomes are drawn from marriages and baptismal fees. The defaulter, the despoiler of the widow and orphan, the envious, the gluttonous, are all regarded lightly. There are those who might hesitate to pick up a ham and walk off with it, which would be a crime and subject to legal action, but who are quite ready to avoid the payment of their accounts. Yet those who evade their grocers are thieves.

Crime and sin have, like everything else, gone out of focus, the perspective has become lost not only internationally, but nationally and personally.

But the proof of man's search for virtue, which is his title to virtue, is in the religious revival that has taken place in the last few years, religious in its widest sense of mysticism, which embraces political beliefs and ethical codes in its search for an answer to the deep spiritual wants of man, who has found that he cannot live by materialism alone.

Even Hitler believes in something. He relies on the stars, on astrology, and directs his actions by them. He believes in virtues of high places, Berchtesgaden, where he communes with the Valkyries, with his German gods, and sees the visions that inspire him.

Man is sick of rationalism. It does not get him anywhere. He knows at last that no one knows anything; that not even a breakfast egg is understood; that no one can make an egg except a hen; that finally, an egg is more wonderful than a Diesel engine or a dynamo.

Astrology, palmistry, spiritualism, and psychoanalysis are all significant of man's effort to seek the truth, of his unconscious revolt from the rational. Numbers have taken up a new place in the minds of people, mystic numbers, such as seven, which have an historic folk-lore past, the seven candles, the seven plagues, the seventh wave, the seventh year in the life of a child, the fourteenth of puberty, the twenty-first, the seventieth.

Man must believe. Faith of some kind is necessary to his spiritual well-being that is tied to physical well-being. His health, then, is dependent on the power of those gods in whom he finds himself able to believe, be they a political system, a superstitious reaction to numbers, an established religion, or a code of semi-formulated ethics that assumes an almost concrete form in what he believes to be right and wrong.

Religion and beliefs are tied by unsuspected strings in our unconscious minds to the folk-lore and mythologies of our ancient pasts. They retain the sexual flavor of Ceres, of Circe,

of the demoniac possession of the Gadarene swine; the pre-
historic rites of initiation at puberty, and the mystic estate of
becoming adult, that is, sexually potent, and able to reproduce.
If God made man in His image, then man makes man in the
image of God.

For some obscure reason, the sexual impulse, which is the
cause of man's existence, each man and woman in the world being the effect of a cause which was a sexual impulse, has been
classified as sinful, and even when canalized into marriage, not
admirable. It is hard to correlate the act of creation with obscenity, or to reconcile such obscenities with the parents we have
loved. The changes in the bodies of men, from their childhood
into their manhood, where their lust, which means strength, is
passed on to their decline and death, are merely phases of existence on varying planes, of varying intensity. Sex must be removed equally from the management of priests who admit only
that it is sinful, and from the hands of psychoanalysts who
grope in the murky depths of the human psyche for the primeval
slime that is unfortunately a part of our heritage.

The fundaments of life are based on man's love for woman;
and woman's love for man, and the children that are the result
of that love. True obscenity, true licentiousness, are the outcome of failure. They are distortions due to the failure of the
human mechanism, but they are no more distortions than the
brutal asceticism of the Middle Ages, or the uncharitableness of
those who judge without knowledge.

Herr Hitler is an ascetic, an eater of grass. By the distortion
of his personality, by his refusal or inability to use those powers
that were put into his loins by God, perhaps he has been driven
to a madness that would put shackles upon the world. Once, a
wife, or even a dancing girl might have cured Hitler and saved
the world. Now it will take the assassin's knife. Let those who
tamper with such things take note, for they are beyond the
understanding of men.

Woman is man's security. She is a refuge, an escape. She is

the opposite from activity, and fear. Where on the outside his blood is charged with adrenalin and his blood pressure raised by the excitements of strange contacts, on the inside, in his home, which is centered round a woman, he gets release. First, the mother, then the wife, but always it is a woman who remains man's tie with the earth, through whom he came into being and through whom he passes on his seed. Without woman, man has no sense of his own reality. Existing, man requires continual proof of his existence.

The relationship of woman to man is different. To her, a man is a combination of child and God. Her children are an integral part of her, a portion of her, that has broken out of her body by a miracle of subdivision. The man who begot them remains associated with them. As they are, to some extent, replicas of him, so is he, by association, a replica of them. But woman, by the active passivity of her reproductive functions, remains the solid foundation of humanity, endlessly subjective in her necessity of rearing her young, and but faintly affected by the motives that govern masculine behaviorism.

What she has learnt of men she knows by hearsay, by the teachings of her mother, by observation and experience. But her knowledge is partly instinctive, and partly acquired, parrot-like, and accepted as phenomena are accepted. Women, being life itself, are apart from it. Similar tastes are cultivated for different reasons, similar acts, performed for diverse motives, and superficial resemblances grow from vastly different roots. Man and woman He created them. Dissimilar but complementary the one to the other, they fulfill themselves in the pattern of their lives, being joined, yet isolated, for no human being can feel what another feels, or view the same sights in the same way, or give the same words a similar meaning. Man lives his days and dies alone. Some more alone than others. A man's search for woman and a woman's for man, or God, are efforts to mitigate their aloneness, to give them such courage that they can bear the burden of their lives.

Oddly, the most envied men, the most successful, are those who have been driven by their unhappiness into success, who have sublimated their misery and used it as a mechanism for escape into a world of active fantasy, a ladder that raised them above the conditions that had become intolerable to them.

* * *

The worst things can, by a kind of overcompensation, have good effects. Today we blame Hitler. But Hitler may prove to be the savior of the world. For the world could be saved by an Antichrist. Its revolt against him would have the same effect as the coming of a new Messiah.

It is, in the end, conceivable that Hitler will have done more for the world than any man since Jesus Christ. In the event of a German victory, it is possible that the world will be welded into a single whole, and might, long after National Socialism has died, remain a single whole. It is possible that if he is defeated, a United States of Europe may come into being. It is possible that by his existence the forty-eight states of the United States of America may be welded into a nation, that the twenty-three nations of the Americas may become a continental affiliation.

The day may come when the world will give thanks for Hitler, when his picture may hang beside the Declaration of Independence as the image of the man who, by its denial, gave that document reality. The day may come when man, having passed through Gethsemane, having been crucified, shall rise again in all his glory.

It is possible that, judged by results, the Christ and the Antichrist are not very different; that disaster may be better than victory, that out of a chastened England a new England, the pride of the world, will arise newly created from the ashes of her cities and the blood of her young men. The future is in the hands of God and in the hearts of men, and by the actions of men will you know them.

* * *

Our most wonderful methods of address have become poisoned by their associations. What could be finer than the "Comrade" of communism, the "Citizen" of the French Revolution, the "Brother" of early Christianity?

How have we become content with Mister, with Mrs., with Miss, with the false gentility of "lady" for "woman," using it colloquially where it was reserved for the worshiper, in "his lady of sorrows," for the lover, in "the lady of his heart"?

By their abuse, and the company they have been forced to keep, great words and great ideas lie dead on the field of dialectic battle, or have been killed by the white-collared fears of social-climbers, who in the splendid isolation of their small positions, refuse to be the comrades of other men, plain citizens of their country, or brothers to any but their blood kin.

In the new world that must come, there must be a new creed in which man will say with humility, "I am the comrade of all men, I am the brother of all men, I am a citizen of all the world." Could this be, there would be need for little more, for a man does not slay his brother, nor steal from his comrade, nor betray his citizenship. Should it come, there would be no need to speak of charity, for there would be nothing else, only faith, hope, and charity.

Chapter Ten

The Liberators

WORLD POLITICS MUST BE REMOVED from the sphere of national amusements and mass spectacles and returned to their place, which is the ancient council house. Public men are public servants hired by the public for public work. They are men dedicated as priests are dedicated. That the public is amused at the antics of its politicians is a reflection on that public and the reason that serious men are unready to enter politics.

Statesmen are not there to make a holiday, for it is they who hold the sacrificial knife. The lives and fortunes of the people of the United States are in the hands of their president and their congressmen and their senators as those of England are in the hands of Churchill and Parliament. These are the wise men of the tribe. But are they? Or are they hunting dogs picked out by the machine for the petty jobs they can retrieve from the woods of national emergency?

One hears continual references to international law. Such references can now be regarded as academic, of interest only to the historian. Nearly all law, international as well as national, lies buried beneath the political avalanche of the last few years and months. New laws will come into being, but whether they are based on the unchanging principle of justice, or that of ar-

bitrary force, remains to be seen, and is dependent on the outcome of the struggle. Laws are tied to the economic, political,
psychological and religious necessities of populations. Laws
which have not popular approval may be enacted but will not
be enforced, except in a dictatorship, where the civil liberties
have been transferred from the people to a single representative
of the people, either by popular vote, as is possible in a crisis,
or have been taken from them by force. But to believe that the
law or legal procedure will retain its exact pattern and form
seems as absurd as imagining that anything else will retain its
pre-war shape. The demand today in religion and politics is not
for the exact interpretations; not for the letter of the Sadducees
and Pharisees but for the spirit.

The world is paralyzed by its fears. The employer's fears of
bankruptcy, the employee's fear of dismissal; the omnipresent
fear of change in all classes. And yet change is the law of life.
It is going on all the time. The loss of a tooth is change, the
growing of a fingernail is change; dying is the last change.

That the world is changing only necessitates our changing
with it, the using of our greatest asset, that of human adaptabil-
ity. No animal is as adaptable as man, none so widely distributed. Man can live, and does, from the arctic to the equator,
can be entirely carnivorous or entirely vegetarian. Yet modern
man beset by his fear of change tries continually to return to the
past he knew, its only virtue being that he was able to survive its
dangers. Man still prefers a devil he knows to the angel to
whom he has not been introduced.

The world is as it is, and man must contrive to live in it.
People still talk of the New Deal as though it were new after
seven years. Those who look back at the past are inevitably fos-
silized, turned into pillars of spiritual salt, by their denial of the
change that must accompany progress. They still search for
scapegoats—Mr. Roosevelt in America . . . Mr. Chamberlain
in England / . . M. Renaud in France—gods to be sacrificed

on the altars of their past security. Yet ideas, like men, die of old age.

Some peculiar value has been placed on men who are consistent by those who have been too lazy to analyze consistency. Imprisoned in the bakelite towers of their consistencies they comb their golden hair and stare with wondering eyes at the changing scene. Constrained by habit, they live enclosed, unwilling to acknowledge the metabolism of political or economic evolution.

A belief in the impossibility of change is an admission of insufficient courage to meet it. The wise man is ready to change his opinion, is open to conviction, but the fool abides with his folly. Change implies a thought process, means reading books, listening to educators, looking at works of art. It implies the conviction that nothing is static, finally settled, or not open to controversy.

Recent figures show that only fourteen million people in America own their homes, only three and a half million farmers own their farms, and only eleven million own bonds and stock in various companies, out of a population of a hundred and forty millions.

These figures may be higher than those of any other country, there is little doubt that they are, but they certainly leave a great deal to be desired. A man is free only when he is independent. A peasant working his own land, living at a low rate without debt, is better off than a business executive living at a high rate and without savings. What a man makes is what he has left over after he has lived. Both, the man who makes ten thousand a year and spends it, and the man who makes a thousand dollars a year and spends it, only making a living. The one lives well, the other badly, and both die insolvent.

It is probable that after the primary wants are satisfied on any family living scale, the bulk of the increased expenditure is for the purposes of economic exhibitionism, wasted in a fantastic desire to create envy, or to impress others who are following the same course. Men who blame nations for the deficits produced by the armament race are engaged in almost as useless a pursuit themselves. Their own unbalanced budgets are the result of similar competitive buying.

*   *   *

There appear to be two main psychological strains in North America. There are those whose forebears came to this country, often leaving comfort and plenty to face the terrors of hardship, Indian warfare and starvation, because they were unable to bear religious persecution, or to change the principles that governed their existence in the old world. And there are the descendants of those emigrants who came to America for gain, because the life here was easier, and the opportunities greater.

This seems, superficially at least, to explain the adamant integrity of one type of American, and the corruption of the other. Nowhere in the world is there such uprightness, such moral force, or a greater spirit of self-sacrifice; and nowhere in the world more crime, more swindling, racketeering, more graft, or exploitation. The extremity of this differentiation is usually in abeyance and becomes apparent only in an emergency which, as it increases in intensity, uncovers those motives and ways of life that were previously hidden. The good vastly outweigh the bad, but in normal times their democratic spirit of tolerance allows evil such latitude that it is able to consolidate itself into politico-criminal organizations that infiltrate the national structure and, by their ramifications, connect the lowest dock-side dives to the government in Washington.

Democracy seems, by its democracy, to be self-destructive— a virgin who, turning her face from the sight of evil, becomes engulfed by the evil which, in her rectitude, she refused to recognize. The time for raising the hem of our academic garment has passed. The time for looking away has passed. The world is stirred up like an ant heap with a stick.

Education has put a false complexion on truth. A false belief in treaties, in declarations of war, in fictitious makings of peace, in theoretical boundaries which can exist only when defended by men and guns, by ships on the seas, and aircraft in the skies.

The failure of education to seek out the truth even when her face is pock-marked, riddled with the sores of social evil and economic failure, has precipitated a war that might have been avoided had all things been regarded as controversial, and no fact or act taken as final. Education, by its harking back to half-developed thesis and precedent, has ignored change and has placed a fantastic value on that consistency which is spiritual death. There has been no limit to educational failure, to second-rate teaching, to cheapness, to sophistry, to the worship of false gods in the temples of learning. The pedagogue has taken the place of the prophet, the correspondence school that of the master. Education has been preached as a means of making a living. The best education has been considered that which brought the greatest worldly rewards. By these standards the education of Al Capone is greater than that of Diogenes, and a villa in Miami vastly preferable to a barrel in Greece.

The price of competitive education, of competitive life in all its modern forms, is now being paid. Inarticulately, the masses of the world have been demanding bread and education, have been crying with the voice of Danton for "work and knowledge." What they receive is state relief and radio programs.

The hunger for knowledge is the greatest world hunger—the greatest world need. With infinite pains after the day's work is done, laboring men with rough calloused hands make pot hooks and hangers; black men in South African mine-compounds work over little books, trying to teach themselves to read. And that these, when they become literate, are fed on Marxism is less their fault than that of a system which justifies Karl Marx to their simplicity, and denies them the teachers they would follow.

Poor men, knowing no security, are helpless in the hands of unscrupulous agitators who qualify their ignorance with half-truths and inflame their envy. They are grown men, but intellectually they are children over-eager for knowledge and without the cerebral equipment to digest it. Capacity for thought comes only with thinking, and the human mind which can be broken open like a flower can also be sealed up.

Yet there have always been liberators of the human mind, men who tried to cut the bonds of ignorance. They exist today, and will continue to exist, despite the fact that at all times so many have ended their lives on the scaffold, or died in penury.

*   *   *

This war, which began in the new Germany as a war for the middle classes against communism, has turned into a war against the classes it was supposed to save. Total war, as it exists in England today, with the regimentation of the country, or preparation for total war such as occupied the last seven years in Germany, allows no time for education. In England this has happened with regret, in Germany with intent, in the newly conquered countries by force of circumstance and German pressure. Contrary to the beliefs of either the extreme left or right, the opinions of conservative reactionaries or of communists, civilization rests neither on the uneducated masses, nor on the comparatively rich but tradition-bound aristocracy. Civilization is bourgeois. It is middle class. It is based on the good-will that exists in the small home, the small shop, and the small town. It becomes lost in the vast mass of those who work for their daily food without security and without reserves. It is equally lost among those who by reasons of their wealth live in another world, that of complete economic security. It is lost in the competition of great cities where men live without civic interest or responsibility.

The much derided small town of a generation ago was civilized. It had a culture of its own. Its life was built round the store, the bank, and the church. It was still rooted in the soil and focused. The standards may not have been intellectually high but they were real and embraced all the members of the community. Man is gregarious, interested in his fellows and helpful to them but still suspicious of strangers. In a great city all men are strangers, rubbing shoulders but without contacts.

The middle class remains the solid backbone of any country, from it are drawn most of the leaders, most of the professional men. It is, by the number of its small concerns, the greatest employer of labor and, by the sum of its small savings, the greatest national reservoir of capital.

It was to the middle class that Hitler made his appeal, frightening them with the bogey of communism. It was they who made up his vast army of technicians, and it is they, or rather their counterpart, in the conquered countries, whom he fears. The really rich he does not fear. There are too few of them. They can be bought by their love of wealth, or intimidated by their fear of losing it.

Education is at a standstill in Europe. Within the Reich it is actually forbidden, or granted only on political grounds. Universities are empty, or turned into barracks for the troops, the faculties thrown out. For this reason education in the United States assumes a new importance. It is not only important to the citizens of America but to the whole world since the culture of the world is now in the hands of America.

The internal poverty of Europe after the last war, when most countries were unable to redeem their war bonds, will be as nothing compared to the poverty which will follow this one. The people will be leveled economically to an extent hitherto unknown, and government management of business, begun in the war, will not, owing to the post-war conditions, be broken down for many years if at all. The pattern that seems likely to come into being is that of dictatorship, resembling superficially that of the totalitarian countries. Dictatorship does not necessarily imply terrorism and may, in the event of post-war disorders, be the only means of preserving order.

*   *   *

Big business may be admirable, but it is hard to reconcile the low wages which show large profits with the altruism that is claimed by the great manufacturer. The efficiency of a big business is dependent on the cutting of costs, of all costs—overhead, raw material, and running costs, in which are included wages and salaries. It is difficult to see why there has had to be so much legislation in all countries to protect the working man from exploitation unless there was some definite reason for such legislation, some possibility that, were it not enacted, the equity on which the relations of employer and employee are balanced would be abused.

Big business is anonymous. The executive is very far removed from the worker. He is unaware of him except as a unit. By its centralization for business reasons, big business has become humanly de-centralized. Distance distorts the human being by perspective. Any man who can use a rifle will shoot another man three hundred yards away. At that range he is not a man. He looks like a toy, a midget. To shoot him is not murder.

Dictatorship is the development of big business to its logical end. It is the final combine that embraces all business, the final merger that brings whole nations onto its payroll without redress. The affinity that is apparent between certain business men, as appeasers, and the totalitarian powers is that they alone can understand and appreciate the full efficiency of the fascist machine. No more arguments, no more strikes, and the god of production served by every man, woman, and child in the country.

Business has a defense when accused of its fascist policy, that is superficially excellent. It says "but where would we be in a totalitarian country—our money would be gone." This is one of those half truths that are so dangerous. Big business neither thinks nor works in terms of ordinary money. It works on power, which is dynamic money, as opposed to money in the bank, which is static money—and power they would retain.

What business would really like is a return to the Victorian standards. What it really fears is socialization of any sort, that is, revolution even though it be bloodless, and fascism seems to them the best deal they can make. Consciously or unconsciously business inclines towards the right, refusing to see the middle course, which is neither right nor left, but a compromise in which the best of both systems is blended and grafted onto the stock of our present social and economic methods of existence,

There is a superficial resemblance between the F.B.I., the C.I.D. and the gestapo. All three are secret police and are partially occupied in dealing with subversive elements. The difference is only one of degree, but in that degree lies the difference between the freedom and the slavery of nations.

No one can say how long the present period will last. When the war is over conditions will still be such, and the time factor so vital, that the democratic form of government by committee and subcommittee, by argument, will be impossible in Europe, and perhaps impossible even in the United States, whether it becomes involved in the war or not.

The small importer, the small retailer, even the small farmer, if they exist at all, will have to exist under a controlled economy of production, labor and distribution. It was the inevitability of this phase and the refusal to face it that helped to cause the delay in the Allied war effort. Chamberlain and Daladier were unwilling to put such a yoke on the neck of their people while they still hoped it could be avoided by a war of attrition.

The modern way of life has gone, and a new way must come. Whether it be good or evil depends on the people. It is conceivable that out of England will come a new formula in which the virtues of the old system are combined with those of the new, as out of England came the idea of the "rights of man" and the organization of constitutional government.

It is impossible to condemn every theory of National Socialism, or communism, for within the putrescence of their forms are contained the germs of new truths, such as the theory of national solidarity, which could be advanced to international solidarity, which means no more than love your neighbor, or do unto your neighbor as you would he would do unto you. When the cloak of political formula is removed, they both encourage youth groups, local customs, arts, and universal service to the state.

That these ideals were used as bait to delude people into accepting such ideologies does not detract from the abstract virtue of those ideals, and does show how willingly men endeavor to go forward, how lost they are in the mental chaos. As civilization seems to be an attitude of mind, culture seems to be a matter of the relationships existing between individuals. As such, culture exists to a greater extent in an African native village, or a collection of Eskimo snow houses than in London, Paris, or New York. In such primitive societies food is never refused to the passerby; a strange native in Africa feeds without question from any cooking pot as a right. In such societies each man has his place, the hunter, the dresser of skins, the maker of spears and hoes, the story-teller, and the midwife. In such a community the vices of a single man affect the others directly, and the outstanding virtues of one man may bring prosperity to the rest. In this sense culture is communal and relatively unselfish.

The now almost extinct Bushman owned as personal possessions only his weapons, clothes, and cooking pots. He killed no more than he could eat. He claimed nothing that he did not use continually. Material civilization with its emphasis on personal wealth has lost sight of the primitive ideal of common possessions, the ideal of the early Christians, and is at last swinging back to it by means of totalitarianism, the possession of all things by the state, which is merely the enlarged tribe, and may in the future come to include the whole world.

There was a time when, if there was only one pear tree in a community, everyone would take an interest in it, protect it, talk about it, and wait with a pleasant sense of anticipation for the time when the pears would ripen. Now no one would care.

They can buy pears at any time of the year. Even the owner of the tree would no longer care, no longer even bother to prune it. But forgotten, deep in the hearts of everyone, the old instincts exist. Every man who plays golf is sublimating his hunting instinct. Every woman who buys a bunch of flowers is trying, with lacquered, helpless fingernails, to get back into the soil that is inseparable from her heredity.

Before we can go forward we must go back, not thirty or forty years, as the reactionaries would have it, to the fictitious prosperity of mass production by sweated labor, but back into the dim ages where man began his organized life, and on those ancient roots graft the tree of modern science and industry. We must go back to the days when men still believed in God, and on that belief graft the new belief in God which is an all-embracing love of man; go back, even in the use of our language, to the simple purity of its roots, back into the thought of origins and implied meanings.

A word in itself means little. It rarely means what it appears to mean. The actual meaning is the implication that is carried by the word. Words as simple as rose, woman, horse, all carry a hundred shades, a hundred memories according to their use and context in the life and experience of those who read them. The word neutrality, which has become a key word, has an implication of sexlessness, of sloth, of apathy. It is strange that so many nations deliberately proclaimed themselves gelded and proved it by their actions. Neutrality has shown itself to be negative, a combination of wishful thinking and a desire to profit by the misfortunes of others; an endeavor to remain anonymous and to assume the protective coloration of disinterest.

Love of pleasure, the outcome of prosperity, has sapped the virility of the democracies, rendering them an easy prey for totalitarians with their cult of a spurious masculinity. Both the democracies and the totalitarians have become unbalanced in the extremity of their views with their worship of pleasure on the one hand and of power on the other.

The pleasure sexuality of the democracies is counter-balanced by the brutal sexuality of the Reich. Normality cannot be induced by either laxness or repression. There is a natural level of sexual relations between men and women, as there is in every other phase of life—a series of compromises and adjustments that will in the end, by trial and error, fulfill their natural ends and produce a form of life suited to modern man into which he will fit because it has been built round him.

The will for good, for happiness, vastly outweighs the powers of evil for evil. For every murderer there are thousands who would not take life, but those thousands receive no publicity and it is upon them, the anonymous men of good will, that the future of the world depends.

It is a terrifying thought that there should be men among us who can subscribe to a doctrine of lies, of forgery and coercion; that some of them should be prominent businessmen, factory-owners, university professors, officers of the army and navy, and politicians who hold the reins of government. It is terrifying that those who cry "it can't happen here" have not seen that it has already happened, in Louisiana, in New Jersey, in Kansas City; that it exists in every big city, in every crooked labor organization, in every political set-up of jobbery and nepotism; that every rake-off and cut, every evasion of income tax, or other law, is a wedge driven into the democratic system.

Though they may grow great, all things begin in a small way, as Hitler did, and then, as power begets power, they change. Laws are rewritten so that those who break the law are operating within it. The running of hot oil, of controlling chain-houses of prostitution, of handling shipments of narcotics, all become easy when justice is under the control of the fixers. The break-down of legitimacy produces, and must precede, the chaos that is the dictator's chance.

Yet there is no need for panic. There is possibly even no great reason to be disturbed. What has happened is logical, it epitomizes all logic, all cause and effect, all evolution. Those whose mental processes were not arrested twenty-two years ago, that is the Germans, are defeating those whose brains have become atrophied by lack of use. Guns for butter, guns to get butter, became a religion, a mania, a philosophy that depends on the elimination of what has been called right, but which if the Germans win may be known as weakness.

The citizens of America must think for themselves and of themselves. They must remember that they are the last great democracy, the country on which the countless millions of despoiled, homeless, and distracted people of Europe depend. Not for help. They are beyond help. But for the knowledge that somewhere civilization still exists; that somewhere there is still freedom of thought, speech, and worship. One country is the hope of the world. What stands between America and this great destiny is not the fifth column whose technique is now understood, but the sixth column, the column of the unready, the column of the wishful thinkers and those who, like a New England professor of history, consider that Hitler has sharp Yankee insight, and that a Nazi triumph in Europe would have no effect on America.

Should the Germans be successful in the battle of Britain it is unlikely that they will move against the United States immediately. Their victory would be followed by disclaiming all interest in this hemisphere, by reconciliations, even by very favorable trade agreements which would slow down all defense activities, prove how right the appeasers had been in their estimation of Teutonic reason, and make fools of the real leaders.

Then, as Germany organized the conquered countries, coordinated the conquered fleets of merchant and war vessels, the tone would change. There would be protests about the immense German minority in the United States, the twenty or thirty million people of German descent in this country who are separated from their fatherland and condemned to live in the chaos of an unorganized democracy; demands for rights; more protests, and at last that finely strung Teutonic patience would become exhausted.

It cannot be said that Germany has no designs on America, the richest democracy in the world, when everywhere one reads of their undisguised envy, when it is reported that: "Before the late Douglas Fairbanks died he had a remarkable conversation with Hitler's Minister of Propaganda, Herr Joseph Goebbels. Intelligence officers to whom Fairbanks told the story are now dusting it off and examining it carefully to see what significance it has in regard to Hitler's future conduct toward the United States.

"Fairbanks and his wife, the former Lady Ashley, were vacationing at Venice one year ago. Goebbels also had come to Venice, and the town was so decorated in his honor that the Fairbanks home was about the only one along the Grand Canal which did not fly the swastika.

"Later at the Lido, Fairbanks was introduced to Goebbels, who called him 'Zorro,' no doubt remembering Fairbanks' picture, 'The Mark of Zorro'. At a dinner, Goebbels sat beside Lady Ashley and became extremely frank about Nazi ambitions, predicting that Poland would be taken in the near future.

"Lady Ashley countered that while Hitler might be able to take some of the war-born states of Europe, his philosophy never would be accepted by the Low Countries.

"To this Goebbels replied: 'Oh, France and Great Britain are tired old men. They will never fight.'

"The conversation then went on to the United States, which Goebbels described as a country of 'niggers and Jews.'

" 'They will never fight,' he said. 'Our political philosophy will sweep the world. When it comes to America we shall conquer you by methods and means of which you know nothing.'

"Later, Goebbels said Germany's greatest shame was the fact that she was without a great fleet, had been forced to scuttle it at Scapa Flow after the World War. Regarding this sorrowful incident Hitler had practiced the philosophy of Gambetta, 'Think of it always, speak of it never.'

"And since Hitler's greatest ambition was to secure a new fleet, he planned to let the British off lightly if they surrendered their navy to Germany.

"Goebbels did not specify whom the fleet was to be used against, but as he left the Fairbankses he made this boastful farewell: 'See you in the United States in 18 months.'

"Fairbanks at first did not pay much attention to the remark, but later got to thinking it over. Finally he decided to report the conversation to intelligence officers."

Germany, however, will never attack America if she is strong. A powerful air force and navy would make such an attack impossible and a big army, fully equipped, even without the navy and air force, would at least stave off the danger while these services are being built up. The necessity for two million trained troops in this country is due only to the time factor, to fill in the two to six years required for the building of a great air force and of a second fleet.

The average civilian is still at a loss when discussing military training. He is still afraid that he may be damaged psychologically by serving his country and being disciplined. It does not occur to him that he is also damaged psychologically by his lack of discipline, or that a year's training may be of immense value to him physically. If conscription is general, no time as far as competitive work is concerned is lost. No one obtains an advantage over any one else, and the free democratic soldier, the man trained to bear arms for his country, is a man worthy of respect, a true citizen. But there still remains a hang-over from the "lewd and licentious soldier" of the Napoleonic wars and a vague objection to the swashbuckling soldier of the last war who, though he saw no active service, allowed his mental development to be arrested by the months he spent in khaki. There is still much talk of the hundred and twenty-six thousand doughboys who lost their lives in the last war. There is no talk of the way those casualties would have been reduced by fuller training, or by better organized medical services. A soldier is trained to kill while avoiding death himself and the heaviest casualties are always among young troops. 62,670 of the casualties were deaths from disease.

The making of a soldier can, for practical purposes, be divided into two parts. The first is psychological. It is the drill which seems to have nothing to do with warfare, the discipline that teaches him to take pride in himself and his regiment. It is this that makes him a trained cog in the machine, makes him mobile, and enables him to be moved as an orderly part of a unit instead of as a member of a mob. Once the movements of close-order drill were battle formations, now they serve no useful purpose save that of coordinating single men into bodies of men. Privates Jones, Smith, Black, White and their comrades lose their individuality and become a Platoon, which again loses itself in the Company, which is part of the Battalion. The Battalion is part of the Brigade, and the Brigade part of the Division. So the twenty thousand-odd men, all of whom are individuals with mothers, sisters, and young ladies interested in their welfare, become a single striking force whose power is dependent first of all on the quality of the discipline and esprit de corps among those men, and secondly, on the efficacy of their equipment and their efficiency in its use. The best equipment is useless without men, but equipment once the factories are organized can be made more quickly than men can be trained.

The shortage will probably be in non-commissioned officers, and officers who are capable of training a modern democratic army, or who understand the basic principles of war sufficiently well to adapt them to the new rapid-moving battle tactic which is the full development of the machine and the abandonment of the machine when its efficacy is impaired. "Save the guns" dates back to the days of hand-forged ordnance. Men who will do no bayonet fighting must be trained in it to obtain the spirit of offensive. The cold steel is generally only an idea, but it is an idea which gets men up to the enemy. Almost always, when it comes to fighting at close quarters, one or the other turns and runs before they actually close in combat.

Being a soldier can destroy no man though he may die of it. Standing by while others fight is what destroys him. An argument against conscription is the question, where are the troops going to be employed? and if they are not going to be employed, why have them?

The answer is that if there are enough soldiers, if they are well enough trained, and well enough equipped, there will be no need to employ them. The threat will be enough.

The man with a gun, a reputation as a good shot, and a trained police dog is not likely to have burglars. Naturally he has the expense of buying his gun and his dog, and the cost of their upkeep.

Adequate defense is insurance. Inadequate defense is an act of faith, or as a senator recently put it, "I'd sooner have them and not want them than want them and not have them."

*　　*　　*

Most countries seem to begin a new war where they left off the last one. The English fought the Boer War according to rules established in the Crimea. They started the war in 1914 as if it was another Boer War, and the war of 1939 was begun by the Allies with the certainty that they could hold it immobile according to the best trench warfare tradition of 1917.

In 1910 the French general staff stated that they were making machine guns to please the public which demanded them, but that they would be of no use. In 1914 the French took the field in the long blue coats and the red trousers of the Third Empire. Their cuirassiers went into action with shining breastplates and long horse tails swinging from their helmets.

In 1940 America still seems to count on the use of cavalry armed with pistols, clinging to the magnificent tradition of such generals as Jeb Stuart and Forrest. It does not occur to anyone, except the German general staff, to think what Stuart would have done if he had had tanks at his disposal. British cavalry regiments when they were mechanized still wore spurs, sounded "stables" on their trumpets when they groomed their iron horses, and "feed and water" for refueling. Most of the British disasters of the last war were due to cavalry generals who thought in terms of the *arme blanche* and the charge, apparently still hypnotized by Lucan's epic tragedy at Balaklava.

Germany has a great number of cavalry but they are employed as mounted infantry. The horse is not a charger but a beast of burden for use in country too close or too broken for the motorized units.

The minds of professional soldiers seem to atrophy more easily than those of other men, and the older officers, who by virtue of their age are the most senior in all countries, retain their childish affection for the horse and the glamor of a military operation seen in terms of horse, foot, and guns. The greatest generals are gunners and engineers who see war for what it is, who see it as a mathematical problem concerned with the complex play between weight of projectile, volume of fire, concentration of strength in men, and the psychological factor of morale.

But if the mechanization of war has changed, the war-heat among men is engendered in the way it always has been, by music, by the rhythm of marching feet and the rattle of rolling cannons. The war dance—by means of the newspapers, the radio and public entertainments—still continues. Parades and martial music still pull on the old battle chords that are hidden in the hearts of the young men. The young braves still wish to prove their courage and the old witch doctors and wise men have again provided them with opportunity.

The change, and there is a change, is that now, as is being seen in England, men are no longer ready as they were to fight for causes which are not fully stated. They are less interested in abstract glory than in the concrete results of war as it will affect their lives personally and those of their children.

* * *

Germany in her indiscriminate bombing of London has made a profound psychological mistake. Germany has now set hands upon America's historic past. Today, with the bombing of ancient English monuments the monuments of America are also bombed.

Shakespeare, Bacon, Raleigh, Wren, Chaucer, Milton, Newton, Wesley, Wycliffe are all American—a part of American culture, welded into it before the separation of the two countries. American liberties were born on the marsh of Runnymede, were confirmed by Cromwell, Lord Protector of England, and carried from England to the Americas, where the Constitution was made on an improved conception of English justice and the religious principles of the Pilgrim Fathers.

What is assumed to be sentimental curiosity on the part of the American tourist is no such thing. It is the interest of a normal human being in the past of his race; its literature, its heroes, its buildings, its cities, and its countryside. There are hereditary roots that have been laughed at, but cannot be denied. The American may have no liking or regard for an Englishman but thinks, and justifiably so, that the monuments and soil of England are partly his.

Until recently there was plenty of cause for disillusion. In the last war Germany was beaten. Clemenceau the Tiger had seen to it that she was stripped of guns, planes, and rifles. Her armament works were wrecked, and bridgeheads forty miles deep were established on the right bank of the Rhine. And then suddenly all was changed. Germany was rearming. Germany was being encouraged to rearm. Not by the man in the street—he was simple enough, having fought Germany once, still to fear her, but by those financial forces that moved, like mistresses, behind the politics of France and England; the shadowy court beauties of industry, economics, and great interests, that have replaced the courtesans of kings. The looseness of a monarch was easily understood by the ordinary common man, but the amorality of international finance was beyond him and he gave up. Immorality can be understood, can even, upon occasion, be condoned since it is explicable. Amorality cannot be explained or understood, and it is the amoral expediency of National Socialism which has roused the democracies to the point where they will die before they bow before it.

It was impossible for the ordinary man to reconcile the events that have taken place since 1933 with the promises of 1918. The world had been promised to him if he was willing to fight for it. He fought for it, and then, having gained the world, it was taken away from him. The world was no safer for democracy. The world was safe for business.

* * *

A personal fear of Hitler is natural since through him our lives are disorganized and our future existence at stake. But a real fear of him is absurd, as he will find his own end, like every other phenomenon. It is a natural law that abnormality produces abnormality, that a super-plus produces a super-minus by the fact of its existence.

Certain conditions favorable to locusts produce a plague of locusts that devour everything in front of them, but owing to their numbers they upset the natural laws of increase and their enemies also increase. The birds that prey on them, with such an abundance of food, rear immense quantities of young, and ichneumon flies, which are usually uncommon, lay their eggs in their bodies, mature in them, hatch out and attack them again in ever greater numbers.

Had conditions not been favorable in Germany, there could have been no Hitler. Had there been no Hitler there might have been no Churchill. Without Hitler and Churchill, England might have been more weakened by her years of success than she will be eventually by her losses in war.

Calamity and disaster are calamity and disaster only for those who suffer them. The ones who follow may benefit vastly. Our persons are without significance except as the bearers of torches. The light was handed to us and must be passed on.

In spite of war, of threatened disaster, life goes on in England. Children play; young men and women hold hands in darkened houses; babies are born. Old people die, while trees grow leaves, and lose them according to the seasons. The park railings are torn down, the parks cut up with trenches, but the birds still mate and sing, still rear their young. The green fields are dotted with stumps and wrecked cars, but they are still green. Church steeples still point their fingers to the skies and hold their bells silent in the lull before the storm of England; but their bells hang in their belfries, and the rivers roll under ancient bridges on their ancient beds. There are still trout in those rivers; they still lie, gently moving in the brown water as they face upstream. Butterflies still fly in the meadows, and the roads now signless, still lead through England. The pulse of England still beats slowly, undeterred, for there are things there that cannot be destroyed. Only the bodies of free men and women can be destroyed, the bodies of free men and women easily, but not their minds which are steadfast. Nor can the sap of the broken trees be stopped from running, nor the seeds in the pitted fields from germinating.

Should the dark cloud fall, should our island be destroyed, there will be no finality in that destruction, for the seed of England is too widely sown, too deeply planted. The death of old England cannot destroy her spawn, nor the razing of her monuments undo the charters of her ancient justice.

Morituri te Salutant.

Chapter Eleven

"The American Way"

THE AMERICAN WAY is not a way of luxury. It has nothing to do with ease, except the ease and luxury that are the birthright of free men and women. It is a mental approach, a deep feeling that permeates the nation. That has, basically, been unaffected by the materialistic trend which has apparently swamped it.

Thoreau was an American . . . an exponent of one of the American ways. He said: "The mass of men lead lives of quiet desperation. Their incessant anxiety and strain is a well-nigh incurable form of disease. They have no time to be anything but machines. It is a fool's life.

"It appears that they honestly think there is no choice left; but no way of thinking or doing, however ancient, can be trusted without proof.

"The nation itself, with all its so-called internal improvements, is an unwieldy and overgrown establishment, ruined by luxury and heedless expense, by want of calculation and a worthy aim, as are a million households in the land; and the only cure for it, as for them, is in a rigid economy, a stern simplicity of life and elevation of purpose. With respect to luxuries and comforts, the wisest have ever lived a simple life.

"Most men are so occupied with the factitious cares of life

that its finer fruits cannot be plucked by them. To be a philosopher is not merely to have subtle thoughts, but so to love wisdom as to live a life of simplicity, independence, magnanimity and trust. It is to solve some of the problems of life, not only theoretically, but practically. What is the nature of the luxury which enervates and destroys nations?

"It is remarkable how easily we fall into a particular route, and make a beaten track for ourselves. The surface of the earth is soft and impressible by the feet of men; and so with the paths which the mind travels. How worn and dusty, then, how deep the ruts of tradition and conformity!

"But if a man does not keep pace with his companions, perhaps it is because he hears a different drummer. Let him step to the music which he hears, however measured or far away. I learned this, at least, by my experiment: that if one advances confidently in the direction of his dreams, and endeavors to live the life which he had imagined, he will meet with a success unexpected in common hours. He will put some things behind; and more liberal laws will begin to establish themselves around and within him. In proportion as he simplifies his life, the laws of the universe will appear less complex, and solitude will not be solitude, nor poverty poverty, nor weakness weakness. If you have built castles in the air, your work need not be lost; that is where they should be. Now put the foundations under them."

Theodore Roosevelt, Jack London, and Colonel Cody were other exponents of other American ways. So were Edison, Brigham Young, Paul Jones, Burbank, Mrs. Eddy, Benjamin Franklin, and Abraham Lincoln. There is no end to the list of American heroes or of their American ways of life, which in each case was divorced from luxury, from what is today known as pleasure, from ease or sloth. The old American culture has not been lost. It has only been covered by a veneer. Under a hard-boiled exterior the American remains deeply religious, full of sentiment and without the cynicism that made the old world

so disastrously tolerant. He remains a perfectionist equally in his demand for the best kind of marriage and the highest skyscraper. He is unready to compromise. He demands the finest in everything, the biggest, the fastest, the most beautiful. He is undeterred by the apparent impossibility of obtaining a cactus without thorns, or raspberries that have the qualities of blackberries. He achieves them. He resembles the child who cries for the moon, with the difference that when he grows up, he gets it.

But his way of life is incompatible with the way insisted upon by Hitler or that which would be imposed upon the Americas by a German victory. Without invasion, without direct threat even, a victorious Hitler means the regimentation of the nation for preparedness.

Lincoln said the world cannot exist permanently half free and half slave, and the situation was summed up by Mussolini when he said, "the struggle between two worlds can permit no compromise . . . It is either we or they." And by Hitler when he said of the war, "It will go on till one or the other cracks. And it will not be Germany that cracks."

Britain is America's first line of defense. That it is three thousand miles away is an advantage. It is the English that are getting bombed. And England, now a fortress, is like a giant pill box which must be taken before Hitler can advance. If England is defeated, the face of the world is utterly changed, perhaps for good, certainly for many years. If she holds out, she is the rock against which the resources of Germany will be shattered. England is not asking for much—moral support and the products of the American factories. What she is paying for them in blood and treasure is beyond all calculation.

Brazil is five thousand miles away, and the United States has guaranteed Brazil. Yet Brazil has not Great Britain's workshops which, in German hands, would make the protection of Brazil impossible. The old measurements have gone with old standards. Hitler has consolidated his gains as he went along by exploiting the workers and shops of his conquered territories. The seventy-ton tanks that accounted for France were products of the Skoda works. The battleships that may one day shell New York City will be the products of English yards if they come into his possession.

While Americans have Englishmen ready to fight for them, it would seem wise to keep them in the field, to keep their guns in their hands, their planes in the skies, and their ships on the seas—both wiser and cheaper. With a British victory there would be no need for rearmament or the sacrifice that rearmament will entail.

Help to England has changed its form in the last few months. It has lost its altruism and become sound common sense. "The Lord helps those who help themselves" is translated into "the Lord is more likely to help the United States of America if it helps England."

The only objection to helping England at this time, when there is no question of sending an expeditionary force to Europe, is that it may annoy Hitler—that such help might produce war between America and the German Reich. Hitler is already annoyed, and the war, though undeclared, is already on. It began when the first of Hitler's agents entered the country. There are new casualties, due to sabotage, almost daily.

At first, it was only the sentimentalists who would have gone to the aid of England. Now, it is only a new lot of sentimentalists who will not.

The report of the Naval Affairs Committee of the Senate is public property. It stated that: "From all the evidence available it appears that the United States can be conquered without military conquest of continental United States. An effective blockade against our foreign commerce can be maintained at points thousands of miles from our coasts and well beyond aircraft range. Our outlying possessions will be captured and used against us as advance bases. There will be nothing to prevent the establishment of bases, by force if necessary, in this hemisphere, from which as well as from aircraft carriers, repeated bombing raids can be dispatched against our highly industrialized areas. . . .

"Under the foregoing conditions, enemy ships, except in the form of raiders, need not approach anywhere near our shores. With the loss of our outlying possessions, our foreign commerce, and subject to continual raids upon our coastal areas, our ultimate defeat is inevitable. It will be only a question of time, depending on how long our national will to further resist will hold out. Without the power to carry the fight to the enemy, there can be no alternative other than subjugation to his wishes."

*   *   *

American foreign policy has followed certain established lines for nearly a century and a half. The present negotiations between Great Britain and America in the middle of a great war follow the policy that gave birth to the Monroe Doctrine . . . and before that, in 1803, to the treaty that during the Napoleonic wars transferred Louisiana from France to the United States.

Mr. Roosevelt and Mr. Churchill are following in the footsteps of Mr. Canning and Mr. Monroe. The vital interests of the countries they represent are dependent on the Atlantic Ocean. A sea is as much a possession, or even more of a possession, than an area of land. There is little doubt that the United States of America would fight for her foreign possessions were they threatened. There is little doubt that she will, in the end, fight for the Atlantic Ocean which is hers, jointly with Great Britain, if it is endangered.

In 1798 England was at war with Napoleon, who was maneuvering to obtain control of the "resources of South America." Jefferson said: "The day that France takes possession of New Orleans fixes the sentence which is to retain her forever within her low-water mark. It seals the union of the two nations who, in conjunction, can maintain exclusive possession of the ocean. From that moment we must marry ourselves to the British fleet and nation. . . . This is not a state of things we seek or desire. It is one which this measure, if adopted by France, forces on us as necessary as any other cause, by the laws of nature, brings on its necessary effect."

According to Walter Lippmann, there were three main points in Jefferson's policy—no revolutionary imperialism must be allowed to establish itself on this side of the Atlantic; this can be achieved only when the Anglo-American forces control the ocean; and thirdly, that to maintain England's and the United States' exclusive possession of the Atlantic he would, if necessary, "marry ourselves to the British fleet and nation."

Jefferson demanded the acceptance of Mr. Monroe's suggestions on the grounds "that while Europe is laboring to become the domicile of despotism, our endeavor should surely be to make our hemisphere that of freedom. One nation, most of all, could disturb us in this pursuit; she now offers to lead, aid, and accompany us in it. By acceding to her proposition, we detach her from the bands, bring her mighty weight into the scale of free government, and emancipate a continent at one stroke, which might otherwise linger long in doubt and difficulty. Great Britain is the nation which can do us the most harm of any one, and with her on our side we need not fear the whole world. With her, then, we should most sedulously cherish a cordial friendship; and nothing would tend more to knit our affections than to be fighting once more, side by side, in the same cause. Not that I would purchase even her amity at the price of taking part in her wars.

"But the war in which the present proposition might engage us, should that be its consequence, is not her war, but ours. Its object is to introduce and establish the American system, of keeping out of our land all foreign powers—of never permitting those of Europe to intermeddle with the affairs of our nations. It is to maintain our own principle, not to depart from it. And if, to facilitate this, we can effect a division in the body of the European powers, and draw over to our side its most powerful member, surely we should do it. But I am clearly of Mr. Canning's opinion, that it will prevent instead of provoking war. With Great Britain withdrawn from their scale and shifted into that of our two continents, all Europe combined would not undertake such a war, for how would they propose to get at either enemy without superior fleets? Nor is the occasion to be slighted which this proposition offers of declaring our protest against the atrocious violations of the rights of nations by the interference of any one in the internal affairs of another, so flagitiously begun by Bonaparte, and now continued by the equally lawless alliance calling itself holy."

At President Monroe's request, Jefferson sent the papers to Madison, who replied: "I return the letter of the President. The correspondence from abroad has gone back to him, as you desired. I have expressed to him my concurrence in the policy of meeting the advances of the British government, having an eye to the forms of our constitution in every step in the road to war. With the British power and navy combined with our own, we have nothing to fear from the rest of the world; and in the great struggle of the epoch between liberty and despotism, we owe it to ourselves to sustain the former, in this hemisphere at least."

It is more than a century since the fifth President of the United States offered some advice to those who would remain neutral. James Monroe said: "The history of the late wars in Europe furnishes a complete demonstration that no system of conduct, however correct in principle, can protect neutral Powers from injury from any party; that a defenseless position and distinguished love of peace are the surest invitation to war, and that there is no way to avoid it other than being always prepared and willing for just cause to meet it."

The conception of isolation is the conception of insulation— is the fairy story of the Beautiful Maiden in the Ivory Tower, the result of a narrow point of view which does not see the world as one; each part of it intimately related to the other parts. If this was true a century ago it is still more true today.

Since prehistoric times men have crossed the Atlantic. Bretons, Danes, Norsemen, Spaniards, Frenchmen, Englishmen, Dutchmen have come here. The ocean is a waterway which joins as much as it separates.

Isolated lines and paragraphs have been taken from the speeches of America's great men, removed from their context, and fed to the American public, to lull them into beliefs never held by the fathers of this country.

Why is it supposed that they never told an unpalatable truth? Why is it assumed that they considered what has come to be "the American way of life"—a way which had not then come into being—before they considered American honor and integrity? Luxury is not compatible with sacrifice. And the time has come for sacrifice.

Even the W.P.A. worker in America lives on at a higher standard of comfort than did employed people in Europe before the war. Willing or unwilling, this high standard cannot last and cannot remain unaffected by the European war, or by the taxation that has just begun. Appropriation will follow appropriation, tax follow tax, super tax follow super tax, of necessity. The luxury of the past, and the apathy induced by it, are going to be paid for in the future. But why should this cause resentment? Luxury has little to do with happiness. It has little to do with Lincoln's Gettysburg address, in which he said: "Fourscore and seven years ago our fathers brought forth on this continent a new nation, conceived in liberty and dedicated to the proposition that all men are created equal.

"Now we are engaged in a great civil war, testing whether that nation or any nation so conceived and so dedicated can long endure. We are met on a great battlefield of that war. We have come to dedicate a portion of that field, as a final resting-place of those who here gave their lives that this nation might live. It is altogether fitting and proper that we should do this.

"But, in a larger sense, we cannot dedicate—we cannot consecrate—we cannot hallow—this ground. The brave men, living and dead, who struggled here, have consecrated it, far above our poor power to add or detract. The world will little note, nor long remember, what we say here, but it can never forget what they did here. It is for us the living, rather, to be dedicated here to the unfinished work which they who fought here have thus far so nobly advanced. It is rather for us to be here dedicated to the great task remaining before us—that from these honored dead we take increased devotion to that cause for which they gave the last full measure of devotion—that we here highly resolve that these dead shall not have died in vain—that this nation, under God, shall have a new birth of freedom—and that government of the people, by the people, for the people shall not perish from the earth."

This is perhaps the finest expression of a public ideal ever made in our language . . . one that is applicable not only in the United States of America, but everywhere—in all places where men are free.

Unfortunately, as with the Bible, such speeches are over-familiar. They were learned parrot-like at school. It is hard to imagine the impact such a speech, or the reading of the New Testament, would make upon an open, adult mind that had never heard them. Repetition breeds contempt as common usage makes things common.

There are things—words, books, and objects—which should be reserved for special occasions. There is something to be said for the attitude of our parents who kept certain things for best. There was wisdom in this, as there was wisdom in their good manners and their conventions which served a purpose—that of acting as a framework for ethical behavior. That tradition has been thrown overboard is without significance, for a new convention, a new ethical and moral code will take its

place—derived from it but more fitted to the times in which
we live.

*   *   *

Mental confusion surrounds everything today. Nothing is
clean-cut. Nothing, neither man nor event, can be accepted
without qualifications. Yet there has never been a time when it
was so vital for a man to make up his mind as there is now,
when the conflicting sources of all current information are such
that it is impossible to know what to believe. The difficulties are
endless. Every paper we pick up presents news which we cannot reconcile with our previous opinions. For example, it was
reported at Andover, New Jersey, on August 19th:

"An out-in-the-open flare-up has occurred among elements
of the German-American Bund, and welding of a sympathetic
relationship between the Bund and the Ku Klux Klan appeared to be the fruits of a Klan 'Americanization' rally at
the Bund's Camp Nordland here.

"The rally was disrupted when six men began distributing
a pamphlet entitled 'an appeal to friends of Fritz Kuhn.'

"The six were arrested and later fined $10 each on disorderly
conduct charges.

"The pamphlet incident came midway in the rally, for which
the New Jersey Klan had rented the camp from the Bund.
Earlier, August Klapprott, camp manager, extended a welcome
to 'the anti-war, pro-Americans who had the courage to attend
this rally.'

"Klan speakers expressed sympathy for members of the Bund
who had been 'persecuted' for their adherence to the doctrines
of Nazi Germany."

From this it appears that the Ku Klux Klan, whose activities in the name of American patriotism have run from the
lynching of *niggers* to attacks on the Jehovah's harmless Wit-
nesses, are now to all intents and purposes affiliated with the

German-American Bund, members of which they consider persecuted. This is the usual paradox reappearing, in which the persecutors represent themselves as the persecuted, and the unpatriotic as the patriots.

Undue emphasis on un-American behavior becomes an ism —Americanism, a word not mentioned in the writings of the great Americans—Washington . . . Monroe . . . Jefferson . . . Lincoln. It becomes a slogan with which to attack racial and political groups, a weapon whose use in the name of America will turn brother against brother and house against house. By such affirmations, subversive activities are camouflaged and Hitler is assisted by that fifth column on which he counts so much.

Again Col. Wm. Donovan and Edgar Mowrer state that: "when all allowance has been made for Hitler's superior armies, his resourcefulness, his daring, and the vital assistance by Germans living within the victim countries, his success can only be explained by another factor. This is nothing less than the presence among his enemies of what, since the Spanish civil war, has been known as the 'fifth column.'

"Since no country has ever been unanimous, a 'fifth column' has existed potentially in every land in every war. But despotic or totalitarian countries ruthlessly suppress it at home while exploiting it elsewhere. It is in a democracy that the 'fifth column' can function most freely and effectively. It remained for Adolph Hitler's genius to raise the creation, strengthening organization and activity of the 'fifth column' in the countries that opposed him to a decisive weapon.

"He said more or less openly that he would do so: 'We need armies. But we shall not use them as in 1914. The place of artillery will in the future be taken by revolutionary propaganda, to break down the enemy psychologically before the armies begin to function at all. The enemy people must be demoralized and ready to capitulate before military action can even be thought of. . . . Mental confusion, indecisiveness, panic, these are our weapons. The history of revolutions . . . is always the same: The ruling classes capitulate. Why? Defeatism: They no longer have the will to conquer.'

"The propaganda machine for creating and sustaining a 'fifth column'—again according to Hitler's confessed theory—is of a double nature. On one side it aims at influencing the masses. For this purpose Hitler in the present war utilizes his radio traitors. Lord Haw Haw for the English, Ferdonnet for the French, and to some extent, particularly in the last two years, Communist agitators whom he tricked or corrupted into serving him. But for the classes he had a much more subtle bait. As he himself put it: 'The results at which I aim are only to be obtained by the systematic corruption of the possessing and governing classes. Business advantages, erotic satisfactions, and ambition, are the three main stops in our propaganda organ."

These are just newspaper clippings. But they are the only sources of information open to the public and from them the man in the street has to form his opinion.

Then in the gossip columns it is said that Riedl, the German air attaché at Washington, is kept on there, despite what is known of his activities, because of his pull with the du Pont family; that the Duke of Buccleuch has been turned out of his post as Lord Steward of the Royal Household owing to his Nazi sympathies; that a fortune has been made out of manipulations of federal philately; that Al Capone is richer than he ever was and is trying to obtain a refund on his income tax; that a judge, now in jail, ruled that sending money to criminals at large is not harboring them; that a well-known refugee replied to some questions about a trailer that had been brought across the Atlantic, "Why, all refugees have trailers nowadays. . . ." (A strange reflection on our civilization when the rich can still say with Marie Antoinette, "If they have no bread let them eat cake.")

These are the things the ordinary man reads in his paper. To puzzle him still more such items are hidden, like the meat

in a sandwich, between articles describing the virtues of ante-
lopes' milk, which is apparently much richer than cows', and
a beauty hint.

All men in high places have enemies who are ready to
spread scandal about them, so the ordinary man discounts
much of what he reads and hears, but still realizes that much
news is written in good faith and must have origins. What are
these origins? How much is truth; how much gossip? How
much propaganda or counter-propaganda?

What is he to make of it all? What is he to believe? Has he
become so used to taking everything with a grain of salt that
he cannot take even the truth without condiments? Has a belief
in an ulterior motive now become so ingrained that an ulterior
motive is sought in all things?

There must always have been such discrepancies, such different reports. But until recently each event or scandal affected
only the limited number of people who were directly concerned
with that particular problem, whereas now all people are concerned with all things.

Religious principles, political creeds, and patriotism are
mixed up with the policies and beliefs of our leaders, whose
virtues and defects have become vital, for on them our future
existence may depend. In an emergency everyone becomes
fanatically partisan, taking one side or the other with all his
strength. And with such a welter of information, misinforma-
tion, speculation, and prophecy, objective thought becomes impossible. So, while trying to sort out in his mind the reported
facts, man in his confusion is turning more and more to those
spiritual truths that are, by their simplicity, less puzzling. But
even here, seeing the failure of orthodox religious thought, he
is beginning to think for himself.

He wonders what would happen to Jesus Christ if he appeared in Germany or France. As a Jew he would be flung into
a concentration camp. As a reformer he would be killed more
brutally perhaps than he was by the Romans. If he came to

England he would be sent to the Isle of Man, or to Canada, as an alien. It is unlikely that he would be hurt but he would be treated as a lunatic and placed under restraint. If he came to America as a refugee, or under the quota, he would be left at liberty. But what would happen if he turned water into wine in a prohibition state? Could he freely send a demon from a hobo into a herd of hogs that were climbing a ramp in a Chicago stockyard? Would he be able to use dust to mix with his spittle for a blind's man's eyes in New York City?

      *   *   *

The democratic constitution of the United States permits the entry into the country of German "National Socialists" provided their papers are in order, as it permits the entry of English "Conservatives." Thus, in certain circumstances, do the freedoms of democracy act against the freedoms of democracy and the principles of democracy become a double-edged sword.

When the U.S. Army transport *American Legion* brought 875 passengers from Petsamo in Finland, 87 came from Germany and tried to spread panic and dissension during the voyage, and were described by Major Frank Burns, of the Army Transport Service, as "extremely pro-Nazi."

Traveling Germans at this time must be accredited by their government, financed by their government, and could come to America for no purpose that was not connected with the plans of that government. Unfortunately, even genuine refugees are under suspicion, since the experiences of other countries have become known. There could be no better disguise for an agent than that of a refugee, with his assumed hatred of the Nazi regime. The stool-pigeons planted in the prison camps have as much knowledge of those camps as the genuine inmates and can talk of the horrors and perhaps show scars said to come from punishments they have suffered. Such scars could easily, and almost painlessly, be manufactured in hospitals under an anesthetic. This war and the methods by which it is being waged must rouse suspicion of everybody, must of necessity breed distrust and hatred; it must result in terrible injustices as the innocent suffer with the guilty . . . as good German-American citizens are forced into subversion by threats of reprisals against their relations and friends at home . . . as men are bought with German gold . . . as others are seduced by their will for peace.

The appeasers, and big business interests, are being seduced by fair promises of trade and co-operation when the war is ended; as all the starving people of Europe are being seduced into a desire for peace at any price by the emptiness of their larders and the length of their food queues.

An August 29th, Mr. Henry Wallace called upon the voters of the United States to "curb" Hitler's designs against this hemisphere. He said, "The nation must face the fact that the dictators have definite designs against this hemisphere.

"Their tactics here, as in Europe, are to divide and conquer. They hope by propaganda and bartering agreements to set one nation against another. . . . Out of the confusion which they have created they hope to build political power and eventually military power.

"Those who stand for business appeasement with Germany," he continued, "are the backbone, even though unwittingly, of the most dangerous of all fifth columns.

"For the sake of a profit in 1941 they would sell out their own future and their children's freedom."

Wallace linked the economic destinies of nations in the Western Hemisphere with the outcome of the present European conflict.

"It is a war," he said, "to prevent the people of North and South America from developing their resources without paying tribute to Europe, and serving a self-appointed master race.

"If the Americas present to the axis powers the same divided front as the democracies of Europe presented them, we shall assuredly walk the same path of destruction and lost freedom."

This can be dismissed as propaganda as any statement can be

dismissed as propaganda. Every advertisement for Nylon stockings is propaganda, every sermon is propaganda, every menu card is propaganda. If I say I love England, it is English propaganda for England. If I say I hate England it is also propaganda. If I say Katharine Cornell is a great actress it is propaganda.

What Senator Wheeler says is as much propaganda as what Senator Pepper says. Both are propagandists. Everyone is a propagandist who dares to state an opinion. Our standards are such that if an opinion we hear coincides with our own it is a truth that should be self-evident to all people of intelligence, whereas if it is contrary to our opinion, it is propaganda for the other side. For no matter how objective we may think ourselves, we take sides on every issue. That we change our minds from day to day, from hour to hour, makes no difference . . . at any given time we have views about everything from film stars to breakfast foods, from presidential candidates to bootblacks.

It is absurd to imagine that big business is pro-German or anti-American, but it is also absurd to think that a business man can see much further than his business. No matter what his business interests are, they are his interests and his views are circumscribed by them. He is held chained to production, to distribution, and expansion. That is his attitude to life, the thing, that by his devotion to it, made him great in business. A captain of industry is a captain of industry and neither more nor less than that. World politics are the sea through which he must steer the ship of his business, and appeasement, either in great or small concessions, is the oil he is ready to pour on the troubled sea of commerce.

The attitude of the church remains even more inexplicable. The church should at least be clear on moral issues. The church all over the world should stand by its principles. Should say either: "Thou shalt not kill," or should proclaim a righteous war against wrong—a Crusade.

Instead, it follows diffidently in the wake of vested interest and armed force. The churches have great powers; suppose they refused to marry or baptize soldiers or the children of soldiers? Suppose they refused to serve with the armed forces as chaplains? Suppose from every pulpit they denounced all war, all aggression, all racketeering, all strike breaking, all forms of force or third degree?

On September the 12th in "News Behind the News" Joseph Alsop and Robert Kintner say: "Private polls show that the greatest Democratic defections in New York are in the ranks of the Catholics. There are probably many reasons for this. One is the new foreign policy of the Vatican, which no longer runs parallel to that of the White House. Then too, there is great opposition to the President among such foreign groups as the Germans and the Italians, many of whom are of Catholic faith. Another is that a great many of New York's Irish think Jim Farley was treated badly by the President. And a third reason is that representatives of the Church were incensed at the refusal of the army to exempt clerical students from conscription. Since Mead is a well-known Catholic, replacement of him by a non-Catholic would create antagonisms." But how can anyone force a man to be a soldier if he refuses to be a soldier and is ready to suffer for his beliefs? Or are they not beliefs? Is it merely that clerical students demand a kind of diplomatic immunity?

Why, long ago, when it all began, were the pogroms and the atrocities of the National Socialists not condemned? It is idle to say that they were not known. They were. It is idle to say that the church is not concerned with politics or temporal things. It is.

But the church dare not condemn evil till evil is publicly condemned. Instead of leading, it follows. It drags along behind the tail of a public opinion that dares neither to worship God nor to condemn Him; an opinion that dares not deny, in case, "after all, there is something in it"; a public that is unwilling to face the issues of right and wrong, that dares not even sin with its eyes open but prefers the half dark of pseudo-ethical morality in a belief that anything is permitted that is not found out.

Either right is everything, or it is nothing. Either it matters immensely, or it does not matter at all. There can be no other way; and the churches have failed us.

What do we know of the new martyrs? Nothing, save that they have existed. Why are we not told of those men who, in the last year, have died at their altars for their faith? The priests, the pastors, the ministers of every denomination who have paid the price? How is it that we have not heard their names?

We have not heard of them because we are not to know of the anonymous holy dead. To know them would disturb men. They would recover from their comfortable religious amnesia, would demand that their churches be cleaned out, that they be given spiritual leaders instead of prelates.

Within the church lies the whole organization necessary for social welfare and the betterment of men—spiritually, morally and physically, but those who would use it are given no power. The church wants no crusades. The church is unwilling to bear the responsibility of its place in the world. And the church is losing its place. Whatever harm was done by the church in medieval times, and there was harm; whatever cruelties have been perpetrated in the name of Jesus Christ, and there have been cruelties, those who did these things did them in good faith. Torquemada sent thousands to the stake and suffered the tortures of the damned for his conviction. But conviction, even in the church, has gone. Conviction, even of God, is suspect as propaganda.

Chapter Twelve

"We Have a Man"

A DEMOCRACY IS GOVERNMENT by the people, that is, by the majority. It has become fashionable to say that the majority is always wrong. And it may be intellectually, but the world does not function on an intellectual basis. The intellectual is the exception, the madman, the dreamer born out of his time. He is not the nation. He represents little in the nation. What he expresses may, or may not, be representative of the nation's unconscious desires, but even if it is, the nation knows nothing about it.

The idea that the intellectual leads thought is fallacious; he merely precedes the masses, walking ahead, as it were, along the road the nation will subsequently tread or, thinking himself on the road, he may be on a by-path.

Neither laws nor ideas can be forced upon a people, except by Gestapo methods. But laws and ideas can be forced upon a government by a people become aware of their necessities. If the majority is always wrong intellectually, it is always right in the expression of its unconscious desires. Without logical reasons it desires those things that are necessary for its survival.

The party system is ineffectual under ordinary conditions because the majority of people see little difference between one party and another. The party that is out promises performance in order to oust the party that is in, and the party that is in avoids performance because it is afraid of being thrown out.

Once in office the political principle of any party is to stay there, entrenched behind its bureaucratic obstructionism. To do nothing is always the safest course. Miss Rose Macaulay has put it very neatly, "The Liberals in opposition were democratic idealists, in office makeshift opportunists, backing out and climbing down. . . ."

Action occurs only when it is forced upon the recalcitrant politicians by the electorate. The politician, like the debutante, is seen in his full glory in the political marketplace. Then he is beautiful, dewy-eyed, and full of promise. The disillusion comes later. One politician turns out to be much the same as another politician. He fits into his place as neatly and inconspicuously as the café society beauty fits into Reno. The main function of a political platform is to detach voters from one party and attach them to another. With this as the primary object, at least some sincerity must be lost as measures which might be good for the country are put aside to make room for measures which will give pleasure to the political audience. There is some danger that candidates are chosen less for their capacity or character than for their lack of it. A blameless nonentity is more easily elected because, although no one wants him, no one objects to him. The man of strong views, of character, has enemies; he has passionate admirers and equally passionate detractors.

All constitutional government is based on a series of checks and counter checks. The English have the House of Commons, the House of Lords, and the nominal power of the king to dissolve the legislature. In America there is a president who holds, with some exceptions, the entire executive power of the government but cannot dissolve the legislature. These systems, which operate at least tolerably well in times of peace, are inefficient in war when confronted by such governments as those of Germany, Japan, Italy, or Russia. Controversy and debate are incompatible with swift or decisive action and result at best in compromise; at worst, in nothing at all.

In England it is not understood that a state governor is not an officer under the president. Nor that the federal and state authorities work supreme in their separate spheres, subject only to certain constitutional restrictions. Congress had to be made pleasing to the smaller states in order to bring them into the Union. They were afraid of being out-voted by larger states and reduced to impotence. This was safeguarded by each state having only two members in the Senate, while in the House of Representatives the representation is according to population. Thus at any given time the two forces of representation may be opposed to each other, and a measure of which the vast majority of the population approves may be checked by the opposition of a majority of states.

Little more than a hundred years ago the chief concern of the legislature in America was to obtain Union. In 1830 the doctrines of secession and nullification were argued in the Senate. On Jefferson's birthday, Webster proposed the toast, "Our Federal Union; it must be preserved." The United States are relatively new. There are still alive many men who fought in the Civil War. The doctrines of its Constitution are not yet fully assimilated or even understood.

Everyone is very willing to acknowledge himself the equal of President Roosevelt, or Mr. Ford, or Mr. Chrysler, or Mr. Sinclair Lewis. But few are willing to agree that the red-caps who carry their bags at the Grand Central are their equals, though there is probably less difference between the mental capacity of the average red-cap and the average man he serves, than there is between the average man and the man of genius in politics, business, or literature. But this is something we do not like to acknowledge.

The paying of taxes and the bearing of arms are both national duties, part of the responsibility that men owe to their country. They are a man's civic responsibilities, which offset his civic advantages. The fundamental difference between National Socialism and democracy is the point of view produced by their respective systems of education.

William White, in one of his articles, describes the way Nazi education works: *

"Hitler came to power in 1933. The boy is only sixteen years old, so he had attended Nazi schools in Germany ever since he was nine. So maybe you'd like to know what seven years of Nazi schooling does to a human mind—even to a boy who, because he is part Jewish—might have reason for being skeptical of what the teachers tell him.

"How did they explain that Germans are superior to all the other peoples in Europe?"

"That is because of the ice age," answered the boy.

Since he has been in America only a short time, his English is stiff and school-bookish.

"What did the ice age have to do with it?"

"It was when the ice receded, two thousand years before Christ—"

"—Don't you mean twenty thousand?"

"No," said the boy firmly, "two thousand. I learned this in school."

"But how did this cause Germans to be superior?"

"Because the first part of Europe to become clear was a region which is now on the old frontier between Austria and the Reich."

"What part?"

"The region where the German Fuehrer was born," explained the Jewish boy. "And after that, the next region to become clear was Prussia. All the rest of Europe was under ice."

"But why does that make Germany superior?"

"Because since these two regions were first thawed out, the German people living in them first learned the use of fire, and how to make weapons for war, and tools to till the soil,

* From the *Register and Tribune Syndicate,* Des Moines, and the *N. Y. Post.*

so of course their German culture would have to be the oldest and best in Europe."

"But if these are true, why is it that in England and France and all over the world, it is taught in all schools that civilization first began in Egypt, and that the Phoenicians first developed the alphabet and writing?"

"They explained to us in our school that other nations are jealous of the German people and so teach false history to belittle the Germans, and puff themselves up," said the boy.

"But did you like it when the Nazis told you that Germans were a superior race, and the Jews far inferior to them?"

"It is not a matter of liking it," said the boy. "You go to school to learn useful things which are true. I am glad I learned this, and why it was, because otherwise I might have had much trouble and not understood."

"Yes, but did you like it?"

"Why should I not like it?" asked the boy. "Since the Germans are superior to all other peoples in the world, even if the Jews cannot possibly be as good as they are, still we German Jews are superior to Jews from Poland or France or anywhere else in Europe, because we have lived in Germany and learned something of German culture."

And this is from a Jewish boy.

What does the genuine, dyed-in-the-mud-and-blood young Teuton think of the world? It is this aspect which has been insufficiently considered. There are millions of children brought up to these beliefs. How are their ideas going to be eradicated? Can they be eradicated? Will the world be safe, even with a victory for the democratic forces, while children brought up like this are still alive? Or will it be necessary to wait fifty or sixty years till they die off? And what about the children they leave behind them? Won't they raise them to their own beliefs? Won't everything start again? Is the world going to be forced to fight a biblical war of extermination—the putting of every man, woman, and child to the sword?

This is what Hitler is ready to do. It is this that is terrifying, for here is something quite different from the old wars which sought only territorial advantages, and ended when they were settled one way or the other.

This is war for land, all the land, belonging to all men, and for the souls of men as well.

The unconscious mind works at rest. In Germany there is no rest. There are only radio programs, work, and military parades. There is no time for contemplation, for the examination of the heart. This, at least, force can accomplish; by the exhaustion of the body it can conquer thought.

It is conquered in Germany by the spiritual exaltation of war. It is conquered in the rest of western Europe by starvation and despair. When the future cannot be faced the present collapses, for tomorrow is built upon the foundation of today.

Man cannot live when his thoughts are out of harmony with his physical existence. He cannot live as a man when thought is canalized by force. Justice remains the abstract ideal of man. The resistance of England, the English acceptance of the terror that is ravaging the country, are due in part to this sense of justice. The English see how they brought it on themselves.

The hope of man is his force for good; his desire for good that is represented by his belief in Jesus Christ. His fears are atavistic fears of devils. His life is a compromise between these two, between the hope which is spiritual and the desires which are physical. Originally, all gods were devils to be placated. Man still feels this and is more ready to placate devils than to worship God. Appeasement is the placation of devils. It is a compromise with evil, a contract with unrighteousness. There can be no marriage between justice and expediency.

Epstein's Adam, which has caused such comment, sums up these two forces, the spiritual force that makes a man reach upwards, and the force of nature that holds him earth-bound. The statue is heroic, sculptured out of an immense block of alabaster. It stands a monument to man's duality, to his ambivalence. The figure is slightly bent, the hands are raised to the shoulders, the neck is thrown back so that the face stares upwards to the skies. Heavy chested, heavy bellied, heavily loined, one feels the weight of the earth, the pull of its gravity on man. It is the Adam who has knowledge. It is Adam after the Fall. He has learned to distinguish good from evil. The figure is nude. It has a horizontal phallus which brings suburban housewives from miles around to stare and titter, women who dare to surround it with an aura of cheap pornography, who are unable, in the smallness of their minds, to understand the conception of man straining at the burden of his sexuality and trying to escape it, of man, held earth-bound by his manhood, striving to reach his God.

Artists of the greatest genius—in pictures, books, sculptures —have concerned themselves with the fall of man. Man is interested and surprised at his fall. The debacle of the Garden of Eden has been repeated in most men's lives. Guy de Maupassant's *"Boule de Suif"* and Somerset Maugham's "Rain" and his "The Letter" are modern examples. The pictures of the Renaissance, the writings of Boccaccio, of Milton, of Dante are older ones.

What is expressed on the face of Leonardo's Mona Lisa? What was meant by Blake's seven designs, illustrating Dante's Inferno? By the innumerable pictures of the Passion, of the Crucifixion, of the Resurrection?

Behind them all is the same theme, the same mystery, the same belief in the humanity of man, the same portrayal of his struggle.

Revolution is part of this. Wars are for aggrandizement. They are without other ideals, and they die as nations become fatigued. But a revolution is born of the spirit. It is conceived in justice, though its parturition may be a "Terror." Desire for war is an induced hysteria, an illness that burns itself out like the fever of France which Napoleon grafted on to the idealism of its revolutionaries. His hardened troops at Waterloo were as good, or better, than any he had ever commanded, but the fever was out of France. She was war-tired. She wanted rest. The retreat from Moscow in 1812 had taken the edge from the weapon.

Hitler has emulated Napoleon. His grand army is camped on the same spot. He too has prostituted the fever of a country, using the maniac strength of its despair.

There had to come a war to end war; a folly to end follies. There had to be a tremendous psychological cataclysm which, dwarfing all issues, leaves man spiritually naked, ashamed, and face to face with the beast which is also man. A war in which man the god and man the beast must meet in the wilderness and there contend the one with the other. In the air, upon the sea and the land, in the hearts of men, this struggle must go on till it is done; till man conquers the beast or till man is conquered and begins his climb once more.

The Jews are rallying. They are forming their battalions. Perhaps we shall see the Children of Israel marching again as they did under their Biblical captains. And though Gabriel Wechsler's plan for a Jewish army was called fantastic, what is there fantastic or un-American about it? In Mr. Wechsler's words:

"There is nothing un-American in the desire to form a Jewish army fighting against Hitler and the evil forces which support him. The American way is to oppose him. You say you want Jews to fight as Americans, but it seems you do not want Americans to fight.

"Americans of Finnish origin have gone to fight against aggression without losing their citizenship, prestige or respect in this country, as have Danes, Norwegians, Dutch, Czechs, Poles and Frenchmen. What is wrong with Jews doing likewise?

"We believe it to be a laudable effort to declare ourselves as a people among other peoples; ready to fight for our beliefs and ideals."

There is something much more fantastic in the belief that

things are normal, that the actions of Germany are not fantastic; in the idea that a whole section of the German population should be degraded, ill-used and expatriated without resentment on their part; in the cynical acceptance of the *fait accompli* however evil it may be.

But today, in spite of our cynicism, of our advancement in the arts, we have fallen into a new heroic age, a new age of myths, of dragons, of angels, and of Crusades.

If eighty million people can be educated into a fanatical belief in National Socialism, other millions can be educated into a belief in true democracy; into a belief in the rights of man, into self and mutual respect. Since Herr Hitler has created a system perfectly adapted to destruction, there is no reason why a great democracy cannot create a system that is based on the highest instead of the lowest human instincts. It would be harder to do, since it is always easier to go down hill than up, but it is not impossible. It is in fact the only possible course to pursue if civilization is to continue. But it requires faith, and belief in the sanctity of human life and endeavor. It must divorce the pursuit of happiness from its material contexts.

The national rebirth of Germany is due to the adoption of a system of direct action which is violence philosophically sublimated into a spiritual reality. The force of destruction is creative inversely in that it creates destruction. National Socialism is the exploitation of this impulse, of this rejuvenation by elimination. It is a religion that produces one thing by means of and through another, strength through joy, life by means of war; that locks sadism and courage in an embrace, and sees gentleness as the mother of all weakness.

Civilization as we understand it is the reduction of all forms of violence in so far as it is possible, and the substitution of reason for brutality.

*   *   *

It is always hard for a native of one country to write about the customs, habits, and government of another. It is, in a sense, an impertinence. What he says cannot be taken as fact for he is unaware of many of the facts. He cannot know the country's history as its citizens know it. He must be biased, entranced by some things, appalled by others. His only measure sticks are the customs of the land of his birth.

For an Englishman to write of America is doubly hard because, owing to the similarity of language, he easily believes in greater similarities than exist. The position of an Englishman in America or an American in England is that of a foreigner in any country who has the good fortune to speak that language very well.

There is in these days the added danger that what he writes is taken as propaganda; that whatever he says has only one end in view—involving America in the war. Quite how this would be done is not considered. England is thick with men, her forces ample to repel an invasion. The most that could be asked of America is what America is already giving, "help short of war" and parallel action where the mutual interests of the two countries converge.

That the new defense measures of the United States which include the Dominion of Canada and a number of islands in the West Indies may one day lead to a great English-speaking alliance is possible. More American help to England will be fully appreciated as only by such help is victory possible, and England's resistance to Germany will be appreciated in America as a proof not only of England's democratic sentiments, but as an answer to those who considered England effete and finished as a power.

The man in the street in America, the ordinary man, has seen no Englishmen. He may have seen some English authors who have come to lecture, some English adventurers who have come to look for rich wives, but he knows nothing of the yeoman of England or the English stock.

The man in the street in England, the ordinary man, has seen no real Americans. He has seen no New England farmers, no horse and buggy doctors, no small drug-store owners, no western cowhands. He has seen only tourists who come to England on a budget, rich Americans who come over for the London season, and expatriate Americans who live abroad because they find their own country too "crude" for their sensibilities. Yet by and large the English and American stocks are one. It was the Englishmen in America who fought Gentleman Johnny to a standstill. It was Englishmen who drafted the Constitution and whose ancestors were the Pilgrim Fathers who came over in the *Mayflower*. There has been since the founding of the first American colony a continual exchange of blood and ideas. Our greatest Englishman today is half-American. Such dislike as there has been between the countries has been due less to their differences than to their resemblances, to the English assumption of superiority without adequate reason and the American overcompensation of boastfulness. England is no longer the mother. Nor has England ever been a good mother. She has always expected to live on the earnings of her children. But England and America are cousins. They share their ancestry, the greater part of their history, and their language. Much of what is lamented in England as American slang is merely archaic English that has come back. From what we hear and read, a new England resembling the America that made the Constitution is already coming into being. In an article, Evelyn Montague writes:

"Britain today is a happy country! That is the strangest thing that has happened to us in all this strange year.

"I am a happy man! My home has been broken up, my child is in one part of the country, my possessions in another. My wife and I are in a third, living in a stranger's house, overtaxed, overworked, uncertain of the future, cut off from most of our small pleasures, restricted in our movements, threatened with invasion.

"But we are happier than we were twelve months ago.

"Twenty-two years of unnatural living are behind the change. They began in 1918 when a million or two of our soldiers came home vowing that there should be no more war for any reason whatever.

"It was natural that exhausted men whose too simple hopes of the millennium had been disappointed and who had been bloodily mishandled by some of their commanders, should feel that way for a time. But the temporary neurosis became a settled principle, buttressed by bad theology, slipshod logic, and plain materialism. It sank deep into British minds and has influenced all our policies ever since, usually for the worse.

"It began to take extravagant forms as time went on. Ignoring all the evidence, we deluded ourselves that a tough revengeful people could be won away from their purpose by our disarmament.

"Our more amiable qualities—readiness to believe other men's word, friendliness towards a beaten enemy—helped to foster the delusion.

"Some of us became ashamed of our own warlike history and of the Empire which it had won for us; the world resounded with our cries of remorse.

"We upheld the League of Nations with promises which we could not perform. We tried to persuade ourselves that we could tame the Italian lion by letting him run about loose, but keeping his food away from him.

"In the end, the British Labor Party got itself into the ludicrous position of demanding that we should fight for the League of Nations, but not provide ourselves with the arms to do it, and the Conservative Party did neither.

"War was the ultimate evil; we admitted no other.

"Disillusion was slow and painful. It began for us in China, it went on in Abyssinia, Spain, Austria, Czecho-Slovakia. With deepening anger the British, one of the great fighting races of the world with a record of victory unbroken since the American Revolution, saw themselves outmaneuvered or elbowed aside when they tried to help the oppressed nations. But they clung to their theory that somehow things could be put right and justice done without violence. The hatred of war was still too strong in them for reason.

"At last came Munich, with its scene of hysterical relief in the House of Commons and its fury of shame in the hearts of many Britons who could not make themselves heard. Happy or bitter, all of us knew then—or very soon afterwards—that the dream was over.

"We took stock of our armaments and set to work to make good the years that the locust had eaten.

"And all through the year that followed, as we tuned up our armament factories, built our air-raid shelters and trained our civilian army, we grew more bitter as we realized more fully how we had been fooled.

"The patience of the Government outlasted the patience of the people. On the eve of war, when Chamberlain made a speech in the House of Commons which suggested that he was ready to condone even the invasion of Poland, Arthur Greenwood got up to reply for the Labor opposition, and Government backbenchers, in an agony of shame and rage, cried out to him, 'speak for England.' Their voices were the voice of England taking charge at last, saying, No more of these hesitations, this appeasement which leaves us in the end nothing but a choice between dishonors. Life is not so precious that we may compromise with tyranny and enslavement. We are going to fight until either this Nation or Hitler is destroyed.

"The Government listened to the voice of England. Two days later we were at war, and over all of us hung the certainty of loss and the destruction of hopes. But we were happy at last.

"We have had bad times since then. We were distressed and worried by the phony war and angered by the retreat from Norway. There were black days when Leopold laid down his arms with a suddenness that invited a harder name, when our troops seemed inescapably trapped at Dunkirk, when Pétain withdrew France from the struggle and left us to fight alone.

"When France surrendered it seemed for the first and last time that we might not win.

"But the good times have outweighed the bad.

"The rapturous ecstasy of the whole British people over the rescue of the B.E.F. from Dunkirk was not wholly, or even mainly, joy at the saving of husbands and sons.

"It was the happiness of recovering our faith in ourselves.

"From that moment this Nation was twice as formidable as it had been before.

"We have had other rapturous moments, when Narvik or Oran or the River Plate showed that we had recovered our ancient knack of striking hard and quick, without waiting to apologize beforehand, when we knew that right was on our side.

"We do not regret our lost Allies; we have more faith in ourselves.

"Public confidence in victory is so complete that in the last month or two ordinary men's minds and talk have turned more and more to what we will make of Britain and the world after the victory.

"The mood of the moment is propitious for such discussion. The common purpose, passionately held, has drawn us all together; Britain has never been so united in living memory as it is today. It is a purpose for which we are ready, quite simply, to give everything we have. Already we have given much—comfort and money, family life, leisure, freedom of personal behavior.

"Comfort, though they have had more of it than most, has never been necessary to the British; if it had been, they would never have colonized the world. Now they are living uncomfortably (and rather liking it, incidentally), and the greed of personal ownership has receded from their minds. They are serving something outside themselves.

"The result has been the growth in unexpected soil—men who used to be preoccupied with their own privileges and possessions—of a new sense of national comradeship and a new conscience. These feelings are beginning to work in ways that may make a better nation here when the war has been won.

"So you see us—excited, interested, confident, frankly enjoying a situation which exactly suits our national temperament.

"We have no exaggerated respect for one of our enemies and the most complete contempt for the other.

"We are busy, pleased with what we have done so far, delighted to find that we can still enjoy discomfort and danger adventurously.

"Do you wonder that we are happy?"

There seems a very simple reason for this. All Englishmen have become united to face the common danger. A nation of individuals has become a tribe again with its leaders and its councils, something in which each man, woman, and child has a place. The fear of death has replaced the greatest fear of all, that of being alone, isolated as an individual.

There is danger. There is righteous cause. The men of England are fighting on their own ground, protecting their fields and cities, their moors and forests. Their women are with them. They have met the solidarity of the Nazis with the solidarity of their own race. They are bound in their loyalties to the crown, the country and one another. They are ready, as the ancient Britons were ready, to wade into the sea and meet the invader. Ready to fight on the South Downs as they did against William the Norman; ready to sail their boats into the narrow seas as they did against Parma. They stand, armed and waiting, as they did for Napoleon Bonaparte. Once again the English people and English history are one. All artificial barriers of class, sex, and money are broken down. It is enough now, in England, to be an Englishman.

Emerson writing in 1850 of England said, "The island was renowned in antiquity for its breed of mastiffs, so fierce, that when their teeth were set you must cut off their heads to part them. The man was like his dog. The people have that nervous bilious temperament, which is known by medical men to resist every means employed to make its possessor subservient to the will of others."

Emerson's book *English Traits* has been forgotten but it is full of truths, and it is doubtful if the English character has changed much in the hundred years that have passed since it was written, or the thousand that preceded it.

The great days are returning. The days of sacrifice and heroes, the days of simplicity when men once more will dare to love, to hate, and to serve. It was Franklin who said "of what use is a baby?" Today we are seeing the use of those babies of twenty years ago. The babies of dead fathers. The new blood spilled is the old blood still. The old call of Nelson still calls, its echo has never died. It was only muffled. "England expects every man to do his duty." That phrase has been mocked, has been paraphrased by men who know no duty, and has been called jingoism, but today in England's greatest hour, it is in the hearts of all Englishmen. They still see the fluttering of the signal flags from the tall masts of the *Victory*. They still think of Nelson, of how he lived, of how he died. He sent his love to Collingwood. He said, "Kiss me, Hardy," and then he died. The sailors, impressed men torn from their homes, black men from the Indies and powder monkeys, little boys who carried the charges for the guns, all cried. Today men are ashamed to weep, ashamed to love, ashamed to show that they care for anything. And because they refused to show feeling, so have they lost feeling. Because they ceased to care for honor they lost honor.

But this destruction of our island, this bombing of our women and children, this destruction of our ancient monuments is going to make a new England. The lion of England has risen from his sleep. Hitler would have done well to let the lion lie undisturbed by the hysteria of his impatience, for, sleeping, the lion might have died.

Nothing is changed in England. The England that we know

is the old England. Its roads and lanes have been trodden deep by Saxons, Danes, Romans, Normans. They are metaled, asphalted, but unchanged. The men who fought at Crécy, who defeated the Spanish Armada, who broke the French at Waterloo, are unchanged. It is the English long-bow men who stood at Dunkerque. It is the English men-at-arms who refused to surrender Calais, and fought till out of four thousand only thirty-six were left. They are the children equally of the Rupert's cavalry and Cromwell's Ironsides, who left a torpedoed ship marching in good order and singing, "There'll Always Be An England."

Here is something that Herr Hitler cannot understand. The tenacity of the breed that no Teutonic fury can break. The tenacity of the bulldog which, for a wager on the part of its master, had all its legs cut off at the joints and still clung to the nose of the bull.

Hitler has engaged the English. He began what will not end till the English have pulled him down. A lesser man than Bonaparte, Hitler will go the same way. It was the Duke of Wellington who saw that if war did not bring new trade, better agriculture and manufactures, it was doomed to failure. Games, fireworks, marches, and spectacles can begin a war but cannot consummate it.

Hitler may have a secret weapon but if he has we have an answer to it, a new faith in humanity and our appointed ends. A demon can be exorcised only by calling his name. A skeleton can be dealt with only by taking it out of its closet. For too long we have evaded truth, been afraid of it, been subject to the taboo and the totem of word and word association. Things have been labeled as nice, as not nice, have been classified as those which could be spoken of and as those which could not be spoken of. And the things we could not speak of have festered in our minds. Why should a man be ashamed of his love for a woman, with its fullest implications? Only if it had not the full implication need he be ashamed. Why should he be ashamed of his lack of understanding of the miracle of life? Why afraid of saying this is beautiful, this is good? Why be afraid of condemning evil? Why sit perpetually on the fence of non-controversial subjects, not daring to be either right or wrong? There seems only one end to life. That is to live it, doing as little evil as we may, doing a little good if we can, and casting at least some of our bread upon the waters. Being not overcome by evil, but overcoming evil by good.

We have a great creed, a great hope, and a great man to lead us. This is our secret weapon. The one Hitler has forgotten. The great union of all men, who are as nearly good as they may be, with each other. Their great readiness to sacrifice themselves for those things that they are unable to express; those small things their mothers taught them when they were young. On that rock will Hitler's legions be shattered. On the simple prayers no longer prayed, but unforgotten.

Chapter Thirteen

"This Freedom"

AN UNCONSIDERED FACTOR in the world unrest of today is the unexploited energy of women of the upper and middle classes. This energy is loose. It flows, undischarged, through all social life. It expresses itself in art, in sex, in bridge, in gossip, in buying things to pass the time, in religion, in social service and in business.

It is quite new, and results not from the enfranchisement of women, but from their release from the duties which have, until the twentieth century, formed the basic feminine pattern: the continuous bearing of children till they were worn out, and the activities which were required of them in the home—the spinning of wool, the weaving of linen, the making of clothes and preservation of food. These burdens have all been taken from them.

Not long ago a woman of forty was a grandmother and sexually worn out. Now, though she may be a grandmother, her sexual instincts and powers, if they are not directly employed, are sublimated into political or social channels, or in a fury of time-wasting. The grandmother of fifty years ago was the mother of ten or more children, she was content to wait on life, to watch it pass on through her descendants. She was com-

plete, fulfilled, perhaps not in the way that the women of today would choose, but nevertheless fulfilled. She was the
mother of men and women; the mother of a multitude. She
was the center of a community, the wife and helpmate of a
man who could not have got on without her. It was in those
days impossible for a man to live without a woman. He stayed
with his parents until he found a wife who took over the necessary feminine functions of his existence which, as such, had
nothing to do with sex.

Neither men nor women are yet conditioned to the new
mechanized world where things can be bought and need not
be made—the shop where the dollar can be turned into the
whim of the moment, to a world where sexual intercourse does
not result in the birth of a child.

To make a thing, time and effort were required, in consequence nothing useless was made, and the things that had been
made were taken care of. Almost everything in the home was
the result of the work of the women in that home. Now everything in the home is the result of the money earned by the
man and spent by the woman.

Women in the upper classes have become a decoration, an
adjunct, a luxury. There is today only a fine ethical line to be
drawn between the earnings of the prostitute and the pin
money of many married women.

Birth control, while accepted widely, and practiced, is still,
as it were, not recognized. Sexual intercourse is assumed to be
non-existent owing to a perverted puritanism which refuses to
acknowledge its existence, though strange as it may seem, practically every adult in the street, in the subway, on the street-car,
or in the drawing room is having, or has had, sexual experiences.

Motherhood, if spiritually a miracle, remains also a natural
and inevitable function. The spurious maternal cult of today
arises, not out of the strength of maternity, but out of its desire
to dramatize a natural process and to exploit sexual fact on a

basis of cash sacrifice. Maternity, if less beautiful than it is rendered in orthodox art, remains an inexplicable miracle; as the bursting open of a flower is a miracle, as the birth of a lion whelp is a miracle, or of a whale calf, an act of God. Never, even by its continuous repetition among men and beasts, is birth rendered ordinary. It is always new, always strange, always sacred.

The future of the race, its culture and ideals, are in the hands of the young. The young women who are the mothers, and potential mothers. The young men who are the fathers, and the potential fathers. They are also the fighters. They are, by their youth and energy, specially endowed for this, for creation and destruction, for the making of the future.

There is a male culture, a thing unknown to women, a residual legacy of the ancient rites of puberty, of the ancient council houses, a masculine pulse, inaudible to women, that tells men what they must do. Above and beyond the instinct of sex there is sexual pride—a direct relationship between a man's capacity to bear arms and his potency. The fire and intolerance of youth are part of youth. Its desire to destroy is a part of its desire to create. Age is neither destructive nor constructive—it is philosophical and content to observe.

*   *   *

There seem to be three sides to the mind of a human being. The first is the "daily mind" that is occupied with social and business acts. There is the "third mind," as yet almost unrecognized by psychologists, which can be called "the race mind." This is the part that actually governs all behavior. It admits nothing but the essentials of life. It is based on reproduction and on remaining alive, without regard to morals, or ethics, or reason. It has one aim only, to live, and while living to reproduce as rapidly, and often as possible, thus perpetuating the genus. It is completely ruthless and atavistic in both sexes.

The second mind, "the unconscious mind," is the rational-

izer, which is fully occupied in translating the demands of the
third mind into such terms that the first can, without understanding them, achieve its ends. It is at once an interpreter and
a liar. It invents the reasons that justify the acts.

Modern life with its circumscription makes the necessary
freedoms impossible. Instincts are perpetually thwarted and
must be rationalized. Life is lived according to Aesop's fable of
the fox and sour grapes. Man is continually telling himself that
he does not want the things he wants; that he does not want
to do the things that he feels it is necessary for him to do. He
is perpetually trying to prove to himself that one thing is as
good as another, as it may be, but it is not the thing that he
demands.

A breakdown or a neurosis is due to the failure of the overworked interpreter; to the situation where fact cannot, in any
way, be made to fit in with fancy, another word for instinct.
Or where man, unprepared for such an eventuality, gets a
glimpse into the workings of his own psyche, when he sees the
satyr dancing to the Pipes of Pan among the roses of his suburban garden.

Since the fall of man is attributed to his eating of the fruit
of the tree of knowledge, it would be as well to make the most
of this disaster; to examine right and wrong, to face them
equally with an unbiased mind, to find out what is really wrong.
Life will become easier when man recognizes his biological
necessities and heredity, when the man, *l'homme moyen sen-
suel,* understands his own sensuality and no longer fears it.
Why should he, since it is part of him, like his hand? Freud
has stated there is no neurosis where there is sexual satisfaction.
This, being an absolute, is impossible, but the hypothesis, by
approximation, works both ways. Sexual satisfaction has a great
deal to do with neurosis. No satisfaction, great unhappiness.
Satisfaction, little unhappiness.

The questions of sex have been shelved too long, have been
treated as though they were things that could be wrapped up

and brought out on occasion only. The sexual instinct in man and woman must be accepted as the weather is accepted. It is rhythmic like the waves of the sea, subject to the seasons, to the thousand impacts of daily life, to diet, to music, to beauty, to play, to work. About it all the other functions of life revolve, as a wheel revolves around its hidden core.

There is little evidence of real free will. The moment of decision is not the man's. It is not made at the moment. It is not an effort of will, but a rising of the human spirit, good or ill, to an occasion. It is the effect of all previous causes, the result of all previous times, and places, and circumstances upon a particular time, place and circumstance. The man does what he does because of what he is, which is the sum of all that he has been, up to that moment. He is molded by every impact he has ever received, shaped by every circumstance which has acted on the original clay of his inherited characteristics; the clay of his body that gives him his form, and the clay of his mind, which is in part the clay of the thousands whose blood runs in his veins.

The product of circumstance, man plays upon circumstance unwittingly, for even his desires are forced upon him. They are not those that he would choose, had he the choice. His illusion of free will is based on his illusion of choice. Man never has choice. Where he chooses between two things, the apparent choice is governed by the facts of his life and birth. The second course, the one that he conceives rational or right by a cerebral process, is also a result of his past, his training, but even though he takes it he rarely takes it in its entirety. He makes reservations, compromises, and tries to leave himself a way out. The upbringing of his childhood, the discipline of boyhood help him, they make his character, prevent him from being completely irresponsible and give him a code to which he approximates where it is possible. But there remains a point beyond which he cannot be driven. A point where, if there is no way out, he breaks. Where he will take life, his own or another's;

will give in to illness, or lie down and die, or drift hopelessly, not caring what happens.

The great difference between modern man and pre-historic man, who demanded immediate action as a reflex to every stimulus, is that modern man can succeed in controlling his impulses provided he has hope which is the cerebral equivalent of delayed action. Which is, in fact, a way out. Religion, work, money, legal redress, the effect of time, are all hope factors. An animal, probably unaware of the future, lives for the moment. Modern man, almost always unaware of the present, lives in hope of the future. The future in which something may happen that will save him.

It is hope that enables us to face the war. To face, with at least some semblance of courage, the intolerable present, because of our consciousness that things will change. This seems to be expressed in a letter I received recently from an English friend.

"Since the invasion of the Low Countries things have seemed quite a nightmare. The break through the French lines at Sedan was, of course, completely unexpected. In fact, it seems to me incredible that having decided on a war of defense (and defense only, as it afterwards transpired) our high command should have neglected to see that the defense was adequate. Once the break-through had occurred and had been consolidated we did not seem to have had any means of dealing with the onrush, and the rest you know. My eldest brother got away from Dunkirk—thank goodness. He lost every bit of clothing and equipment except the very things he was wearing, as did they all. The men did marvels—with bayonets, rifles, bare fists against tommy guns. It does seem pitiful that the democracy which we prize so much should send her sons forward to fight with inadequate weapons in its defense. Shall we ever be enlightened enough to give them weapons with which to fight the first battle instead of the last? As it is they have to use their flesh and blood against steel. And it is always the way.

"But France asked for an armistice. I had such faith in the French and they actually did wonders, but it seems as though their defense theories (chiefly their Maginot Line) having broken down they had nothing to replace them. And England is left to carry on alone. What will the end be? I do not doubt that we shall win finally—I firmly believe that Hitler made his big miscalculation in believing that the bomber could beat the battleship and that this is the mistake which will beat him. Let us hope so in any circumstance. But meanwhile it will be un-diluted hell. I am content that it should be so. I feel that we in England should pay with our blood and tears for our crass stupidity of the last twenty years. Having given the best that we had to beat these people, having beaten them at tremendous cost, we neglected the duties imposed by this colossal victory, imposed by the stupendous total of killed, maimed, wounded; through this neglect we are now fighting the same people over the same ground, having been beaten there the battle is to be fought and won on our own island. For twenty years we were prepared to listen to any half-baked theory, to the international-ists, the adventurous politicians, provided always that they would tell us what we wanted to hear. And we did not want to hear anything which could shake our complacency or disturb our "peace at any price" attitude. We had more than our share of the world's goods and we honestly believed ourselves justi-fied in this, because we thought we should use them to better advantage than our neighbor and yet we were not prepared to purchase the means of guarding our possessions. Surely the history of these twenty years has shown us that the democracy we are fighting for has failed? If statesmen had attempted to remedy the position we should not have tolerated them in office. And so we and our heritage were exploited by the dishonest statesmen like Baldwin, who were prepared to feed us with the lies we wanted in order to stay in office.

"American opinion seems to me to have reached our own pre-Munich state. Let them beware of the complacency which again overtook us after Munich and which continued right up to the invasion of the Low Countries through eight vital months of war.

"I hope you are not bored by this letter but it might interest you to know the feelings of a very ordinary Londoner, as London is preparing to move into the front line. It cannot be long now. In fact by the time you receive this letter the issue will probably have been decided one way or the other. Pray for me and for us all! At the risk of seeming melodramatic I am not afraid to die—only to live if we were to be beaten.

"How bitterly France has paid for her spell of international-ism, her Popular Front, forty-hour week and intervention in the Spanish war! I was rather contemptuous of the Poles in Septem-ber—they had spoken so proudly and yet their resistance had crumpled so quickly. And yet the Poles so far have made a better showing than anybody—better even than France. I sup-pose you have heard all the atrocity talk about Poland? The one which really makes my blood run cold is the account issued by the Vatican about the sterilization of 300,000 of them—men and women. Could the mind of man devise anything more brutal in a campaign to exterminate a race?

"Enough of this.

"The English spring, now fast turning to summer has been its most beautiful this year. This May and part of June have been perfect. The lilac, the may, laburnum and now the roses have never been more heart-breakingly beautiful as if circum-stances had conspired to make us all realize how much we love our Island home. And the nights, with the searchlights some-times managing to give them an extra touch of beauty, so that the sounds of sirens and aeroplanes do not seem real.

"You would be interested to see England too at the moment, from the point of view that we have not been invaded for nearly a thousand years. Machine gun nests appear at odd corners—our main roads, parks, golf courses, commons, have been turned into traps to catch planes trying to land there.

Soldiers appear from nowhere asking for an identification card."

*   *   *

To complete the picture of the new world and new humanity which appear to be coming into being, I quote at length from "Light Beyond The Strife" by Wickham Steed, published in *The Christian Science Monitor,* Magazine Section, Aug. 17, 1940.*

"The light of Republican France is the last to have been extinguished—with the complicity of Frenchmen of little faith. Can the light of England, of Britain, of the British Empire and the British Commonwealth burn on brightly, and alone? This is the problem to which thoughtful minds among us are addressing themselves.

"Of our resolve to keep our light burning there can be no question. We wish to see what can be done to nourish its flame so that it may shine upon peoples now in the darkness of bondage, rekindle their faith and their hope, and presently illumine a new civilization beyond the present strife. And it is here that we pause and ponder.

"It is not only in the field of mechanical invention for destructive purpose that war stimulates thought. It quickens perceptiveness in other directions. If our faith be unshaken in the purity of the flame that burns within us, and of its value as a light to the world, we perceive, almost as a revelation, that this faith is now more completely divorced from any material care than it has ever been in our history. We feel that "nothing else matters," nothing except our will and our power to withstand and to prevail against the worst the enemy can do. But we feel, too, that the burden of proof is upon us, that we shall not convince the rest of the world of our moral and spiritual steadfastness unless we break the sequence of Adolf Hitler's triumphs and give his victims reasonable cause to persist in

* Republished by permission of the Trustees of The Christian Science Publishing Society.

passive resistance to him. Without the victory of our cause there can be no light beyond the strife.

"But what if Britain be materially ruined by the struggle? It is at this point that the new light begins to shine, that the spiritual quality of the struggle itself becomes plain. We need material supplies, and food, to carry on the fight, but we are not conscious of needing or wanting or caring for anything else. Our lot may be poverty, even penury. All we have may be consumed. Nothing matters if all we have been and are, all we can be and are determined to become, shine forth in glowing spirituality.

"So Britons see this war as a civil war of mankind, as a war for the redemption of the human spirit. For the better part of two generations we have talked and thought in terms of economics, of the "social question," as though the thing that chiefly mattered was to raise the material standard of life for our people. Now we are approaching a point at which there may be only one standard for all, and a low standard at that, if it be measured by former conditions of ease and comfort. We have come to feel and to believe that the rights and liberties of men and women, as men and women, are more important than economic prosperity, and that our possessions are of value only if they can be used to check and to overthrow the foes of the spirit of man.

"A big employer of labor who is actively connected with two of Britain's basic industries—mining and munitions—and who has the confidence of his workmen, writes this of them:

"They are working and will continue working to 'deliver the goods' as never before in our history until we have beaten our enemy. They are not willing to talk about the mistakes of the past. What they are asking today is for courageous leadership. The time for smooth things and fairy tales has gone. They expect, nay, demand the truth. Let it be told, no matter how unpalatable it may seem. They'll stand it and give that extra ounce of effort which means so much. . . . They know that, unless we win, all their privileges, unions, and freedom of speech and right to bargain are gone—and gone forever. They are in complete agreement on compulsory military service. It has swept away class distinction and the sense of unfairness. The hundred percent excess profits tax makes them feel that capital has made a real sacrifice. They loathe the tyranny of force but frankly face the issue that only by force can Naziism be beaten.'

"This is true of our workmen. At the other end of what used to be called 'the social scale,' a member of the House of Lords, who has been Governor General of a British Dominion, demands that our internal union in this hour of trial be accompanied by determined personal effort 'by breaking down what remains of privilege and patronage, based upon relative affluence, to consolidate our social structure on the foundation of a common patriotism, with resulting contentment and mutual confidence.' He calls for this effort 'as the outcome of the trustful comradeship which this war is daily engendering.'

"If one result of this struggle is to bring about a constructive social revolution inspired by 'trustful comradeship,' it will have done more for Britain than decades of 'class struggle' and political agitation could have done. The very prospect of it is light beyond the strife. And in it there may be the foundations of a policy that will help to redeem Europe. Naziism has no saving idea to proclaim, no lofty aspiration to offer. It has one method—force; one principle—the right of the stronger. Its only doctrine is that a German race of rulers shall be free to rule the earth as they will. We believe that our faith in freedom and brotherhood will prove stronger than the strongest force Hitler can bring against us.

"I see in the consolidation of our internal unity, by equal effort and sacrifice, the beginnings of a new and better order that may fill England and other nations with hope. Soon or late men will turn away from the tyranny of mechanized force and will set about the essential task of making mechanism their servant, not their master. If, even as we fight, we can lay in ourselves the foundations of this new freedom we shall serve others besides ourselves. Some of us had already understood, in theory, the anomaly of looking upon territorial frontiers as lasting barriers and divisions between nations, while the very meaning of space and time was being changed by mechanical and natural scientific means of movement and communication. Now most of us are beginning to understand it in practice. This understanding prompted our offer to France of a Franco-British union. Hitler, the 'mechanized Attila,' has swept across frontiers and made a mockery of national sovereignties and sovereign neutralities in a way that puts their full restoration beyond the scope of practical statecraft. He has taught us a lesson he never intended to teach—that if the world is to be saved for peace and freedom, all peoples who care for freedom must learn that they are members one of another.

"It is not a small thing that the Dominions and Colonies of 'the British Empire,' and even the peoples of India, should have made it plain that this war is their war as much as ours, that it is a war of faith, and of faith in the virtue of freedom for the human spirit.

"Is it nothing that the people of the United States should be with us at heart and in material support? In these things I see light beyond the strife, a light that no Hitler can put out. It reminds me of the magnificent vision of our Victorian poet, Tennyson, who wrote nearly ninety years ago lines which today seem filled with the spirit of prophecy:

" 'Men, my brothers, men the workers, ever reaping something
        new;
    That which they have done but earnest of the things that they
        shall do;
    For I dipt into the future, far as human eye could see,
    Saw the Vision of the world, and all the wonder that could be;
    Saw the heavens fill with commerce, argosies of magic sails,
    Pilots of the purple twilight, dropping down with costly bales:

Heard the heavens fill with shouting, and there rain'd a ghastly dew

From the nations' airy navies grappling in the central blue;

Far along the world-wide whisper of the south-wind rushing warm,

With the standards of the peoples plunging thro' the thunder-storm;

Till the war-drum throbb'd no longer, and the battleflags were furl'd

In the Parliament of man, the Federation of the world.' "

Chapter Fourteen

"The Shape of Things to Come"

THERE ARE STILL MANY who think that the aftermath of this war will in some way resemble that of the last war, that matters will be arranged somehow, that drafts, loans and credits will in some miraculous way settle matters in the old pattern, or at least something that resembles the old pattern.

There seem, at the moment, to be only three possibilities, a Nazi victory, a British victory, or a stalemate of some kind.

The broad principles of what a Nazi victory would mean are not hard to understand, a Nordic hegemony centering in Germany with other races in varying degrees of subjection, with their intellectuals exterminated, and all colored people reduced to the sweeper class. Mechanical progress would go on, machines would be improved, but a dark age, comparable to nothing the world has yet seen, would cover Europe, would spread over Africa from the Mediterranean to the Cape of Good Hope.

For America, accustomed to receiving news from abroad, there would be only a vast silence. No questions would be answered. There would be no neutral sources of information.

That the mind refuses to grasp this, that it seems inconceivable, does not render it impossible.

South America would become a German colony. The German infiltration was begun there three generations ago, and the figures of totalitarian populations, possibly inaccurate, are: Venezuela, 4,000 Germans; Brazil, 900,000 Germans, 2,000,-000 Italians, 200,000 Japanese; Paraguay, 20,000 Germans; Uruguay, 10,000 Germans; Argentina, 200,000 Germans, 3,-000,000 Italians; Chile, 200,000 Germans, 40,000 Italians; Bolivia, 3,000 Germans; Peru, 3,000 Germans, 20,000 Italians; Ecuador, 5,000 Germans; Colombia, 3,000 Germans.

The United States of America would be caught in the trap of totalitarian trade, of internal dissension fostered by German agents whose duty it is, "To confuse by propaganda, to divide by corruption, and to paralyze by intimidation." These are Hitler's words.

Dorothy Thompson, one of the best informed American columnists, suggests in her article entitled "The World of Germanica" that Germany's plan is to join all Europe into one gigantic customs union with its financial and economic control centered in Berlin, and a commercial center in London under Nazi dominion. This intricate and gigantic economic machine would include four hundred million skilled workers within and without the Reich, and all the industrial resources of the conquered countries. What are now known as countries would become simply language groups, and even those would be likely to disappear as their languages lost commercial significance and became localized patois or dialects.

In all countries, including the United States, contacts have been established for many years with industrialists and business men who are sympathetic to the National Socialist movement. Those unwilling to agree to Nazi principles would be subject to boycott and intimidation. The methods of the racketeering parasite will be embodied into the new system of economic control. No business will be done with firms whose directors are not favorable to National Socialism, no advertising placed with pro-Ally or democratic papers.

The daily press in the United States gives evidence that pressure of this kind is already at work, that those in favor of fascist reaction and appeasement are already coming out into the open with obstruction and defeatist arguments. The Germans expect, by their possession of the British Isles, with its forty millions of people, to be able to blackmail the colonies that are still faithful to the mother country, and to obtain possession of the British fleet, or as much of it as is left after the action which inevitably will take place, by threats of retaliation on the wives and families of the officers and men.

Reprisals, as a form of blackmail, have become the order of the day; Franco's reprisals on the relations of deserters from his ranks; German reprisals on Jewish families and relations in Germany and on those of such Germans as preferred exile to life within the Reich, national reprisals on all Jews for the murder of vom Rath in Paris; reprisals on individual Hollanders for actions in the Dutch East Indies; reprisals by Japan for imagined insults; reprisals on Americans and English, on Czechs, on Poles, on Norwegians, Belgians, on prisoners-of-war, as a means of attacking those who are out of reach.

A British victory will mean that what is left of England in men and material will become something quite new. Luxury, the Bond Street—Claridge's—the Savoy—Vogue—Elizabeth Arden luxury—will have gone forever from England. Ascot, Newmarket, Cowes, Henley, the Eton-Harrow match, the 12th of August, fox-hunting and the London season, will be things of the past and of the not-so-good-old-times. The upper-class, as such, with its hunting, racing, and shooting, will have become submerged in an immense middle-class.

Dictatorship, begun in the war, will be carried on for the reconstruction. The vast forces of the army and navy, with remembrance of their treatment after the last war, will refuse to be sidetracked into unemployment relief. The Empire will insist on a direct representation, on full equality with Great Britain, and a real British Commonwealth will come into being which will make all who live under the British flag equal. There may even be mass migrations of whole industries to the Dominions. Some Dominions, such as South Africa and India, may break away from the Empire completely. Other possessions, that are liabilities, may be abandoned. Politically, a new system seems likely to arise, a socialist state combining the best characteristics of both the totalitarian and communist ideologies which are in no way to be despised.

At present, the war aims are summed up in the defeat of Hitler and all that he stands for, which is, in fact, a euphemism for Germany and all that Germany stands for. Nominally the British are pledged to restore the European *status quo,* which means, with some variations, those boundaries that were established by the peace of Versailles. Actually this is impossible. There has been too much destruction, too much death, too many enforced movements of minorities, and too many massed flights of civilians. Russia and communism probably will remain intact and ready to encourage revolution. War with Russia would seem to be impossible, not only economically, but because men would refuse commitment to further wars; and despite their disclaimers, the working men have a lingering admiration, not for what has happened in Russia, but for what was attempted there.

There are no experts today who can pierce the mist of events to come. But through the mists, certain probabilities stand out, looming against the darkened sky. The first probability is that the political evolution of the world has passed beyond the period of constitutional monarchy, and what has been somewhat loosely described as the democratic form of government. Whatever the outcome of the war, governments are likely to become autocratic. In the event of a German victory, the form is obvious, its pattern will conform to that already in existence in central Europe. In the event of a British victory, the form is less clear. All that is certain is that the disaster of war will leave all Europe in a state of starvation and chaos, every form of administration and communication will have broken down, and in such a state of emergency the demand will be for quick strong action which can only come from individual leadership. There will be neither the time, nor the desire, for that debate which characterizes a free constitutional government. A United States of Europe is possible, an affiliation of states each ruled by a dictator, or a governor with dictatorial powers under a greater dictator. In this case, the outward form would remain somewhat similar whoever won the war. But it seems likely that in the event of a German defeat the people will at least have representation and the right to elect their leaders.

There is also the possibility that nothing as orderly as this will happen. There is the possibility of complete breakdown everywhere, of famine and disease, of armed bands of soldiers living by plunder while there is plunder, of communism profiting by the earlier phases of disintegration, breaking down and becoming anarchy, of men ceasing to be men and becoming animals crazed by fear and lust, destroying all things in a suicidal orgy. Should the war go on indefinitely, as it may, should an epidemic, such as the bubonic plague that has made its third known appearance in history, spread from Asia, complete anarchy becomes a definite possibility.

It is a certainty that the old forms of personal life, of individual business operations, have gone forever, and that inevitably the Americas will be forced into the world pattern of controlled trade, heavy taxation, and the disciplined regimentation that alone can save humanity. It is probably too late now to save democracy intact. It is now a matter of saving life and the remnants of our civilization.

Zones of influence have come to stay. In the event of a German victory there will be the German zone, including most of Europe and Africa, with an Italian zone, subsidiary to it, around the Mediterranean, a Russian zone of Eastern Europe, Asia

Minor, Iraq, and India, a Japanese zone of the East Indies, China and Australia, a United States zone of all the Americas from Greenland to Patagonia.

For a time, while being consolidated, these zones might have external peace. They would, of necessity, have it, because internal dissension would make war impossible. But there would be friction where interests clash, between Russia and Germany in Eastern Europe, between Japan and Russia in Eastern Asia, between Germany and America in Brazil.

War preparations would continue in these zones (it is idle now to speak of countries, since individual nations will have become counties, states, or departments, in the new scheme), and all efforts will be concentrated on defense or war programs. Germany's aim of world dominion has never been disguised. The other zones will arm against Germany, may even combine, and, at a later date, destroy her. And then, finally, unless this state of affairs lasts too long, long enough for whole nations to be absorbed by forced migrations or starved to death, there will be a break-up of nations again into their racial parts, that will entail further wars of adjustment, and further destruction.

More immediately there remains the possibility that Germany, weakened by attacks on England, and by British counterattacks from the air and the blockade, may be overrun by Russia. This would put the political clock back to the hours that preceded the outbreak of war, when Russia and Germany were expected to attack and destroy each other, with the difference that only Germany might be destroyed, and Russia, stronger than ever, would absorb the countries that Germany has conquered.

By the enforcement of National Socialist principles, underground communism must inevitably be strengthened, since despite their apparent working resemblance, the two ideologies are still diametrically opposed to each other. Repression must build up resistance. Hatred of National Socialism in a democratic country as yet unconquered, produces a desire for real democracy which is socialistic in principle. But hatred presses further, writhing under the conqueror's heel, goes further and demands communism.

Europe is divided into two camps, that of those who support the Nazi principle, and that of those who hate it. The outcome of such hatreds must end in a series of revolutions and civil wars. Having nothing further to lose the people will become completely reckless and seek revenge for their sufferings wherever it lies nearest to their hands. There are only two main political tendencies today. Every country must tend, in its government, either to the right or to the left. Even a middle course will be off center and incline one way or the other.

Within a year it seems likely that Britain will be faced by the choice of attacking Germany, with Russia as an ally, or of attacking Russia, with Germany as an ally. Within a year Herr Hitler will no doubt, if he has not yet beaten England, again present himself as the savior of democracy from Bolshevism. The war will then be complicated or simplified, according to the point of view, into one of ideologies again.

Hitler has a million men who will if necessary die for him, throwing away their lives in a desperate effort to achieve a decisive result. He has, by education, produced them out of his ant-heap civilization. They are the fighter ants whose function is to protect the worker ants. Germany is fighting a fanatically inspired crusade for what she believes to be right.

The only answer to such a crusade is a counter crusade for what we, the others who are not German, know to be right. It is war not only to the last man, but to the last idea. And it is the last idea that will count the most.

Peace in our time seems an impossibility, and the mere cessation of war, a period of respite, too much to hope for. The end of the world has come, in the sense that it is the end of the world we understood, at least in part. Because it has come slowly, over a whole generation, instead of according to the accepted Biblical formula, few believe that it is here. That the dead have not risen in their graves may be merely that there are not yet sufficient dead.

* * *

The United States of America is not at war, but how many Americans have died so far? What are the unpublished casualty lists of death by bombs, by engineered accidents? What are the possibilities of further deaths, of whole areas being shattered by explosions in factories, of whole city blocks being destroyed by fire?

As the war has already attacked America psychologically in a war of nerves, so it has already attacked it physically by the death of American workers and the losses of American capital by sabotage.

The Christian Front, the Silver Shirts, the Ku Klux Klan, the communists, the Bund, have all been laughed off. Father Coughlin, William Dudley Pelley, Earl Browder, Fritz Kuhn, and William Bishop, have been taken lightly. The newspapers, afraid of alarming the public, have concentrated on the dramatic, emphasizing, for example, the sex life of Kuhn to the exclusion of his political significance. The Dies Committee appears somehow to have become discredited, and it is not public knowledge that the German-American Bund has fifty-eight branches, with a membership of two hundred thousand persons, nor that a German-American paper is said to have stated that:

"To give America our souls, as many of our fellow countrymen have done, is a mistake, no one can force that; to become German-American mongrels, who do not know where they belong, nobody could ask us. We are and remain Germans, Germans in America."

These organizations cannot be taken as civil organizations. They are, from the beginning to the end, military. Anyone who has seen the Bund march past in column of route must compare them very favorably with the National Guard. In fact, the Guard shows up very badly by comparison. It remains unfortunately true that, from the quality of their close order drill, the efficiency of troops can be very accurately gauged. The public is regrettably misinformed on the methods of fifth column activity on military lines. Pathetically confident, and entirely unaware of how a very small armed force could take possession of a great city, or how by the co-ordination of a number of such forces, all the great centers could be captured and resistance paralyzed.

According to General Karl Haushofer, president of the Geopolitical Institute at Munich:

"No race has greater claim to rule in the United States of America than the Germanic race. Our vision of a Germanically dominated Western Hemisphere will not be obscured by the red-, brown- and black-skinned races who populate almost half of America. When we will be ready to assert ourselves as a world-power, we will be able to count upon the millions of Germans who have helped make the North American continent the wealthiest on the globe. Never shall we forget that a substantial portion of the United States does not need to be made German. It is German! A strong, determined army of occupation under dynamic National-Socialist command can be recruited overnight in certain parts of the United States. The job of taking over North America will be comparatively simple."

This is an extract from Pierre van Paasen's article "Whom Hitler Reassures" in Red Book. He goes on to say, in 1932 "I was the guest of a Nazi official high in the propaganda section of the party at Munich. After a strenuous day of calls on prominent sympathizers and leaders, and endless discussions with these men on the rebirth of true Germanic *Kultur* with Hitler's imminent assumption of supreme power, my host suggested that we finish the evening in a cinema, where one of Hollywood's latest successes was attracting huge crowds.

"The picture, I recall, was one of those lavish musical comedies dealing with American high life at the peak of the pros-

perity era. It showed homes built and furnished with an elabo-
rateness inconceivable to almost any class in Germany. In this
picture were scenes emphasizing the fabulous wealth and extravagant spending of a financier, the hero of the plot. He controlled railroads, mines and automobile factories, and with a
single word could panic the stock exchanges of the world.
Hollywood's imagination had run riot in this film. Yet the story
was to a certain extent realistic, and unmistakably characteristic
of America's wealth and easy living.

"I asked my host why, after he had been talking so intensely
all day about Germany's future greatness, he had taken me to
see an American movie. To my amazement he replied, with a
grave expression on his face: 'Germany's greatness lies in
America's wealth. Your country is the most powerful country
in the world today. It will determine the political fate of Germany.

" 'We don't go to see American films merely to be enter-
tained. We study them. We want to feel at home in America
when we get there.' "

Law and order in the minds of men are represented, in civil
life, by the police force, by the cops who pace their beats in
every city. But there is no reason why, at a given time, every
policeman should not be shot on the street. That he is armed
will not save him. He will have no time. His assassins will be
young men who perhaps are standing near him staring into
shop windows with girls by their sides. Every now and then
they will glance at their watches. The moment is approaching.
It has come. They move towards the cop. "Can you tell me—"
He looks around. They open up and he falls down.

All over America, at that moment, thousands of police are
falling down. The watches of the assassins have been synchronized for latitude. At that moment, other men, who have been
loitering in the vicinity of armories, of police stations, of power-
houses and radio stations, storm them with bombs and sub-
machine guns carried in suitcases, violin cases, and in women's

shopping bags. At that instant, all over the United States, other young men who have been grouped in homes, in gardens, clubs, and places of amusement, jump into their autos and proceed to the armories and police stations that have been taken by the first storm troop divisions. In a few minutes those who are still offering resistance are defeated by these reinforcements. A few moments later the young men are out, dressed in the uniforms of the National Guard and police, armed with their weapons, or still in civil clothes but disguised with the stars of American legal authority.

The new policemen take up point duty, carry off the bodies of the dead policemen in screaming ambulances. Some take into protective custody the heads of such departments as might interfere with their activities, while others take possession of all public utilities, power-stations, radio and railroad stations, water-works, and harbor facilities. The third line, the larger forces, begin to "fall in" in the streets, and move off in orderly columns. The airports are seized. Reinforcements proceed by air and car to Washington, from New York, Philadelphia, and Baltimore. The President is seized, if he has not already been murdered. The public offices are held by storm troopers. In a couple of hours America is bound hand and foot.

This is not fact. This is fiction, the invention of a novelist who was once a soldier. It may be that measures have been taken to prevent all this. But if no measures have been taken, it could happen today, or tomorrow.

The following is an article by Colonel William J. Donovan and Edgar Mowrer:

"Adolf Hitler's blitz-conquests of Poland, of Norway, of Belgium, Holland, Luxemburg, and France are military masterpieces.

"In all secrecy and with incredible speed the Nazi leader built up a unique military machine, beside which all other armies in the world were obsolete. Basing his organization upon experience acquired in Spain during the civil war, Hitler placed at the head of his mobilized masses a modern "airplane plus tank" spearhead. The German masses were not particularly impressive. They did not need to be. It was the spearhead of 50,000 men that beat France.

"To his superior striking power the Nazi leader added surprise and audacity. Equipping dive bombers with noise makers sounds childish, but against green troops it worked. By striking suddenly, fiercely and without regard for his own immediate losses, Hitler gained an initiative he never lost.

"Yet no amount of genius would have accomplished what the Germans accomplished in so short a time without two other elements. These were the Germans abroad and sympathizers in the victim countries.

"Everyone understands the role played by the Sudeten Germans in the destruction of Czecho-Slovakia. While claiming to be loyal citizens of the new state, an active minority of the Germans was really working for its destruction.

"As in Czecho-Slovakia, so in Poland. There a tiny minority, probably about a million in all, while claiming to be loyal to Warsaw, were preparing to stab Poland in the back. Directed by the German Gestapo, organized into political groups, the Deutsche Vereinigung and the young German party, the minority leaders found means of terrorizing or otherwise inducing practically all the Germans to become spies and agents. As industrialists, commercial travelers, waiters, barbers, taxi drivers, they wormed their way into Polish life. Some 10,000 were actually trained in special camps in Germany to be forerunners, agents and guides to the invading army columns. The Germans were more quickly informed of the Polish military movements than the Polish commanders."

Here is a further article by J. W. T. Mason, United Press War Expert:

"Germans hidden in barges seized the Moordyke bridge in Holland which enabled the German invaders to turn the Dutch defenses from the south. This was decisive. But 120,000 Germans resident in the little country occupied a considerable share of the Dutch armed forces and made conquest that much easier. The 120,000 occupied their leisure in propaganda and espionage for the Nazis. Two hundred and fifty enjoyed extraterritorial privileges as members of the German legation in The Hague alone, without counting the officials in the various consulates. Fifty or a hundred so-called newspapermen spent most of their time wandering the country bent on strategic and economic research. German servants nearly everywhere carefully amassed bits of conversation or copied private papers.

"When Hitler finally struck, the 120,000 turned on their placid hosts and, where they could, shot them down."

The security of the United States of America is challenged. Its commerce is challenged. Its possessions are challenged, its way of living, its integrity and ideals.

There is the grave danger of the British fleet falling into German hands or being scuttled. There is danger of air attack from Greenland, Iceland, Alaska; from South America, from Mexico, where air bases are said to have been constructed. But these are not immediate dangers. They are so indefinite that the men of America are still talking of stocks, and the women of stockings. They are real enough to be dangerous, but distant enough to lull the country into a temporary sense of security.

First Europe—then America. By isolating each country, Herr Hitler has become the master of Europe. Who will care, once England has fallen, about America? Who will mourn America?

Hitler was financed by England and France. German tanks and planes were constructed with American machine tools and run on American gasoline. America has only just stopped selling war material to Japan, her greatest potential enemy. American war industries acknowledge themselves handicapped by German control of patents—and the country sleeps.

The Achilles' heel of America is business. In her desire to make a deal, without considering the result, America has sold a man as big as herself the stick with which she will be be-

labored. In a country that has an automobile for every five people, the army still moves on horseback; having the greatest in-
ventors in the world, its air force is inadequate; equipped with
the finest factories in the world, it is unable to turn out war
material at the necessary rate; and with the largest number of
motor vehicles in the world, it has almost no reserves of rubber.

It is assumed that America can catch up. But can she, even
with her riches in skilled men and factories? Do these, totaled
up, equal the combined factories and technicians of Germany,
Czecho-Slovakia, Belgium, Austria, France, Holland, Denmark,
Norway, Sweden, Switzerland, and the output of her allies,
Italy, Japan, and Russia? How many Americans have considered these questions? How many, even now, believe that
America is in danger, or that the American way of life will be
changed?

The vast majority of Germans in the United States are good
citizens, but within that majority are hidden the minority who
are not good citizens, who already are rejoicing at the conquests
of their Fuehrer. How many Germans are in the United States
regular Army and Navy? How many Germans are in the National Guard? How many in key positions in the civil life of
the nation? How many trained German soldiers are there working in various capacities in America? Every male German who
was over seventeen in 1918 and has since emigrated, is a trained
soldier. How many German officers and non-commissioned officers are here? How many have come in on passports forged
by the government of the Reich, or stolen by the Gestapo from
Jews and political prisoners?

There is talk of next year, the year after, but why should
Germany wait when everything is ready to her hand? A hundred men would suffice to capture most American towns, from
five hundred to two thousand, the largest cities. They are here.
The question is, are they organized? And if so, what counter
measures can be taken? The Bund may be another red herring,

a stalking horse for real activities. Its real use might only come later after the blow has been struck.

All Hitler's plans have been based on such methods. His whole success from the beginning has been built up by the employment of small bodies of highly organized men in synchronized surprise attacks. He is a master of timing, his people, the masters of disciplined precision. Unquestionably the State Department has foreseen this possibility. But the American public has not. It imagines itself secure. It refuses to see the straws in the wind, the Nazi propaganda distributed in the New York subways, the swastika flag raised in New Orleans, the windows of a schoolhouse broken in Minneapolis. It refuses to listen to the men who try to tell it. Walter Winchell is believed only when he talks of a forthcoming café society divorce. The Winchell column against the fifth column is taken as propaganda, which it is, propaganda for the safety of America. We are the alarmists, because we are alarmed.

Against this inertia, those who would save America are battling, and the American people, whom they would save, are fighting back. It is no longer a question of fifty obsolete destroyers for England, or a thousand planes, or ten thousand, or of all assistance short of war, or even of war itself. It is a matter of seeing facts and situations as they are, with hope for the future, but without wishful thinking, without belief that something, God, or nature, or business, will happen to save democracy without personal effort. God was abandoned long ago, nature has been continually thwarted, and business men, practical men of affairs, have successfully brought about the present situation.

It is up to the common man, the man in every street, to heal himself, to heal his parochial affairs, the corruptions that surround him, and to turn politics into government. It is fantastic that men should still be swayed by political programs, believe Democrats to be white, and Republicans black, or labor white

and capital black; impossible they should not see the infinite
graduations of political and religious opinion, and recognize
both the good and the evil in all things; impossible that they
should still believe in a universal nostrum, a formula that would
cure all ills; impossible that, having minds, they should be unwilling to use them, and like cattle, wait upon events.

It is incredible that men should live lives sublimated by films,
dulled by puerile radio scripts, and that they should not see how
little the essentials of humanity have changed over the centuries. The facts of life have been wrapped in false mystery for
their bewilderment, when the facts are mystery enough. Children are conceived and born as they have always been conceived
and born, men die as they have always died. Pleasure remains
what it has always been, sensuality in the form of fine raiment,
music, food, women, and wine. Every parallel is perpetually before them, and standards have been lowered rather than raised.

The Romans demanded gladiators, and would not have been
satisfied with a gloved fight reproduced on a film. The Greeks
demanded Hetaerae, and would not have been satisfied with
Broadway blondes. They feasted for days, garlanded with
flowers. They made spectacles, they ate peacocks' tongues that
came from living fowl, and could not have been put off with
canned goose livers. They raced chariots and horses whole-
heartedly, they gambled, they hunted the bear and the wolf, the
stag and the lion on horseback, instead of playing games or
shooting small birds with guns. They lived and died more fully
than men can or dare today. Pleasure has made no progress. It
is the shadow of what it was; and with pleasure, so have other
things become shadowy and nebulous. Honor and integrity have
gone also, and each thing, each vice and virtue, has become
anemic and without conviction.

Motives have not changed, but the blood has grown thin.
By the fear of missing something, everything is missed. The
psychological urges that activated man a thousand years ago
still function. His feelings in love, in hunger, in death, remain

the same. Only the methods have changed; but character continually duplicates itself. There are men alive today as virtuous as St. Francis and as vicious as Nero, women as good as Esther, as wicked as Messalina. Biblical characters were characters before they were biblical. They were men and women who lived long ago, but lived very much as we do, dwelling in houses, walking, talking, eating, making love, picking flowers, and harvesting crops. The women did needlework while the men conducted business in their work-shops and on their farms.

Nothing is new. Each thing, each invention, thought, or idea, is the result of a previous thought, invention or idea. Everything is derivative. The British mentality as represented by Shakespeare, Bacon, Kipling, Wells, Dickens, Scott, is representative also of what preceded them. They were derivative, the result of their period, and they influenced future thought which inevitably precedes and must result in future action. The writings of Nietzsche, of Goethe, the music of Wagner, are part of the German spirit, representative of it and activating it. Voltaire, Jean Jacques Rousseau, Racine, and Emile Zola are part of France, as are Robespierre, Guillotin, or Murat. The heroes, and the poets, even those who invent machines of execution, are part of the culture of a country, and become embodied in its emotional heredity.

The fox scarf has replaced the purple of Tyre, but the orchid corsage remains a gift of flowers; jewels retain their ancient purpose, and their implication remains constant. The call girl has replaced the brothel, the golf match the tourney, but the vanities of the flesh remain a part of the fleshly heritage. The saint, the seer, and the fratricide are still among us. Boys still delight in swimming naked through cool water. Maidens still delight in fine garments. Men still enjoy the rush of wind in their ears as they gallop through the morning on a horse. The philosophy of Greece still stands, as do its art and that of the Renaissance.

It is the derivations of life, whose roots are sunk deep into the prehistoric past, that give life its meaning, the fact that to all of us things have been handed on, often unconsciously, from father to son, from mother to daughter for incalculable centuries. From its stupendous geological antiquity comes a feeling of continuity that joins all living things, man, beast, bird, insect and plant, into one explicable pattern that must, since it cannot be influenced, be accepted. But by the invention and perfection of machines, the form of life has changed more quickly than man could adapt himself to it. There is no longer a way of life. There is only business. It is no longer what a man is, but the money he makes, that counts.

Once there were shepherds and wheelwrights and tinsmiths. They were master tradesmen, skilled, and accustomed to a way of life which was highly specialized. They made a living, and they lived a life that was enclosed within the pride of their callings.

The old days are not to be mourned. Things are better for everyone than they were then. But *a way of life* must come back, for by losing it man has lost his grip upon reality. The carpenter got satisfaction from buying whole trees, sawing them, and waiting for them to season. The vintner was happy treading the grapes with his feet. He had gathered them, he would make wine of them, mature it, sell it, and drink some of it himself. The housewife carding wool had dreams of the blankets she would make, thoughts of those they would cover, and memories of the sheep from which it had come.

What relation is there between a sheep and a department store, or between a can of corn on the shelf and corn growing in the fields? How does sliced bacon, wrapped in cellophane, compare with the home killed pig that has been home cured? The slaughter of any beast is a rite, it should be conducted with panoply, with an audience that waits, half afraid, for the rush of blood. The farmer kills his beast with regret. The children who have petted it cry. Everything is real. But what has a packing house to do with reality? What happens to the soul of a man who sticks pigs for eight hours a day, for five days a week?

Business has come to stay, modern production has come to stay, but somehow men must get back to the soil from which they spring. There is legitimate profit in trade, as there is legitimate usury. Capital, which is the crystallization of past energy into gold, is entitled to the dues of that energy. As there could be no coal had there been no vegetation to make it so, there can, speaking generally, be no accumulation of capital that has not been earned by effort. The simile fails where the practice fails, in that capital becomes fecund in a direct ratio to its bulk. Capital makes more capital, whereas coal does not make more coal.

The undeniable envy or resentment that the worker has for those in possession of fortunes, is not directed towards those who have made their fortunes themselves. The so-called self-made man may by some standards be vulgar, but, again speaking generally, his capacity cannot be questioned. It is the play-boy and the glamour-girl that are the main cause and excuse for Bolshevism in that they are non-producers, and that, living in luxury, they have no means of producing the money required to live in luxury.

Man is beginning to demand that all men produce actively. He is discovering that he can only respect producers, and man wishes fundamentally to respect his fellows. The legislation of the last thirty years has been largely directed against the inheritance of fortunes. That this has been so is because the people so willed it.

The man who has made a fortune is not much put about if he loses it. He knows that he holds in his brains the secret for making another. He is ready to take a chance, to go forward. He is a progressive member of society; but his son is different. He has no confidence in himself, and his abilities are concentrated on an effort to retain that which he has. It is the inheritor who is reactionary, because he dare not be anything else. It is the inheritor who is in such demand on a board of directors, not only for the capital he can put into the business, but because of the cagey way he will cast his vote. The others, the men who are makers, know that he is a saver and will act as a brake on their dreams of over-expansion.

The successful man is usually remarkable for the simplicity of his life. He often resents even the front that he has to put up to prove his success. He is too busy, too interested in his work to understand fully those ways of passing the time that are known as amusements. In this lies probably the only envy he arouses, that having the means of amusement, having the money for great houses, for entertainment, for yachts, racing stables and show girls, he does not use it. It is forgotten that had he cultivated such tastes he would have had no success, that he has preferred the pleasure of work to the boredom of play.

The laws of cause and effect, of diminishing returns, function in business and society as they do in other ways. By and large, with notable exceptions due to what we term luck, illness or accident, a man obtains about what he is entitled to in terms of happiness or success or health; but whatever he gets he must pay for. The heiress pays for her mink coats and jewels with the unhappiness of three or four marriages. A slim figure is paid for by starvation and exercises, a love of cream cakes, by adipose tissue. The business man pays for his success with the hardening of his arteries, the playboy, with the destitution that stalks him from hot-spot to hot-spot.

In searching for historical precedents, the prophets have been forgotten. It seems to have occurred to no one to bracket Dorothy Thompson, Walter Lippmann, or novelists like Wells, Sinclair Lewis, and Upton Sinclair, with Moses, Elijah, Job, Isaiah, Malachi, and David. Like the ancient prophets they state facts that no one wishes to hear. They prophesy events that because they terrify are deliberately ignored. In 1936, Churchill warned England. In August, 1940, Pershing warned the United States.

Chapter Fifteen

"The Prophets"

HISTORY REPEATS ITSELF not only in the prophecies and the warnings, but by the fact that they are not heeded and that the prophets remain without honor in their own countries and homes. The columnists, the novelists, and the radio commentators, are regarded as entertainers. That they draw big salaries instead of living on locusts and wild honey, does not make them less great in a civilization that regards earning capacity as a test of worth, but that, in an emergency like the present one, disregards its own standards.

They, at least, have no political axe to grind and nothing to gain by their crying in a hostile wilderness. They spend their days searching for news, analyzing it and interpreting it. They alone are in the position to see the small cloud no bigger than the hand of a man that will become a storm of destruction. They give warning of it. That is their purpose, their work, the method by which they have attained pre-eminence. They are expert, as the naval and military leaders are expert, as the Department of Foreign Affairs is expert, as the President, elected presumably because he was the man most fitted to lead the country, is expert.

The failure of many experts is now manifest, but the advice

of experts, since they at least are the best informed in the nation at any given time, remains good counsel.

The democratic system is like a man who buys a watchdog and then prefers to bark himself, or to stop his ears to the barking of the dog he bought. The direction of affairs is not left to those who were elected to direct affairs. The barking is not left to the dog that was trained to bark. Simile can be piled on simile, parable on parable. "It can't happen here," is cried by country after country as it happens.

No one denies the number of foreign agents in the country or the number of aliens who owe no allegiance to the United States, and who profit by her prosperity while they despise her freedom. But the most dangerous fifth columnists are Americans, as were the Poles, Norwegians, Belgians, Frenchmen, and Englishmen in their own countries. Fifth column activities are an inside job. They are the burglars who are guests in the house of democracy, who walk at liberty through the house in tuxedos, immune from interference. It is they who will take the jewels while the servants chase the petty thief who has run off with the silver.

A non-belligerent America could help England without the declaration of war, using as a precedent the principle of German and Italian non-intervention in Spain. Today the declaration of war has little to do with actual hostilities. It has become little more than an archaic diplomatic formula, satisfactory in Ambassadorial circles, but irrelevant and inexplicable to ordinary men who associate war with the explosion of projectiles and the wounds and death that follow such explosions.

There is some danger in continual reference to precedent, to analogy, to generalizations or particularizations. There is some danger in everything, in every opinion, or lack of it, unless it is regarded as elastic, controversial, and subject to change. The fear of a wrong thought or opinion tends to stop all thought and opinion. Silence is not necessarily indicative of wisdom. It can also be due to vacancy, to spiritual emptiness. But there are certain resemblances between the statesmanship of the last two centuries and the more recent moves of commerce. There has been a great amalgamation of small nations into greater ones, as there has been of small stores into greater stores. In 1940 we have seen the greatest amalgamation of all times, in the nationalities swallowed by the German Reich. But with the older amalgamations, those of Scotland, Ireland, and Wales with England, and of the smaller German states into the modern Germany that came into being after 1870, of Brittany into France after the French Revolution, there exists a counter feeling of ardent local nationalism which resents being swallowed up. There is a feeling among the people themselves, the common men, that such great countries were too big for them to belong to.

A great country is not personal, and men must have personalities. They still cling, in their hearts, to their local tribes and local leaders, who spring from their own roots and have the same blood in their veins. In France, there have always been Normans and Bretons and Gascons, racial types who disliked and distrusted each other; in Ireland, there have been for centuries the Celts of the south, and the Scots of the north; in Scotland, the highlander and the lowlander. In England, until recently, Yorkshire was a language, and even today, a Yorkshireman will say he is a Yorkshireman before he says he's English.

The racial strain still clings to its own, still tries, despite national absorptions, to retain its local language and culture; still lives parochially, as indeed man must. The travelers are few, and most men still live and die within a few miles of their birthplaces, still live among men and women that they have known all their lives. As in commerce, where many prefer the small store, where they get personal service, to the great store where added efficiency cannot compensate them for a feeling of anonymity, so do peoples cling to their minority tribal groups.

These are signs of the times, the pull towards great mergers for efficiency and the pull away from them for humanity.

In the days of Rome's greatness, *Civis Romanus sum* was enough. The day must come when, after passing through the fire of these times that may last for centuries, it will be enough for a man to be a citizen of the world, enough for him to be a man. That will be his justification and his passport. But a melting down must precede the recasting. It is merely unfortunate that we are those who, by the accident of our birth, were born to be melted.

Here is something beyond the understanding of vested interests. Here are the things that may cause revolution, the mass desire of men for a purge of their holy offices and a mass anger at the leaders who have led them into the slough of materialism and abandoned them there.

Here is the real fear of the statesmen, of the men who hold the weakened reins of power. It is not evil that they fear, for there is nothing behind evil but hope of gain, which they understand and with which they can deal, but the possibility that the horse of public docility will suddenly burst its bonds and demand justice and the right to live.

The sufferings of the world, its crucifixion, must be justified. A slow cold anger is arising. The dictator's phrase of exhausted patience has been adopted by the man in the street, the common man who is tired of things as they are and begins to see that his cynicism and tolerance were a form of despair. Yet there is no despair in his heart. There is even little fear, only anger and hope and newly arising faith.

The fear of death and change is being superseded by the fear of reaction, of an attempt to put things back. Man has become conditioned to the idea of change, to the knowledge that things cannot be put back, that change is inevitable, and he demands that such change shall be for the better, that, if material standards are to be less good, they must be compensated for by greater spiritual values. He is ready to suffer, but he must know the cause. He is ready to die, but he must know the reason that his life is demanded of him. Man can no longer be shanghaied by the doped oratory of the political meeting, or robbed of his liberties by the strumpets of vested interest who appear to pander to his comforts.

There is talk of alarmists. There are men who describe this as "a moment of excitement and hysteria," who, in the name of common sense, are trying to silence the voice of public sentiment, to delay action till action will be too late; who, ignoring the conscription of Germany, point to conscription as the reason for French failure, who call conscription undemocratic when that most democratic of countries, Switzerland, has had it since the days of William Tell. These are the men who, in the name of freedom would send half-trained boys to war, who, out of sentimentality, seriously suggest that men of forty and fifty could be used as first line troops. These are the men who, for inexplicable reasons, perhaps because they are incapable of constructive reasoning, obstruct all positive suggestions.

Many public servants, members of Parliament, senators, congressmen, appear to be elected because of their political machines, wealth, personal beauty, or success as go-getters. Their intellectual capacity, integrity, education and knowledge of the world are considered irrelevant.

More brains are to be found among the radio commentators and the columnists than in the Senate, but because the views of these men and women are objective, because they do not tell the public what it wants to hear, their views are discounted, and their cry of "Wolf" lost in the jingle of appropriation dollars.

By the distortion of analogy, of word, of fact, men have come to confuse discipline with totalitarianism. It is lack of discipline that causes men to break the law. It is because of their lack of discipline that Americans are a notoriously lawless people. In their fear of coercion, and fear of being dictated to, they destroy their own freedoms. Because they will not respect the notice that tells them to keep off the grass in their parks, they destroy their parks. Because of their love of freedom they have become the thralls of gangsters and racketeers.

The danger of this point of view is more apparent today when slogans have, owing to the urgency of the moment, replaced thought. Compulsion of any kind is labeled as dictatorship, and private soldiers write to congressmen if the top sergeant is rude to them. The label of communism is attached to any suggestion of equality, even if the leveling be upward instead of downward. The desire to raise up, to educate, is almost as reprehensible in the eyes of some men, as the cry, "soak the rich." The fullest liberty to all men would be anarchy and chaos. Claims that attacks are being made on civil liberties are used by subversive elements whenever matters requiring the employment of men or money by draft are discussed.

To obtain the full use of our liberty, as men, we must be ready to bear the duties and disciplines required of us, which can alone justify the existence of the liberties we claim so glibly. We have come to think of liberty as a commodity that we can obtain without payment in kind and in service, that national honor and integrity can be achieved by appropriations of money alone.

*   *   *

In war there are so many unknown factors, so many apparent irrelevancies that cloud events. The Barbary apes that roam at liberty on the Rock of Gibraltar might prove vital to its retention by the British. Italian bombing, if it did no more than destroy the monkeys, might cost the British the mastery of the Mediterranean, owing to the old superstition that as long as the apes remain, the rock will be held by the British. This is a superstition, but one of such importance that the apes draw government rations and have an officer whose duty it is to see to their wants. He is the "Officer in charge of the apes." Superstition or no superstition, the loss of their apes might affect the morale of the garrison.

Old fables, old victories, old names, and traditions have become a folk-lore whose existence is of paramount importance. The Fighting Fifth, the Buffs, the Gay Gordons, the Foot Guards, the regiments of Light Infantry, the Death or Glory Boys, the Green Howards and the Black Watch, are all British regiments whose courage is a part of their past.

Tradition makes men bold, and where is there a greater tradition than in America? Men with great names, or men serving in great regiments become great as the mantle of the past covers them. The defects of aristocracy are offset by its capacity for sacrifice in time of danger. The defect of plutocracy is that men have accepted privilege without its counterpoise of service. Every advantage carries with it the implication of a duty. Old customs that seem ridiculous can be factors on which the issue of a battle rests. Materialism has tried to sweep away those psychological characteristics of the human race that are so deeply imbedded in it as to be indivisible from it. Cabinet Ministers touch wood. Great ladies refuse to dine at a table set for thirteen. Famous lawyers turn their money when they see a new moon. Feminists who went to jail in the cause of woman's franchise are upset if they break a mirror. Few believe in ghosts, but fewer would live in a house reputed to be haunted.

Heredity, tradition, folk-lore are all forgotten, but they remain a fundamental basis of behaviorism. A belief in luck approximates a belief in God, and man's actions only appear rational because the main effort of his life is to rationalize them, to save his face before others whom he cannot believe to be as irrational as himself. He lives by deep inexplicable instincts, by forces that govern him, that drive him to save himself at all cost, to eat and reproduce himself. And all human activity can be enclosed and covered by the continual repetition of this cycle. Man works to live, he exhibits himself for sexual reasons, he marries to have children, and he dies. In this, man is like every other animal, his acts as unconscious as those of an animal. Only in his spiritual aspirations, in his desire for an abstract truth, and his thought of tomorrow, does man differ from the beasts of the field, or the fowls of the air. Whirled through the round of his business and social life, man is almost unaware of his personal existence, and needs continual reassurance of it.

Man is driven to war when ancient hidden chords of his personality are struck. War is irrational yet war exists. The birth of a baby is irrational, or the growth of a plant. There is actually no relationship between rationalism and life. Rationalization has no real place in the mind of man. It is an invention calculated to explain miracles by giving them scientific names, and to replace the comforts and absolutions of the medieval church.

There is a tide of life, an evolution of it, public and personal, on which man rides. The East has developed a passive acceptance of life, while the West actively resists it. Both attitudes are fostered by religion, but there must come a new culture of active acceptance, of cooperation with life forces. The holy man of the East insulates himself against life, insulates himself against pain by suffering till he can feel no more. By religious exercises he becomes separate from humanity, almost unaware of it. In the West, men force their own pattern on life, refuse either to acknowledge its pain or glory, and divorce themselves from those mysteries of existence which render it tolerable. Ignoring the little things, counting always on tomorrow, without evidence that it will be better than today, they go on, fearful of change, even of the final change that must, in the end, come to them. Living not as men, but as beasts, without contemplation, resignation, pleasure, or hope.

The child says, "When I am grown up," the boy, "When I am twenty-one," the young man, "When I am married," the mature man, "When the children are grown up and I can retire." And at all times, with their hopes of the future, their contempt of today and fear for the tomorrow that they look forward to, they achieve nothing. Possessions are found to mean little, once they are possessed. One of the greatest shocks to refugees who are not in actual personal danger, and have food and housing, is how little their possessions meant to them. With the cessation of fear, for one who has been in fear, the actual feeling of life is compensation enough, provided the necessities of life are still available. Memory animals have, but true memory, with the capacity for fitting the events of the past into a pattern, is the gift of God to men. It is in this that the old find comfort in turning over the pages of the past days, seeing the relation of cause and effect in retrospect, and the functioning of a plan that dwarfs, by its immensity, the conceptions of their youth.

The events of today force thoughts upon man as they have never been forced before. Speeded up by mechanization, things which should have taken hundreds of years take a generation. The impact is so great that the spectacular is given greater value than it warrants. The melodrama overshadows the drama. In a hundred years, the effects of the destruction of the library of Louvain will be felt, while in a hundred years the death of a thousand boy pilots will be no more than an instance of the heroism of youth. Those who loved them, the mothers, sisters, wives and sweethearts, will be dead.

But their deeds will not be dead, nor will the epic of Dunkirk be dead. It will live forever by means of the magic word, by means of learning, by means of the songs that men will sing. This must be done by the written word, the tale, the saga, by painting, by sculpture, by poetry and prose. It has been said that nothing is done by talking or writing, yet without talking or writing nothing can even be begun. But the truth must come back, and the attitude of mind that can accept truth, that will prefer Steinbeck's "Grapes of Wrath" to songs like "Little curly hair in a high chair," and that will refuse to accept the cliché, for the cliché has contributed its part to the present disaster.

The cliché is the apt word which, because it is so apt, has

been over-used and has lost its significance. From the "dull thud" describing the fall of a murdered man, to the words "equality," "liberty," and "brotherhood," it has destroyed the power of our language. Great biblical texts, great words spoken by great men, are, by continued quotation, removed from their context of emotional impact. It is the emotional impact of "Mein Kampf" that struck the German people a blow from which they may never recover. It was not the words or the reasoning, it was the words with their lack of reasoning, the impassioned written oratory, and the lies driven home with such sledge-hammer blows that they seemed greater than the truths expressed by other men.

There are words that people fear that are connected with the taboos of morals, of good taste, and false pride. There is the word "beauty" which no one hears today. Where is the boy who dares to say, "This is beautiful"? He will substitute another word, "fine," "swell," "grand," or "not bad," if he is English. We have become timid even in our expressions. Women are called ladies. Natural functions and even parts of our own bodies are given Latin names. If we dare not name a thing, how can we think of it, or employ it? There is a perpetual substitution of words for words, of approximate meaning for the real meaning, of a substitute life for a real life. The belief that one thing, even if not as good as another, will serve as well, has disturbed the balance of existence.

Foch said, "War is won in the soul." It was he who said, *"Ils ne passeront pas,"* and by the phrase, "They shall not pass," their passing was stopped. He said, *"On les aura,"* and they had them. It is the magic word that will be the final answer to Fascism. It is the "word" that they fear, the writers of the "word" that they destroy. The pen is mightier than the sword, the prophet mightier than the captain.

Figures of speech that would not so long ago have been considered melodramatic, or savoring of revivalism, are now on all men's tongues. Self-consciously they repeat them, ashamed to find themselves truthful at last, but relieved to find the same words in the mouths of other men. Melodrama and revivalism are parts of the life pattern. They have been condemned because of their apparent vulgarity. To be melodramatic is to create a scene, to speak seriously of God, or of good, or evil is to make your hearers feel awkward and embarrassed. Emotion is classed with religion and sex, all are conversationally taboo. Yet the highest points of human existence are those that touch upon these things, and the jokes about them, no more than a defense mechanism fostered in man by his fear of such realities.

The mind and body are one. The vast spiritual unrest today is due to this fact and the refusal to recognize it. True rationalization becomes simple by the acceptance of all things while striving perpetually towards the best. But artificial barriers and totems have been erected to bar the progress of man towards his appointed ends.

Acceptance must be tempered by curiosity and wonder. The child's "Why?" must go with us all the days of our lives, and there must be a reversal of the educative system which has taught us to accept its teachings without questions. The acceptance of fact need not eliminate curiosity concerning fact.

By the half-hearted acceptance of God we have lost Him. By questioning the existence of God, He will be found everywhere, at every street corner, in every field and mountain, on every road, in every home, for that which is strange and beautiful is God. The love of a man for a woman, a blue bird's egg broken by the wayside, a discarded an rusting in the ash dump, are all equal examples of His power, the power of change, of force, that remains inexplicable and wonderful. Why should a bird sing, or the frond of a fern uncurl, or iron become encrusted with rust? These are things no man can answer. He can only wonder.

Today man stands before his God, stripped of illusions, of

hope, stripped of all things but those impulses of his heart and mind that force him to choose between God and Mammon, between good and evil, between fighting, and perhaps dying, for his freedoms, or living, and perhaps dying, as a slave. He is stripped of all things but his decision, of all things but his belief or disbelief.

Chapter Sixteen

The End

NOTHING IS UNNATURAL. The murderer, the criminal, the drunkard, and the nymphomaniac are all products of their heredity and environment—of their circumstances.

Events are like men. Storm, fire, flood, wars and disasters are all conceived in the womb of past days, and born suddenly when their time is come. Cause and effect are not wonderful. They are easily understood mechanically, as action and reaction. An object can be warmed by friction. Water is heated by the addition of sulphuric acid, owing to the chemical change that takes place when they are mixed. The miracle occurs not in the material reaction, which is perceptible and easily related to fact, but in the laws that govern such reaction, not in the laws of cause and effect, but the fact of cause and effect.

There are diagrams illustrating the human fetus at all stages, or the germination of an egg, which give the illusion, by their nomenclature, that they are self-explanatory. But they are not. They explain nothing.

Even death, which is accepted as definite, is in no sense definite. It is a medical approximation describing the state of a body in which the heart has ceased to beat and the lungs to breathe. Long after what is technically known as death, bodily functions continue, changes take place. Even the putrescence and corruption of the flesh is a form of life, since it is change. Therefore, in a sense, even stones live, they change continually as they are worn down by the action of the elements. The heart of a frog goes on beating for many hours after it has been removed from the body. The Russians are said to have separated the head and digestive organs from a dog and it continued to eat, to digest food, and evacuate the refuse. Was the dog dead? Is the frog dead while its heart still beats?

The three great mysteries remain, those of birth, of reproduction, and of death. All are equally inexplicable, all equally remarkable, and all a part of the experience of all men.

Would a cynical world a few years ago have believed that a statesman like Reynaud would have cried, "Nothing can save us but a miracle"? That Lord Halifax should appeal to God, and that Winston Churchill should in the House of Commons say: "If we are now called upon to endure what the French have suffered, we shall emulate their courage, and if final victory rewards our toils they shall share the gain—aye, freedom shall be restored to all. We abate nothing of our just demands. Czechs, Poles, Norwegians, Dutch and Belgians, who have joined their causes with our own, all shall be restored.

"What General Weygand called the Battle of France is over. The Battle of Britain is about to begin. On this battle depends the survival of Christian civilization.

"Upon it depends our own British life and the long continuity of our institutions and our Empire. The whole fury and might of the enemy must very soon be turned upon us. Hitler knows he will have to break us in this island or lose the war.

"If we can stand up to him all Europe may be freed and the life of the world may move forward into broad sunlit uplands; but if we fail, the whole world, including the United States and all that we have known and cared for, will sink into the abyss of a new dark age made more sinister and perhaps more prolonged by the lights of a perverted science.

"Let us therefore brace ourselves to our duty and so bear ourselves that if the British Commonwealth and Empire last for a thousand years, men will still say 'This was their finest hour.' "

These are the signs. By a strange completion of the cycle we are back in mythological times.

"And I saw one of his heads as it were wounded to the death: and his deadly wound was healed. And all the earth was in admiration after the beast. They adored the beast, saying: Who is like to the beast? And who shall be able to fight it? The beast is like to a leopard, and his feet are as the feet of a bear, and his mouth as the mouth of a lion. And the dragon gave him his own strength, and great power . . . The four angels are loosed, prepared for an hour, and a day, and a month, and a year, to kill a third part of men. For the power of the horse is in their mouths, and in their tails. For their tails are like serpents, having heads; and with them they do hurt."

*   *   *

The days are come which were prophesied by Jesus Christ, who, foreseeing the destruction of Jerusalem, cried, "Woe unto them that are with child and them that give suck in these days."

Man has revolted from the mechanics of his civilization and has gone back into the distant past for his gods and devils. Ancient prophecies have become true, ancient war cries, long buried, spring loud to the lips of men. Once again it is, as it was at Agincourt and Crécy, "St. George and England!"

The days are come when men, at loss for comfort, raise their tattered war standards and call upon their saints to lead them.

These are the days that give the lie to Freud's masturbations, to the Church that would call for the recrucifixion of Christ were He to appear again. These are the days that proclaim once more the immense spiritual forces that have raised man from the beasts, by his beliefs alone and by his capacity for sacrifice.

If the naturalist is uncertain of the point where man emerges
from the beast, where man becomes man, I am uncertain where
man ceased to be man and becomes God. The Virgin Mary, the
Mother, is all mothers; God, the Father, is all fatherhood;
Jesus Christ, being in all men, is all men. The Holy Ghost is
the spiritual power that supports men, raising them above their
circumstance into belief.

To be whole, man must go back beyond the dogmas that are
preached to him, beyond the intoned prayers of the prelates,
beyond the painted images, the candles, the decorations, the
altars, to seek the truths that are within his heart and judge
them.

Behind all dogma, under every creed, there is truth. In the
hearts of all men, all women and children, there is truth. In
every home there is the Book of Truth, whose virtue has been
stolen from it, by preaching, by proselytizing and interpretation. Let each man read secretly and alone, for the hour is
come.

"Love justice, you that are the judges of the earth. For God
made not death, neither hath He pleasure in the destruction of
living things. For He created all things that they might be; and
He made the nations of the earth for health." It is written:
"Our time is as the passing of a shadow and there is no going
back of our end; for it is fast sealed and no man returneth. . . .
Let us fill ourselves with costly wine and ointments: and let
not the flower of time pass by us. Let us crown ourselves with
roses before they be withered: let no meadow escape our riot.
Let us oppress the poor just man, and not spare the widow, nor
honor the ancient gray hairs of the aged. But let our strength
be the law of justice: for that which is feeble is found to be
nothing worth."

It is further written that: "The fruits of the desire of thy
soul are departed from thee and all fat and goodly things are
perished from thee, and thou shalt no more find them. The
merchants of these things, who made rich, shall stand far off

from her, for fear of her torments, weeping and mourning,
and saying Woe! Woe! that great city which was clothed with
fine linen and purple, and scarlet, and was gilded with gold,
and precious stones, and pearls. For in one hour are so great
riches come to nothing: and every shipmaster and every one
that sails the lake, and mariners, and they that work at sea,
stood far off. And they cast dust upon their heads and cried
out weeping and mourning, saying Woe! Woe! That the great
city in which all were made rich, who had ships at sea, by
reason of her prices: for in one hour she is made desolate.
The voice of the harpers, and of the musicians, and of them
that play on the pipe, and on the trumpet, shall no more be
heard in thee: and no craftsman of any kind shall be found
any more in thee: and the sound of the mill shall be heard no
more in thee: and the voice of the bridegroom and the bride
shall be heard no more in thee: for the merchants were the
great men of the earth, for all nations have been deceived by
thy sorceries."

*   *   *

"Little children it is the last hour: And as you have heard
that the Anti-Christ cometh: even now there are many anti-
christs: Whereby we know it is the last hour. Who is the liar,
but he who denieth that Jesus is the Christ? He is the Anti-
Christ who denieth the Father and the Son."

These are the words of God; some of the words that have
been misunderstood and forgotten. They are beyond meaning,
since to each man their meaning is different; as to each man,
in his mind and heart, the conception of God is different. In
that difference, because of it, lies the true concept of omnipo-
tence, of power.

There must be a new conception of God, a new understanding of God the Father, that appeals to the desire for a father
in all men, that makes them, as they grow older, think back to
their childhood and the earthly father who carried them high

upon his shoulder. The father whom they loved and feared, the jealous god of their homes, who protected them from all danger and all evil.

There must be a new conception of the Virgin Mother, who by her motherhood became the mother of all living things, the mother woman, on whose breast men would rest their heads to weep; the everlasting womb, which all men unconsciously wish to re-enter; the everlasting earth from which all men sprang and to which all will return, the vast earth that is female and comforting.

There must be a new understanding of the Holy Ghost, which is conscience, which is no more than the knowledge that man has of good and evil; no more than the almost visible aura that surrounds old men and women who have lived their lives righteously, who have sinned—for those who have not sinned are less than men—but who have sinned no more than they need, who have hurt no one needlessly. The very old, with old tired eyes that have seen all things and are ready to die.

There must be a new understanding of Jesus Christ, the Son of God, partly human and therefore partly explicable to man.

Such blasphemous explanation as this, such rationalization of God the Father, God the Son, God the Holy Ghost, and the Holy Virgin, with the ancient gods of man, with his fear complex, his Oedipus complex, with his new knowledge of evolution, detracts in no way from the magnificence of the creation of God; nor from man's faith in himself, through his belief in God; nor of his identification of himself with God, through the spirit of God, that he recognizes within himself; nor in his belief in virtue. Neither does it remove the grandeur from the works of God, the tall mountains, the trees, the little rivers, and the great waters, among which he moves. Rather does it renew hope as it destroys dogma which would bind man in its bureaucratic, religious conceptions, with its demand for temples, as though the God who created the world needed housing in an office, with its clerks to interpret him, when the flight of a bird through the firmament is interpretation enough, and when the love of man for man proves the spark of divinity that is indestructible in his heart.

That Jesus Christ, the Son of Man, was a carpenter, makes him real. He was a handler of tools, a young man who delighted to stand up to his knees in curled pine shavings, who cut his hands on chisels, who delighted in happiness and good company; a man who called to the children to come to him, who talked to prostitutes on the street corners, was friendly with publicans and cursed the hypocrisy of a priesthood that followed the letter of the law and denied its spirit.

Of what importance is the Virgin Birth when the mysteries of conception and birth remain miracles that happen daily? What matter whether Christ walked upon water as God, when He trod the hot sands of Palestine as a man? Why this splitting of hairs about a man who refused to split hairs?

The rights of man are indistinguishable from the rights of God. Man's existence, as man, rests on his concept of an abstract God, on a plan that is irrevocable and unending, in which he plays his part, as every living thing plays its part, all miraculously interwoven, the one with the other, in the immense tapestry of living things.

Man's existence as man is dependent on evolution, that of man, that of God, as man evolved from brute beast to man; his greatest concept a belief in his own creator.

Modern thought has not destroyed the Almighty God; on the contrary it has enhanced His majesty, His mystery, but it has destroyed the medieval concept of religion, destroyed a church that was organized on a temporal basis with entirely irrelevant moral views, a church that served God with its left hand, and Mammon with its right, and that evolved a process of spiritual intimidation to serve its own purely physical ends.

That modern science can trace the track of storm changes nothing. That modern medicine can alleviate the pains of childbirth does not alter the method of that birth. That modern

botany gives the greenness of plants the name of chlorophyll
does not make them more green.

*   *   *

A long time ago a young Jewish man went up a hill which is
near Jerusalem and turning to the multitude that followed him
said:

"Blessed are the poor in spirit: Blessed are they that mourn:
Blessed are the meek: Blessed are they which do hunger and
thirst after righteousness: Blessed are the merciful: Blessed are
the pure in heart: Blessed are the peacemakers: Blessed are they
which are persecuted for righteousness sake: Blessed are ye
when men shall revile you, and persecute you, and shall say all
manner of evil against you falsely for my sake. Rejoice and be
exceeding glad: for great is your reward in heaven: for so persecuted they the prophets which were before you."

St. Paul said, "Though I speak with the tongues of men and
of angels, and have not charity, I am become as sounding brass
or a tinkling symbol . . . And though I bestow all my goods to
feed the poor, and though I give my body to be burned, and
have not charity, it profiteth me nothing. Charity suffereth long,
and is kind; Charity envieth not; Charity vaunteth not itself, is
not puffed up . . . seeketh not her own, is not easily provoked,
thinketh no evil, Rejoiceth not in iniquity, but rejoiceth in the
truth; Beareth all things, believeth all things, hopeth all things,
endureth all things. . . . When I was a child, I spake as a child,
I understood as a child, I thought as a child. But when I became
a man I put away childish things. For now we see through a
glass, darkly; but then face to face. Now I know in part; but
then I shall know even as I am also known. And now abideth
faith, hope and charity, these three; but the greatest of these is
charity.

"Behold, I show you a mystery; We shall not sleep, but we
shall all be changed, in a twinkling of an eye, at the last
trump; Then shall be brought to pass the saying that is written,

Death is swallowed up in victory. Oh death, where is thy sting? Oh grave, where is thy victory? The sting of death is sin; the strength of sin is the law."

*   *   *

Passionately conceived, passionately written, these are the opinions, the views of a single man. Serving some purpose or no purpose they stand from the first word to the last as a conviction, a view, one of the many hundred million facets of the collective human mind that waits today, aghast, facing tomorrow.

THE END